Enterprise.com

Enterprise.com

Market Leadership in the
Information Age

JEFF PAPOWS

PERSEUS BOOKS
Reading, Massachusetts

Library of Congress Catalog Card Number: 98-87765
ISBN 0-7382-0064-6

Perseus Books is a member of the Perseus Books Group

Jacket design by Suzanne Heiser
Text design by Heather Hutchison

1 2 3 4 5 6 7 8 9-DOH-02 01 00 99 98

Perseus Books are available at special discounts for bulk purchases in the U.S. by corporations, institutions, and other organizations. For more information, please contact the Special Markets Department at HarperCollins Publishers, 10 East 53rd Street, New York, NY 10022, or call 1-212-207-7528

Find us on the World Wide Web at
http://www.aw.com/gb/

CONTENTS

FOREWORD

Geoffrey Moore

Interesting books often live at the intersection of an older paradigm giving way to a new order, and the one you have just picked up is no exception. When Jeff Papows and a whole lot of the rest of us entered the computer industry more years ago than we care to count, the dominant paradigm was the stand-alone computer, be it a mainframe or minicomputer dedicated to back-office transaction processing, or the newly arrived PC dedicated to office automation applications. The boundary between information inside and outside the computer was well defined, with the focus of systems being to improve the productivity of relatively autonomous functions.

Today that paradigm is giving way to a new order that is centered on collaboration rather than autonomy and in which borders are being deconstructed in order to achieve new levels of coordination and competitive advantage. None of the old-style computing has gone away, but now it has been merged with communication in ways that are redefining the nature of cooperation. The early manifestations of this change first showed up at the workgroup level, beginning with the local area network (LAN) and e-mail and getting a huge boost from the introduction of Lotus Notes. More recently a similar manifestation of this change has engaged at the enterprise level, beginning with wide area, network-based e-mail, electronic data interchange (EDI), and the introduction of the Internet.

In both of its manifestations, as the communication infrastructure took a major step up, this change invited communities to explore what new forms of transactions might be enabled. And that is largely where we are today—exploring the domain of what is possible and seeking to develop new practices to leverage new capabilities.

The evolution of new practices is a recurrent theme whenever new technology stimulates market development. At the outset, progress is made through the isolated efforts of intrepid individuals, often working in pairs—with a hands-on practitioner leading the close-up development and a visionary securing the resources to support that effort. Because the rest of the market hangs back to see if the early outcomes warrant an ongoing commitment, these individuals work without a safety net. Individual companies, with equal boldness, then support the practitioners and visionaries who have defined the new practices—companies like Price Waterhouse (for Lotus Notes), Amazon.com (for Internet retail commerce), and Cisco and Dell (for Internet business-to-business commerce). In this first phase, there is no sustainable market, just an outcropping of projects, each forging its own way.

The technologies of collaboration, however, have passed beyond this phase. They have crossed the chasm into mainstream market acceptance. The question is no longer whether there will be a market for them but rather, What kind of market will it be? Will these technologies remain relatively complex to deploy and maintain, in which case they will settle into niche markets, or will they simplify and commodify, leading to mass market deployment? The former has been the outcome in the case of project management software, geographical information systems, and video conferencing, the latter in the case of word processing, relational databases, and Internet Protocol (IP) networks. There is no right or wrong outcome here; but the difference in impact is an order of magnitude, and so it is the latter possibility that truly bears watching.

In technology-based market development, mass markets emerge spontaneously. They are what academics call self-organizing systems, meaning that they are not shaped by some external creator but rather find their shape as the laws of natural selection are applied to millions and millions of independent events. This is Darwin at work, with the organisms that can replicate the fastest and defend their territory the best winning out. And, as in evolution, here too environment plays a heavy role. For instance, the Macintosh OS was long acknowledged to be superior to the Microsoft OS (or Windows), but the latter was born in the IBM PC environment and raced ahead to ubiquity as a result. And a similar tale could be told of the race between Motorola's 68030 microprocessor and Intel's 80386. It is not a dominance of species so much as one of ecosystems that matters in the end.

And that notion—that competition can be conceived and potentially managed at the ecosystem level, and not just at the level of individual battles—is what makes this book important now. The idea itself is already in circulation, thanks to books like Michael Rothchild's *Bionomics* and James Moore's *The Death of Competition*. The question going forward is, To what extent can technology-based infrastructure influence the outcome? Evolution is always about competitive advantage. Can we harness systems forged at the intersection of computing and communication to generate new forms of collaboration that will prevail over alternative economic forces? Or is this some form of overreaching bound to be brought down by local forces that resist being co-opted into some higher-level game?

The answer is not obvious, and most organizations are pursuing a range of options, hedging their bets across whatever portion of the spectrum feels most comfortable. Moreover, they are anxiously watching each other to see how their peers are making out. This too is evolution at work. We congregate in herds, flocks, schools, or tribes to learn from each other, support each other, and buffer each other against whatever change comes next. Much of life is spent milling about, muddling through—not the most elegant form of behavior, perhaps, but the one for which evolution thus far has selected.

Muddling, I would argue, is a primitive form of collaboration. It is rooted in a kind of incidental communication—not point-to-point telegraphing of clear intentions, but rather ambient circulation of bits and pieces of lore. How are we doing in the ABC account? How far ahead or behind is our competitor? How will the stock market react to the latest news? Will consumers really go for our new offer? These are the crucial types of questions that business decisions are based upon, and they are inherently ambiguous, indeterminate, and, well, muddled.

The fundamental way to answer all such questions is to "ask around," and it's here that we come full circle to the information systems at the heart of Papows's discussion. Groupware and the Internet are both superb media for asking around. They're optimized precisely for the ambient circulation of bits and pieces of lore. As such, today's advanced Web-based messaging and application platforms have the potential to accelerate an organization's ability to come to grips with the ambient circulation of information.

These metaphors of chasing and grappling that we use and hear so frequently are all about finding an operative context. That is the real challenge in business decision-making, and that is why these new collaborative technologies pique so much interest.

As an executive at Lotus for seven years and its president and/or chief executive since the company's acquisition by IBM, Jeff Papows has been at the center of collaborative technology development in the 1990s. It is hard to imagine someone more qualified to address this technology's impact and future. So—timely issue, informed author, serious outcomes at stake: What more do you need except for me to wish you good reading!

PREFACE

Life in the software industry is so intense that committing the time and effort to write a book on the business implications of the World Wide Web and the collaborative technologies catalyzing its greatest impact was not the most intuitive extra project to take on. Staying ahead of an industry that moves as quickly as ours is already more than a full-time job.

However, it has become clear to me that we are all now engaged in a change of monumental proportions that will have broad social, political, and economic implications, greatly affecting our lives and times. In fact, it is my conviction that we are in the early years of a fundamental change in the way that our civilization works. Seemingly basic conventions and terminology such as customers, communities, culture, and even competitors will take on new meaning as we begin to come to grips with the truly borderless, twenty-four-hour world enabled by today's technology.

Having said that, I should also say that I've been around this business long enough to know that our industry has often forecasted far-reaching changes and advances that have never materialized. Expert systems, artificial intelligence, pen computing, social interfaces, the Apple Newton, and other projects all either totally or substantially failed, despite great initial promotion and enthusiasm.

Nevertheless, no one technology can possibly compare to the broad, order-of-magnitude significance of the networked world we are entering. To me, the potential of the World Wide Web is exciting, incredible, and a constant source of wonder. As Lotus's chief executive officer and (since Lotus's 1995 merger with IBM) a member of IBM's senior management team, I feel privileged to have a front-row seat at what I think is the best and longest-running show in town.

So, the question remains: Why invest the time and energy to add my perspective to your bookshelves? It's certainly not the monetary incentives; all proceeds from my efforts will be donated entirely to higher education. No, the reason is actually much more personal.

Like many industry CEOs, I do a lot of public speaking and talk to literally thousands of business professionals each year. Time, however, is always at a premium, and even with the breadth and frequency of these interactions, there has always been a degree of frustration that comes from the lack of opportunity to discuss the complete range of issues raised by today's information technology.

For me, this book is that opportunity. In my travels around the world, it has become clear that not everyone sees the significance of a world hurtling toward perhaps a billion networked computer users. And, of course, not everyone shares our insiders' zeal, excitement, and expectation. Logically, not everyone has to. However, the business implications—and, to a lesser degree, the personal ones—of missing out on or even arriving late to this great digital celebration spell serious disadvantage or, at the very least, important missed opportunities.

More specifically, my goal for this project is to convince readers—be they corporate executives, information technology (IT) professionals, or my many friends and colleagues within the IT industry itself—of the critical role that technology has already played in global business competition. More importantly, all that has happened so far is really just a warm-up act for the far greater changes to come. Rather than dwell on today's mind-numbingly complex range of technologies, I have chosen to focus directly on the business value of IT and its ever increasing impact on market leadership. In an industry full of many myths, misconceptions, and exaggerations, I hope to present an objective and realistic assessment.

Toward that end, I've enlisted David Moschella (among many other qualifications, a columnist regularly analyzing the IT industry) as a safety net for my own objectivity. This text has been a responsibility that, like most things in my life, I have taken very seriously. I was determined to avoid any specific product or company bias and not to let my own position, responsibilities, and industry relationships slant my opinions in any way not well supported. Like many things, this is easier said than done. David has been an ample ally in this attempt at objectivity—and in other regards. He made significant contributions.

I'd also like to mention Stephen Fenichell's contributions to the quality of the final work you hold in your hands. Steve's editorial scrutiny was clearly value added.

So, for you the reader, it's my hope this book will heighten your interest in this great new phenomenon that is reshaping our world, and that I
have succeeded in clarifying the importance, direction, and impact of the
many dramatic changes to come. Ideally, the topics I have selected will
excite and motivate you to get more involved in what will soon be the
largest of all industries. Our society is changing; we are participants in
and witnesses to a quantum leap in the way the world works and commu-
nicates. Welcome to it.

Jeff Papows

ACKNOWLEDGMENTS

Enterprise.com was an effort born of my desire to get out an important message with respect to the quantum leap in the way civilization will work in the network-centric and Web-based era we are now firmly engulfed in. Information technology will revolutionize all facets of business, from planning and strategy to manufacturing and from human resources to customer commerce and customer service.

Irrespective of my zeal to fully communicate the wealth of ideas, best practices, and prescriptions associated with these social, cultural, and economic changes, the putting together of this book was no small task. And just as relationships—business-to-business, company-to-company, supplier-to-customer, as well as those within the enterprise itself—will come to be increasingly important in the new era described in this book, so, too, were relationships an important part of getting this book to press and in your hands. There are a number of people I really do need to thank.

First, let me thank my family, who put up with the endless late nights and weekends when I wasn't available for other pursuits. As always they supported me in the intangible ways families do, despite the incredible demands my day job and career continue to place, and have always placed, on them. My agent, Owen Laster at William Morris Agency, did a tremendous job in educating, supporting, and representing me, and ultimately in selecting Perseus as publisher. I have grown to value and respect tremendously the people at Perseus, and I am thankful for the great advice and counsel that both Owen and the staff at Perseus have offered. My thanks also to Andy Grove for putting me in touch with Owen to begin with.

There were of course a good number of my direct staff at Lotus who at various points found an extra hour here and there to contribute to my efforts. My thanks for their help and, as always, for their never-wavering support. In particular, I would like to thank one individual at Lotus whose consistent support and encouragement were a catalyst both for taking on this effort in the first place and for the quality effort that resulted: Bryan Simmons, Lotus's vice president of corporate communications, is truly one of the most amazing people I've worked with in this industry. He is a study in both integrity and professionalism, and he is always there to offer encouragement to anyone pursuing his or her dreams. I should also thank John Thompson of IBM for his never-wavering support

So my thanks to all the amazing individuals delineated here and to the others too numerous to mention who one way and another made a contribution along the way.

Jeff

CHAPTER 1

THE NEXT WAVE

In the midst of our current wave of economic prosperity, it's difficult to recall the time, not so long ago, when the conventional wisdom maintained that the American free-market economic model was obsolete. The true beneficiaries of the global revolution in information and communications technology were said to be Asian-style partnerships of government and business set up along the lines of the *chaebols* of South Korea and the *kieretsu* of Japan.

Today, Asia is in turmoil while the United States, now in its sixth year of steady economic expansion, shows every sign of providing the new model for the global future. Unemployment is at its lowest level since the mid-1980s. Inflation, astonishingly, has remained in check. And, perhaps the best evidence of American competitiveness, there has been an unprecedented stock market expansion. Indeed, compared with the rest of the world—particularly, of course, Asia—the U.S. economic position has not looked this strong since the 1960s. To a degree almost unimaginable less than a decade ago, the American economy has become the envy of the world.

How do we explain America's extraordinary economic success of the past several years? No less an authority than U.S. Federal Reserve Board Chairman Alan Greenspan has publicly stated his conviction that the prolonged, heavy investment by American firms—as much as $2 trillion, by some estimates—in information technology (IT) is the main cause of the unprecedented combination of low inflation and high GDP growth that we are experiencing. The visible benefits of this investment are finally showing up on corporate balance sheets. A less obvious benefit, but an equally important one, I will argue, has been the internal, structural transformation of many enterprises and industries in response to the new advances in IT.

Absurd as it may seem today, not long ago American business was commonly blamed for being "shortsighted," "greedy," and "hollow." Fortune 500 multinational enterprises were widely considered the worst offenders—a collection of bloated behemoths and dinosaurs whose perverse penchant for restructuring, reengineering, and downsizing was denounced as exemplifying the worst excesses of an outmoded laissez-faire system.

American managers were widely regarded as being obsessed with Wall Street and with their companies' ever fluctuating stock market valuations. Their shortsighted fixation on quarterly profit forecasts and results led senior managers (so it was said) to spend too much time with investors and traders and, by implication, too little time with customers and partners. This checkered outlook was widely perceived to be the very antithesis of the broad vision that U.S. companies needed to compete with the juggernauts of Asia. The decline in U.S. spending on research and development seemed, at the same time, to provide persuasive quantitative evidence that corporate long-term prospects were being sacrificed for short-term gains.

Even the most globally successful American companies were often criticized for being too small or too "hollow," a critique typically accompanied by ominous warnings that our excessive reliance on offshore manufacturing in Asia and other places would soon come back to haunt us. This notion of "hollowness" extended far beyond manufacturing and was, in fact, most often used to describe America's ongoing evolution toward a service-oriented economy.

A popular wisecrack of the time captured the mood: If we all charged money for doing each other's laundry or watching each other's children, our economic growth figures would surge. For many reasons, high-value services such as entertainment, health care, and finance were disregarded while fast food, gas stations, and day care were emphasized.

Not only U.S. management took it on the chin. American workers were seen as increasingly falling behind the standards of the rest of the world. Here, the frequently deployed epithets were "unskilled," "spoiled," and "disloyal." There was certainly ample evidence for this view: In math, science, and literacy skills, Americans consistently ranked below other industrial countries. In view of the widespread predictions that our economy would be increasingly information driven, it was natural enough to assume that declining educational achievement would result in an increasingly noncompetitive workforce.

Today, the tables have turned. With the Dow Jones over and again hitting new all-time highs, while Asia sinks into turmoil, it has now become clear that a critical relationship exists between heavy U.S. investment in information technology and the global competitive resurgence of the United States.

According to some rough estimates recently published in *The Economist,* an amazing 42 percent of the investment capital base in the United States now goes into IT annually. Take a moment to absorb that remarkable statistic: *Nearly half of U.S. capital investment is now spent on enhancing information technology.* It might come as an equal shock that according to *Business Week*, fully 35 percent of growth in the U.S. GDP during the present recovery has been associated with growth in information technology.

That's a mind-numbing number. Take a quick breath, sit back, and consider its staggering social significance. Not since the golden age of railroads in the late 1880s and 1890s has one industry had such a profound impact on the entire national economy.

THE WEB AS ACCELERATOR

Since it arrived on the scene as a full-fledged cultural and social phenomenon in late 1994, the Internet and its graphical interface, the World Wide Web, have come to dominate virtually all conversations about the future of technology and, by extension, the future of business. It is safe to say that the World Wide Web is simultaneously overhyped and undervalued. Looking back—not very far back—the scope of today's information technology revolution is staggering. The accelerating speed of the evolution of hardware, software, and communications easily justifies the term "web years"—meaning cycles of change lasting three months at most, in contrast with traditional business cycles that typically lasted a year or more.

While major media coverage has, understandably, mostly focused on the Web's potential for transforming the consumer realm, the Web's real and as yet largely untold story is the great as yet unmined potential that lies in the realm of business-to-business applications and commerce.

Undoubtedly, the Web's increasing ubiquity will bring about significant shifts in the consumer sector. But over the next few years, business-to-

business commerce will substantially outgrow business-to-*consumer* activity on the Internet.

Over the past decade, information technology has become *a*, if not *the*, defining element in business itself. Once confined mainly to intracompany activities, computerized interactions now reach across business, social, political, and geographic boundaries, compelling new ways of working, communicating, and organizing activities in both the commercial and personal realms. The once arcane realm of information technology is drastically redefining all of our core competencies and helping to construct new visions for the future.

One of the most powerful concepts of the nineties has been the notion of an enterprise's "value chain." The value chain—an idea originated by Harvard Business School professor Michael Porter (the author of books on business competition and strategy, a former Lotus board member, and also my friend)—is the complex web of links between an organization and its suppliers, sales force, purchasing and distribution channels, clients, and customers.

As Michael has shown, businesses benefit from enhancing and integrating the links among and between the key players in their value chains, utilizing a technique called "value chain innovation." But once enterprises have learned to do this, What comes next? In the next century, the central repository of enterprise value will no longer be a *chain* but a *space*. This amorphous realm is what technologists have presciently dubbed the "marketspace."

The very notion of a value chain can be considered, from an evolutionary standpoint, the last vestige of the industrial era and the beginning of the postindustrial economy, with the Internet and the World Wide Web providing the catalyst for the next stage of enterprise evolution. The links in these chains are being rapidly broken up and replaced with a wider, broader, less orderly matrix of relationships, stretching far beyond the traditional boundaries of the enterprise—in fact, girdling the globe itself.

THE MARKET-FACING SYSTEM AND THE MARKET-FACING ENTERPRISE

The Web offers companies the opportunity to deliver either all or substantial portions of their business activities directly on line. However, successfully developing a market-facing system (MFS)—a component of information technology that creates a consumer experience defined by be-ing on line—requires an unprecedented blend of business knowledge and technical capability. The challenge of developing and properly imple-menting market-facing systems is likely to alter, if not entirely eliminate, many of the traditional lines between operational and information systems resources. Although a successful alignment of business and technology goals has long been considered a business necessity, the advent of MFS has meant that forward-looking, technology-enabled enterprises must move beyond *alignment* toward *integration,* creating a tremendous need for managerial and organizational innovation in order for these Web- and Net-based systems to attain their full potential.

Realizing the ultimate promise of business computing over the next decade will mean enhancing and integrating not only the links, sometimes still remote, between organizations and their customers, clients, suppliers, and partners, but also the links between the enterprise and the population at large. Most firms' key clients, customers, suppliers, and partners are apt to be located just about anywhere and everywhere in the world; this fact alone will compel a wholesale shift in organizational resources to an ex-ternal and market-facing focus.

The time will come—sooner rather than later—when an enterprise's primary connection to the outside world will be its World Wide Web site and its collaborative and messaging-reliant extensions. This new breed of organization—I'll call it the "market-facing enterprise" (MFE), with thanks to IBM senior strategist John Landry, who coined the term—will have radically evolved from the old industrial and early postindustrial style of business model into something entirely new and different.

Before any such radical transformation can be completed, however—and there is no reason to think that it will happen any time soon—the competitive implications of such a sea change in the global communica-tions and business environments are likely to outstrip any challenges that the information technology industry, or indeed private enterprise itself, will have faced up to by that time.

THE THREE WAVES

Without confronting the significant changes that information technology has recently wrought in the operations of large and small organizations, it's become nearly impossible to comprehend the roles that network computing, the Web, and Internet-based communications will play in redefining the modern enterprise. The information technology industry has rightly been accused of making many dramatic claims for business benefit. And the long anticipated, much discussed return on investment (ROI) has often failed to materialize. Nonetheless, we have seen a significant impact of one form or another through what I believe have been three distinct waves of change in our industry. Let's spend a minute getting a sense of these three waves, because the current wave is changing our lives.

Wave One: The Back Office (Automated Accountants)

The first wave, which lasted through the late 1960s and even the mid-1970s, was characterized by the then radical deployment of mainframe and minicomputers to automate and organize a wide range of back-office functions, including customer accounts, payroll accounts, and rudimentary database management.

During this "back-office" wave, computers served business as highly efficient calculators and record keepers—in short, automated accountants. To perform these essential and previously labor-intensive functions, the first generation of IT managers employed centralized mainframe computer systems and hierarchical database management systems to track inventories, compile human resource data, and perform other basic accounting and general ledger tasks.

Since many of these "legacy" systems automated manual tasks—and were employed almost exclusively for internal administration—their overall impact on a company's competitive position was relatively slight. Any enhancements in productivity that derived from this mode of office automation were largely ignored by senior management, whose decision-making processes remained almost entirely unaffected by the technological revolution taking place in the back office.

Wave Two: The Front Office (Knowledge Workers)

With the advent of the personal computer in the 1980s, however, computing leapt from the back to the front office, where it began to automate a large number of clerical white-collar tasks. This shift was still of minor concern to senior management—except insofar as eliminating and/or streamlining clerical functions helped the bottom line. However, during this second great wave of IT innovation, the foundations of today's "integrated enterprise"—heavily reliant on networking and "groupware" culture—were laid. This would later explode into the third and current wave of computing.

Once company-wide office computing was handled by so-called "client/server systems"—consisting mainly of interconnected local area networks (LAN), organization-wide electronic mail, and document management systems, as well as corporate and departmental database systems—the efficiencies attained and the reorganizations required by these systems began gradually, if inconspicuously, to alter the fundamental nature of work, and of organizations themselves.

Applications directed at so-called "knowledge workers"—successors of the old "white-collar workers"—tended to concentrate on personal productivity enhancement products such as word processing, spreadsheets, desktop publishing, and graphics presentation. It was, in fact, Lotus's own "1-2-3" spreadsheet that became the industry's first killer application, detonating the PC explosion that generated this second wave. At the same time, the business impact of office productivity was—self-deprecating as this may sound—a virtual drop in the bucket compared with the impact of the current and next (third) wave of computing.

While an individual knowledge worker's experience on the desktop might have been enhanced by the first and second wave of systems, it was not until the widespread deployment of electronic messaging (e-mail), voice mail, databases, and other forms of information infrastructure that these often controversial, often underappreciated IT investments bore fruit. These innovations prepared the way for the "$7 \times 24 \times 365$ enterprise": the seven-day-a-week, twenty-four-hour-a-day, 365-day-a-year corporation, which was obviously a major leap forward.

Wave Three: The Virtual Office (The Global Marketplace)

The rise and global spread of the Internet and the World Wide Web, beginning in 1994, launched the third wave of the information technology revolution—the virtual office wave. The Net and the Web (in combination with the newly enhanced networking capabilities of the integrated enterprise) have resulted in a quantum leap in the evolutionary pace of organizational change.

The Web and the Internet are accelerating the transformation of enterprises, both large and small, into globe-spanning market-facing enterprises, even as these same firms ceaselessly confront (whether they like it or not) the competitive realities of constant, universal access to the global marketplace.

KNOWLEDGE NODES

Like a movie star who is catapulted to fame and fortune by one big hit movie after a decade of laboring in obscurity, it was the huge success of the World Wide Web, the graphical interface for the Internet, that caused the Internet to explode into public consciousness.

Consider these four terms, today in constant use but either little known or nonexistent a few years ago: intranets, extranets, the Internet, and the World Wide Web (WWW). These four elements, which combine to form the cyberspace world, are all of immense strategic importance in defining the competitive position of companies today and tomorrow. Let's look at them more closely.

1. An *intranet* is a secure, internal network that employs the power of digital information technology to promote the sharing of information and knowledge among employees of a single company.

2. An *extranet* employs similar technology to reach beyond the walls of the corporation outward to external communities in order to link businesses with suppliers, customers, and other businesses.

3. The *Internet* is the public information highway, a vast network of interconnected computers. Originally developed by the U.S. government to protect military installations from nuclear attack, today it is open to anyone with access to a computer equipped with a modem.

4. The *World Wide Web*, the fastest growing entity on the Internet, was created in 1989 at the European Laboratory for Particle Physics to provide easy access to pages of information through "hypertext" links. These provide any computer linked to the Web with instant access to information published on any other computer on the Internet, whether it be down the hall or across the world.

It's critically important to recognize that each of these four "knowledge nodes"—intranets, extranets, the Internet, and the Web—is not a separate area of information technology but an integral component of the same great wave of the information technology revolution. All four are in con-

TABLE 1.1   Enterprise Solutions Framework

4. Extended Enterprise	Customer and Supplier Transactions	Marketing Communications	Ecosystem Development	Market-Facing Systems
3. Integrated Enterprise	Enterprise Data Systems and Apps.	Enterprise-wide Communication	Enterprise Knowledge Management	Enterprise Process Innovation
2. Automated Work Group	Workgroup Data Systems and Apps.	Workgroup Communication	Workgroup Collaboration	Workgroup Process Innovation
1. Empowered Individual	Data Creation Access and Usage	Information Access and Authoring	Training, Education and Expertise	Workflow Integration
	A. DATA	B. INFORMATION	C. KNOWLEDGE	D. WORK

stant collaboration (*not* competition) with each other. And the continual interaction among all these domains is rapidly creating today's and tomorrow's global cybermarket, or marketspace.

Whether their products are books, cars, PCs, financial services, health care, or travel, industries across the board have been forced to rapidly reinvent themselves to be able to survive and thrive in this brave new environment. Long-established and well-established value chains are being suddenly thrown into chaos and flux. Companies will need to compete and adapt, or wither away. The wealth of information being managed by today's information technology—whether the network be inter-, intra-, proprietary-, or Net- and Web-based—now ranges from raw data and simple text to in-depth expertise and complex workflow systems.

As a general rule, the most advanced enterprises are moving steadily upward and to the right within the framework shown in Table 1.1.

THE MARKETSPACE

To remain competitive in the cyberspace market—from now on, I'll call it the marketspace, as do some technologists—enterprises will need to maximize their organizational know-how. This will require a new culture of information *discovery, distribution,* and *application.* Establishing a culture of effective knowledge management (KM)—(see 3C on Table 1)—

goes to the heart of such issues as individual and management incentives, merit recognition and rewards, and job definition and description.

Knowledge management requires an entirely new level of workgroup and even company-wide cohesion. Collaboration, or rather collaborative technology, is the fundamental DNA, if you will, of knowledge management. Messaging is still the killer application of collaboration, so it's fair to say that knowledge management is messaging-centric. Nonetheless, knowledge management is about broader technology-enabled capabilities centered on three elements: creation, discovery, and distribution. Each of these elements is central to the successful implementation of knowledge management practice.

Over the next decade, the historically *internal* focus of most information systems will shift toward more of an *external*—market-facing—emphasis. But the cultural changes that this trend will impose on organizations and cultures are likely be at least as profound, challenging business and government leadership at nearly every organizational level to keep up with the new environment.

A growing need to work closely, cooperatively, and collaboratively with customers, suppliers, partners, and other allies will become the defining factor of enterprise innovation. Meeting this challenge will raise new challenges of trust, security, and openness, particularly when it comes to sharing intellectual capital and other forms of corporate know-how.

The corporate restructuring of the last decade is likely to have been merely a first stage—an opening salvo—signaling far greater changes to come. The critical need to effectively integrate information technology with more streamlined information flows will reshape the boundaries in many industry sectors.

Over the last decade, most companies focused on refining their specific value propositions, typically through restructuring or reengineering themselves into leaner, flatter, smarter organizations. But over the next decade, many of these strategies will need to be substantially updated. In the coming years, adaptability and flexibility are likely to replace restructuring as the core necessity in industry.

In the past decade, developing a robust *internal network* became a mission-critical infrastructure issue for most organizations. Although enhancing such internal capabilities will still be an indispensable requirement, over the next decade the development of an overall national and global information infrastructure will become an even more important factor than internal information system upgrading—due to the demands of rapid industry convergence. When the most important new network usages are external to the organization, companies will be increasingly dependent upon the capabilities of a public infrastructure likely to vary greatly by country.

Networks have powerful critical mass effects, in that the more people who use them, the more valuable they become. Thus, the value of any one company's technology investments is directly dependent upon those of the related information technology ecosystem they participate in externally. In other words, the broader use and ubiquity of the connections, the more powerful the benefits.

Even as companies have been compelled to redefine themselves and their core activities in the context of digital networks, whether they be *intranets* (internal corporate networks) or *extranets* (networks that reach beyond the traditional boundaries of the organization) a broader message has by now become clear: *What your company can do with technology is inseparable from what your customers, suppliers, and partners can do with technology.*

SOCIAL INTEGRATION

Over the last decade, individual companies more or less controlled their own technological destinies—which for all practical purposes meant that each could define its own strategy. But over the next ten years, as Web usage becomes ever more pervasive, companies will need to adapt their technology strategies to external, national, regional, and even global social norms. Transaction processing, taxation, privacy, security, and cross-border concerns will be only a few of the areas that will require clear and cohesive social and government support.

All these issues have one great theme in common: interdependency. Consider the following:

- Implementing *market-facing systems* requires a seamless merger of business and IT leadership.
- *Knowledge management* will demand that an organization reward and incentivize formalized sharing, and perhaps even penalize information hoarding.

- *Organizational collaboration* will see to it that no company will stand truly alone.
- *Industrial convergence* will create conditions where key capabilities for meeting the needs of one's clients and customers may lie outside a current industry's core capabilities.
- *Public infrastructure* requirements will mean that any one company's market-facing capacity may be only as good as the means that society provides for its competitors.
- *Critical mass* means that what you can do is dependent upon what everyone else can do.
- *Social integration* means that conducting business electronically will require new laws, customs, and procedures that no one company could ever hope to establish on its own.

In sum, if the previous era was primarily defined by individual company competencies and value creation, tomorrow's era will be defined by tapping into codependent cycles of improvement and evolution. So now the great question facing all of us is: *What do these momentous changes in business priorities mean for tomorrow's global business competition?*

THE GLOBAL PICTURE

Contrary to utopian claims heard in the media, as well as on the Internet, neither the Web nor the Net are likely to change the world overnight. Among many features of modern life not likely to be radically altered any time soon are the integrity of national borders and the pervasive power and influence of sovereign states.

Every day, up-and-coming universal technologies are touted as bringing about a "borderless" world. Even a truly and fully integrated global marketplace, however, will be forced to accommodate a rich diversity of national and regional laws and customs.

Personally, I don't consider this a terrible prospect. The Internet is, after all, only the latest link in a long chain of critical technology innovations—from the Industrial Revolution to the discovery of electricity to the more recent inventions of the automobile, the telephone, and television—that have exerted tremendous global impact without altering the fundamental divisions among nations and cultures. The nearly universal desire to maintain a diversity of commercial, governmental, and cultural institutions is, I'm convinced, not likely to evaporate, nor will these age-old distinctions be eroded any time soon.

In many key areas—security, encryption, taxation, censorship, ownership, and regulation are a few examples—the need for effective cooperation among local, state, national, and international governments will provide a critical challenge to the new and rapidly evolving breed of global, market-facing enterprises. Given the vast differences in expectations between the full-speed-ahead information technology industry and the more cautious, bureaucratic public sector, significant conflicts are not only likely but even desirable. In the ongoing give-and-take between public and private sectors and between regions and nation states, the much vaunted "localization" of the global marketplace is likely to occur. From my point of view, that localization will be a net plus for the planet.

More worrisome than any financial and/or political conflicts that may lie ahead are the deep divisions and schisms within the information technology industry itself. The technologies involved are so powerful and so pervasive, and the competitive stakes so unimaginably high, that IT vendors undoubtedly feel compelled to position themselves to maximize profits as best they can from the growing importance of their products and services.

Looking back, we were fortunate to have inherited today's universal Internet standards and protocols from government and university initiatives not concerned with generating profits. In contrast, even though IT industry efforts—UNIX is one example—often operated under the banner of open standards, they often resulted in frustratingly incompatible systems and disharmony all across the communications spectrum.

As an industry, our current challenge in the near term will be to combine the competitive drive and high levels of innovation in the IT industry with the Net's culture of open standards and "interoperability," that is, with the capacity for separate information systems and networks to seamlessly communicate with each other, regardless of proprietary nodes of protected knowledge. Given the "type A" personalities that drive our industry, myself included, this combination of competitiveness, innovation, and openness is not a given.

As with any period of major social, cultural, and technological change, significant shifts in competitive leadership are likely to occur over the next few years, even months. Just look back at what has happened in financial services, retailing, transportation, telecommunications, and most other major sectors over the past fifteen years! Is there any doubt that the next decade will be even more turbulent?

Future business leaders will undoubtedly use computers to create new businesses, transform existing ones, and restructure many of today's long-established industry practices. Just as the computer, telecommunications, and consumer electronic industries are rapidly converging (due to their shared digital foundation), so will a common cyberspace create new overlaps among the major non-IT sectors, including manufacturing and distribution, banking and financial services, wholesale and retail sales, publishing and media, entertainment, insurance, and health care.

As we enter this third, Web-enabled wave of IT innovation, "the virtual office wave," the list of new challenges to business is so long that it's possible to overlook the important role that nations and governments will play in the coming transformation. The IT industry will be compelled to accommodate and anticipate as never before the needs and desires of government entities and other industries—in particular, the telecommunications industry—in the construction of the infrastructure for this wired and wireless world. Here are some key questions that lie ahead on the road to a true global marketplace:

- Which countries will develop inexpensive, high-bandwidth systems?
- Which nations will provide or enable nearly universal citizen access?
- Which states will do the best job of updating existing bodies of law to accommodate new technological capabilities?
- Which states will have the most capable, creative, and enthusiastic citizens and entrepreneurs?

Over the next decade, the answers to these questions are likely to determine who will be the global leaders of tomorrow. Recent history has shown that technology leadership and global economic success are often inseparable, whether the players be nations or enterprises. Although it may take a decade or more (not that long, in my view) to fully resolve these questions, the Internet and the Web have already taught us the enormous benefits to be derived from early market leadership.

CHAPTER 2

THE NETWORK-CENTRIC
ERA AND THE
CHANGING WORKPLACE

In October 1991, a serious forest fire broke out on a thickly wooded series of hillside ridges in Oakland, California—a suburb of San Francisco. By the time the flames were extinguished, the fire had destroyed over 3,000 homes and closed a substantial portion of the community to the public. Oakland, in short, was a disaster area.

Among the first outsiders to enter such a disaster area—closely following the arrival of key emergency personnel—are usually the insurance adjusters. Within days of the Oakland fire's swath of devastation, a small team of programmers from the Fireman's Fund insurance company (a subsidiary of Allianz, the largest corporation in Germany) had set up shop in a local hotel to support their teams of adjusters. They commenced their mission by developing an impromptu collaborative software solution to the urgent problem of how to deal most expeditiously with what was likely to soon become a flood of emergency claims.

The morning after the fire, a local newspaper published a list of addresses—residential and commercial—that were going to have to be written off as total losses. The programmers took that list and mapped it, via a network-based system, to the company's "legacy" (preexisting mainframe-based) systems, thus enabling the company to determine which total losses had been insured by Fireman's Fund.

Armed with this timely information—which no rival company had as yet at its fingertips, digital or otherwise—Fireman's Fund officials were able to move quickly to "lock up" sufficient rental properties in the area. This enabled the company to immediately provide customers who had either lost their homes or were shut out of them with an updated list of available housing options. It also enabled the company to reach out to customers who had suffered substantial losses and to settle claims quickly and accurately.

During times of crisis like this, the true tenor of an organization is often projected to a public broader than its immediate community of customers. Impressed by the speed, efficiency, and innovation of the impromptu collaborative software solution that his traveling team of programmers had evolved in the field in a crisis situation, the then CIO (chief information officer) of Fireman's Fund, Virgil Pittman, embarked on a quest to enable his organization to enjoy comparable networking capabilities across its diverse lines of business.

Rival insurance companies had settled upon a strategy of achieving growth by acquiring other business. But Pittman decided that he could best contribute to the growth of Fireman's Fund's core business by developing state-of-the-art information technology to better manage the business they already had.

A study conducted under Pittman's guidance concluded that field underwriters spent 65 percent of their time manipulating data, and just 8 percent performing risk analysis—an activity at the core of the insurance business. Each of the Fund's thirty-eight offices, meanwhile, followed its own distinct set of processes and systems. And each had developed its own style of forms and correspondence, resulting in—to put it mildly—a certain degree of organizational confusion.

With no central repository of policy information to draw on, and with no knowledge of prior interactions with any given customers, underwriters were forced to go into the field to sell and manage policies. And with the exception of random personal connections, field operatives had no direct access to expert opinion on a wide range of policy options. What was the solution to this problem?

The collaborative network solution developed by Fireman's Fund—dubbed "COMPASS" for "Commercial Profit Acquisition and Support System"—automatically consolidates policy information while simultaneously performing many of the more labor-intensive aspects of the risk analysis process. Because the system can be readily accessed by every employee in the company, its benefits not only accrue to underwriters—its primary users—but also to claims adjusters, loss control specialists, and other knowledge workers.

Supported by a network-based redesign of its entire underwriting system, Fireman's Fund quickly achieved its growth targets without resorting to costly outside acquisitions. In two years, the volume of premiums underwritten rose from $1.5 billion to $2 billion.

The success of COMPASS vividly illustrates an adage recently coined by business consultant Michael Hammer, the intellectual "godfather" of enterprise-wide "reengineering": "The real point of reengineering," Hammer maintains, "is no longer so much about getting rid of people—it's about getting more out of the people you have." And the technological support for reengineering came, as it turned out, from an unlikely source: the evolving digital communications network.

THE DAWN OF GROUPWARE AND THE NETWORK-CENTRIC ERA

When Ray Ozzie, the visionary programmer who developed the Symphony suite of office products for Lotus, first conceived of collaborative network-based software in 1984, PCs had only just landed on a relatively small number of desktops in the United States, at least by today's ubiquitous standards. What made Ozzie's "Lotus Notes" so revolutionary was that Ozzie so vividly envisioned—and actively prepared for—the day when desktop-based computers would constantly "talk" to one another via a high-speed digital network.

This radical notion helped lay the groundwork for the second great wave of computing: the movement from the mainframe to the desktop PC, which coincided with the transition of stand-alone PCs and workstations to PCs linked by a network. Ozzie, who had helped to develop one of the first computer networks as a graduate student, was intrigued by the idea that if a group of PC-based workers in an organization could pool and share information, they could create a form of "collective intelligence" for the group, not to mention for the enterprise as a whole.

From a strict applications standpoint, "groupware" faced extraordinary challenges, not the least of which was that multitasking at the platform level (a prerequisite for even the most rudimentary PC-based network to function) was still not widely available. Microsoft's Windows 1.0 was just hitting the market, and multitasking—a key Windows feature—faced an uncertain future.

Without drawing too heavily on scarce Lotus resources, Mitch Kapor, Lotus's founder, supported Ray Ozzie's networking dream by founding an independent entity to develop the project. Ozzie dubbed this entity Iris— a name as floral as Lotus.

An irony not lost on anyone at Lotus was that their original "killer app" product—the 1–2–3 spreadsheet, first introduced in January 1983—had been widely credited with jump-starting the PC revolution in the first place. Ray Ozzie's dream (coupled with a wealth of other industry events, innovations, and catalysts) was destined to take the PC revolution to its next logical step: enhancing the personal productivity not only of individuals working in isolation, but of teams and groups working together and as a whole.

At a time when PCs existed as stand-alone, isolated "islands of intelligence," the notion of groupware was to some extent an attempt to address a growing problem that the PC revolution had inadvertently created: In too many organizations, too many disconnected knowledge workers remained locked in their offices and glued to their keyboards, staring at their individual screens, unable to easily or seamlessly exchange, coordinate, or replicate information without jumping through hoops and creating new channels.

LAN

The launch pad of the network era was the introduction of the so-called "file server" or "host" mainframe computer, connected to the local area network (LAN), which linked any number of "clients" (PC- or workstation-based) scattered on desktops throughout the enterprise. File servers permitted programs and data to be stored centrally and accessed by clients from their desktops.

During this preliminary phase of development, most network applications that required significant processing power—database query optimization, for example—typically resided on the server. A program for, let's say, graphics generation would ordinarily reside on the individual desktop PC. The basic problem with this configuration was that—like the PC itself—it enhanced personal productivity at the desktop but accomplished too little of value to the group, the team, or the enterprise as a whole.

Jim Manzi (who replaced Mitch Kapor in 1986 and who was at Lotus as CEO until June 1995) backed the development of Lotus Notes to the hilt, at a time when many skeptics within the organization remained unconvinced of its ultimate value. Where groupware was concerned, Manzi was a true believer, and he worked tirelessly and successfully to get Notes past the classic start-up phase of a business and into the anchor accounts that gave it the beachhead of its eventual success. Once Manzi grew the business near to this early goal, he recruited me to run the Notes division as a business unit—that is, to take the product to widespread commercial distribution and to create an industry around the first collaborative groupware product.

I joined Lotus in 1993, just as the then current version of Notes was slated to be shipped. Despite important progress at several Fortune 500 accounts, the Notes business was still something of an incubating infant. Notes revenue at that point was measured in the single-digit millions, as compared to the multibillion-dollar industry that groupware was to become six short years later, catalyzed by its defining and still central product—Notes.

My first challenge in my new capacity was to expand the market for this wonderful and powerful product—and create an enduring new product category—at a time when no one knew what it was or what it could do. In fact we struggled internally for a number of months just to come up with a concise elevator speech to describe the product and category. It was some time before we coined the term "groupware," or were able to effectively communicate what it was.

Despite the growing popularity of LANs, by the late 1980s a number of questions hovered over their successful implementation:

- How do we take full advantage of this more distributed form of intelligence?
- What sort of information would or should be transmitted over these networks?
- How should that information be properly processed and/or stored for future reference?
- How could all this collaboration and network-based interaction function in an increasingly disconnected, mobile world where lap-

tops and airplane seats were fast replacing the digitally connected desktop system?

The more a new breed of knowledge managers began to ponder these problems, the more it became clear that the nature of information, as well as the processes employed to manage it, would need to be fundamentally altered.

Mainframe Myopia

When I joined Lotus in 1993, my recent experience in the computer industry had been, to be blunt, a mixed bag. In the 1980s, I'd held a series of senior executive positions with Cullinet Software, the first U.S. software company to go public on the New York Stock Exchange. Not surprisingly, with software clearly embodying the wave of the future, the company received a sky-high stock market valuation following its much sought after initial public offering.

In many ways, Cullinet was the prototype for a successful software company start-up. But the company remained overly preoccupied with the speeds and feeds of its flagship product IDMS, a mainframe database management system. Despite the evidence of the strength and breadth of the PC revolution taking place in front of our noses, the company remained stubbornly convinced that big systems, big software, and direct sales to the Fortune 1000 were all that really mattered. Cullinet utterly ignored—to its peril—the small and medium-size business markets and the complex distribution channels that would eventually allow a "bottoms-up" approach to dominate the software industry. In short, Cullinet never got beyond blue suits and direct-touch selling.

Ultimately, this myopic market view (combined with the emergence of cheaper, simpler, client/server-based relational database technology) quickly unseated this once hugely successful market leader. Toward the end of my time there, I found myself involved, along with a few other principals, in a number of strenuous efforts to sell the company (which we ultimately did at a hefty shareholder premium).

The lesson I learned from this experience was that because of its narrow, short-term focus and its failure to confront the realities of the PC and the networked PC revolution, a once high-flying software icon had all too quickly become a footnote in IT history. My Cullinet experience was followed by a four-year tenure as president and chief operating officer of another publicly traded software company (Cognos Incorporated, a development tools company), where I enjoyed a very good run that culminated—after a number of years of solid financial performance—in a highly successful secondary stock offering. As I recall, the market capitalization of Cognos grew by some 400 percent during those years.

Lotus Notes, Object Stores, and Documents

My tenure at Lotus coincided with a critical time in the development of its second make-or-break venture. The Lotus 1–2–3 spreadsheet—which had become a huge success, a "killer app" in computer industry jargon—was beginning to run out of steam, just as Lotus was getting ready to ship Notes.

As competing products began to erode Lotus 1–2–3's once dominant market share, Lotus found itself embroiled in a full-fledged war with Microsoft in the market for so-called "office suites": comprehensive software solutions that combined spread sheets, word processing, presentation graphics, and personal databases. The war continues to this day, as Microsoft has grown to enjoy a dominant, nearly 90 percent share in the office suite market, with the remaining fraction divided between Lotus and Corel.

Back in 1990, the good news was that we had a fantastic product to ship: the then pending version of Notes. The bad news was that we had no well-developed market to ship it to. We desperately needed to find new sources and users who would grasp its value and help bring this powerful product—our second "killer app"—to realize even a modest percentage of its virtually unlimited potential.

When I arrived in 1993, it was clear that Lotus Notes was likely to be something of an acquired taste, and the first question we faced as a marketing team was, What *was* Notes? Quite frankly, answering that seemingly elementary question with any degree of precision proved to be as difficult as it had been, some years before, to explain the 1–2–3 spreadsheet to the first wave of knowledge workers. Notes was a product whose singular strength was its virtuosity and flexibility, which just happened to be precisely the same quirky characteristics that made it so difficult to categorize—hence the aforementioned struggle to invent the elevator speech.

In any event, it was Lotus's task to try to explain Notes to potential customers. One fundamental concept underlying Notes was, and remains, the *database* or, more accurately, the *object store*. A database is a repository of information, more often than not a collection of data stored in digital form as computer files—"notes"—that can be viewed and organized in a panoply of different styles, forms, and formats.

The Notes object store differed from the database management programs of the time by defining the *document,* as opposed to raw *data,* as its central currency. And it was a good deal more flexible. For the most part, Notes databases—like the digital hearts stored at the center of most networked or collaborative software solutions—reside on *servers:* high-performance systems—often UNIX or NT workstations, or even mainframes—equipped with substantial storage capacity.

Users or "clients" are "served" by these servers via the network—in most cases, a LAN. Clients working on their PCs can easily access the applications or object stores located on the server, while also maintaining their own personal copies of selected databases in the form of replicas stored on their personal hard drives.

Structured and Unstructured Systems

To put the network-centric era and the evolving process of groupware into a broader context, let's take a look at how information technology evolved from the early days of front-office automation, which ran roughly from the mid-1980s to the mid-1990s (see Table 2.1). This evolution can be characterized in part with reference to the difference between structured and unstructured systems, a difference that has much to do with the central currency of a system, be it data or document. In the first two waves of the IT evolution that I discussed in Chapter 1, the document emerged as the central currency of information systems. The current wave of information technology, however, is in part the result of a revolution in structured systems and has everything to do with data and advances in the way IT structures and processes information of this type.

Structured systems have been around longer than any other group of processes and systems outlined above, dating back to the dawn of IT history in the 1940s and 1950s, when data was laboriously encoded in primitive punch card systems in order to facilitate manual processing. As ad-

TABLE 2.1   Enterprise Computing, Circa 1987–1994

3. Integrated Enterprise	Enterprise Data Systems and Apps.	Enterprise-wide Communication		
2. Automated Workgroup	Workgroup Data Systems and Apps.	Workgroup Communication	Workgroup Collaboration	Workgroup Process Innovation
1. Empowered Individual	Data Creation Access and Usage	Information Access and Authoring	Training, Education, and Expertise	Workflow Integration
	A. DATA	B. INFORMATION	C. KNOWLEDGE	D. WORK

vances in technology and lower costs began to make *unstructured systems* more affordable, mainframe computers moved up the intelligence ladder from exclusively performing back-office functions—such as payroll, general ledger, and inventory—to the so-called "self-service" structured data systems of the mid-1980s. The most familiar of these systems are bank teller machines, stock trading systems, on-line medical records processing, retail point-of-sale systems, travel reservation systems, credit authorization services, general record processing, card-key-based security systems, credit card calling services, and automated ticket purchasing.

The key to the operation of virtually all *structured systems* was *database management software,* typically but not always *relational*. Indeed, *relational database technology* was the digital backbone that propelled the far-reaching reengineering of business processes that characterized the 1980s and early 1990s.

The ability of database management systems to enable more rapid access to vital business information became more widely appreciated as the notion of using a common information repository to drive an ever widening array of business functions began gradually to catch on (as reflected by the astronomical growth during this period of database companies such as Oracle, Informix, and Sybase). In fact, in the present era, proper database management strategies have become key enablers of a wide range of enterprise innovation. As emphasis has shifted toward making greater use of this captured information, we've witnessed the proliferation of "data warehouses" and even more specialized "data marts," which attempt to "mine" transaction data to derive broader business patterns and more targeted market and customer profiles.

Whereas the vast majority of *back-office systems* process *structured information*—because the primary thrust of just about any database management system is that data should be entered in a consistent way in order to facilitate future processing—*front-office systems* tend to deal with *unstructured* information, typically rendered in text or document form. Although computers can readily search, proofread, or reformat text and documents, they're not very good at analyzing, classifying, or otherwise adding value to unstructured information. In short, *unstructured text* is generally designed for human, not machine, use.

THE CHANGING NATURE OF WORK

The advent of groupware was destined to ultimately transform the very nature of work itself.

Mostly Structured Work

In most companies, *work* remains an inherently *structured* process—or at least it should. Organizations want and need work performed in a certain way, at certain times, with maximum predictability, manageability, and consistency. But highly structured systems are not always the most effective means of managing *all* work. In the end, most work is not "highly structured" but in fact turns out to be "mostly structured." The challenge for most organizations today is to effectively combine *structured data* with unstructured *information* and to produce an efficient and effective "mostly structured" work process. In fact, this efficient combination of structured data and unstructured information has been the unspoken goal of much of reengineering and restructuring of business processes that has taken place over the past decade. Consider, for example, the knowledge-empowered customer service representative who's been provided with complete access to all relevant customer records (structured data) along with the capacity to generate specialized streams of service value (unstructured information), whether that be a field service visit, a price quotation, or the registering of a customer complaint.

One thing e-mail and database management have in common is that they tend to require and facilitate substantial *organizational change.* In part the dynamics are simple and obvious. In these systems, information tends to flow more horizontally and less vertically. In other words, the ubiquity and informality of communication due to e-mail and collaboration changes the organizational culture as communication moves away from the traditional command-and-control or hierarchical model.

- Electronic mail enables the flattening of organizations and the breakup of rigid country-specific management structures.
- Effective database utilization likewise requires the strategic reorganization of functional barriers between *sales, marketing*, and *customer service* departments.

In both cases, substantial business and cultural changes are required before meaningful benefits can accrue. It's only a small stretch to claim that many organizations today are being reshaped from the bottom up to take advantage of the third great wave of rapidly evolving information technology: the integration of internal data networks (intranets) with the Internet and the World Wide Web.

Workgroups, On-Line Discussion, and Collective Intelligence

The first generation of collaborative network solutions fostered by groupware seamlessly supported the exchange of information among *workgroups*, physical or virtual, formal or informal. Typical applications included e-mail, electronic calendars, and on-line document repositories. Once employees learned how to share information on line among themselves, however, more innovative team members quickly discovered how to put this information into proper perspective and how to unleash the incredible power of networks.

The second stage in the evolution of networks was ushered in by team members who learned to leverage each other's once private expertise through on-line discussion groups. These informal, casual exchanges of information ultimately enabled everyone involved to engage in mutual discovery and decision-making via the connections on enterprise-wide *intranets*. These internal proprietary networks eventually evolved into digital repositories for an organization's *collective intelligence*: broad databases accessible to the enterprise as a whole.

Groupware-empowered departments learned how to make more effective group decisions. The old derisory term about a decision seeming as if it had been made "by a committee" rapidly went by the wayside, as a joint "networked decision" was frequently found to be superior to the old-style, top-down, command-and-control-based, hierarchical decision made unilaterally by a "superior" from on high.

Indeed, once the decision-making style evolved from "top-down" to "bottom-up," organizations as a whole discovered that some layers of management were expendable—hence the new, leaner, flatter, smarter organizations based on the more collaborative network model, as opposed to the more rigidly structured, old-style, hierarchical chain of command.

Workflow

Providing people with the capacity to vary and alter the decision-making process according to case and need quickly enhanced ordinary e-mail and turned it into a sophisticated tool for managing *workflow*—a concept at the core of many of the most successful reengineering efforts of the past and present. *The essence of workflow is the provision of electronic support for business processes previously accomplished by means of laborious manual procedures.*

A good example might be the hand transmittal of employment applications by an office messenger from one department to another. Such a labor-intensive system might be replaced in the new networking era by an "applicant tracking system" or ATS.

An ATS enables all of the paper-based personnel applications to be scanned into the group database so that human resource managers can review them as a group simultaneously or even comment jointly upon them, as they would in a meeting. This joint review is possible even if—and this is the truly nifty, not to mention enterprise-enabling aspect of workflow— all of those managers are scattered in different offices around the country or even around the world.

Suddenly, issues of time-zone synchronization and face-to-face contact become essentially irrelevant. Each person charged with making a decision instantly finds himself or herself on the same page, so to speak, although that "page" remains digital in form.

Learning Tools

In recent years, the literature of business management has been flooded with glowing testimonials to the urgency of converting sluggish behemoths—hog-tied by hierarchical bureaucracies, suffocating under a barrage of useless data, and confounded by mixed signals—into leaner, flatter, smarter "learning" organizations. Such converted organizations will be invigorated and rejuvenated by easy access to relevant and timely information from a wide range of internal and external sources and will be poised to embrace and implement change. Only in a genuine learning organization, many management experts agree, can genuine reengineering take root.

Such learning has been greatly facilitated by the most recent revolution in communications technologies. This revolution has witnessed services spring up like weeds in a meadow to meet the increasing need for richer, more timely knowledge. These services range from e-mail, voice mail, pagers, and cell phones to overnight delivery services such as Federal Express. And, more recently, e-mail itself has expanded to include various forms of task management, discussion groups, shared reference materials, file exchange, and other forms of electronic collaboration. In short, *unstructured information* has seen an unprecedented explosion in tools, usage, and volume.

Longer Work Weeks and Shorter Vacations?

For better or for worse, advances in information and communications technology have been largely responsible for what appears to be today's lengthening work week. Once it became possible to work effectively from the road, at home, or even while on vacation, the marketplace (especially in the United States) began to incorporate these capabilities into its everyday expectations. Checking for "can't wait" voice mails and e-mails during the family holiday has become an increasingly common feature of modern life.

In sharp contrast, however, to the popular depiction of this humdrum reality as a nasty intrusion on our personal and private space, I would argue that this isn't necessarily such a bad thing. The ability to check messages remotely can certainly intrude on one's personal life. But it can also extend or even enable our often too brief recreational time. In other words, at times it may be better to work occasionally while on vacation than not be on vacation at all.

THE CHANGING
NATURE OF MANAGEMENT

As work changes, so does management.

Four Dimensions of Change

Major improvements in management have been made along four dimensions: asynchronous communications, authentication, information dissemination, and mobility.

Both voice mail and e-mail provide what technologists refer to as *asynchronous communications:* Messages can be sent and received at any time, without any direct connection between sender and recipient. Beyond eliminating wasteful versions of what was once commonly called "telephone tag," asynchronous systems are now utterly essential for effective global communication across the world's twenty-four time zones; they are easily an order-of-magnitude improvement over their most direct predecessor: the fax machine. Asynchronous communication is also required for the twenty-four-hour organizational responsiveness that many industries must increasingly provide, virtually as a matter of course.

A less publicized but perhaps equally important aspect of both e-mail and voice mail is that they can be *saved.* They can therefore provide useful, permanent data histories and, if necessary, official *authentication*—a mission-critical application for brokerage houses, to take just one example. In addition, both voice mail and e-mail offer broadcasting capabilities, which facilitate rapid *information dissemination*.

E-mail and voice mail likewise contribute to *mobility*, since messages can be received and answered from virtually any time or place. Perhaps the greater boost to mobility has come from the widespread use of cell phones, pagers, and laptop computers. Many of us know that, armed with various combinations of voice mail, e-mail, cell phones, pagers, portable

PCs, and when necessary, the odd trip to Federal Express or Kinkos, we are capable of working productively almost regardless of time or place.

Not long ago, *Business Week* pegged the number of U.S.-based "lone eagles"—professionals who work virtually wherever they wish—at 10 million. Collaborative software solutions have enabled a good many of these 10 million "lone eagles" to fly—and to increase their efficiency without losing any of the benefits of face-to-face contact. As the Information Highway opens up and broadens its scope, that number is likely to climb higher.

Direct Reports and a Changing Management Philosophy

From a management perspective, more efficient communications systems have enabled the growth and superior firepower of today's flatter, leaner organizations. After all, what does a "flatter" organization really mean, other than that most managers have more direct reports? Companies with advanced e-mail cultures like to assume that important communications will be responded to within a maximum of twenty-four hours, regardless of time or location. Within truly global organizations, the positive effects of this change can be even more pronounced, as time-zone differences are actually leveraged into a competitive advantage.

Take, for instance, the fact that it's become the norm for executives in global organizations to expect that if you send a message at 5:00 P.M. from New York to Sydney, you will have a response waiting for you by the time you arrive back in the office the following morning. The efficiencies in this utilization of once worthless "downtime" are obvious.

Such quantum improvements in efficiency and responsiveness have become far more important since the pervasive use of word processing over the last ten years has led to a dramatic surge in the quantity of *unstructured, text-based information* landing on workers' and executives' desks—not to mention their digital desktops. This trend has occurred at a time when many businesses have drastically reduced and in some cases even eliminated any number of traditional forms of secretarial support. Here's a classic example of a *technology feedback loop*, in which information technology generates more information that requires even more technology to cope with it.

Having more direct reports implies greater communications requirements and often greater geographical dispersion. Like most of the readers of this book, I have grown accustomed to working in environments where a manager's direct reports are often in different locations, increasingly in different countries. Running companies on a global scale without today's communications tools would be entirely unimaginable. Case closed.

The international implications of improved communications technology have gone far beyond mere efficiency to affect the very nature of many companies' management philosophy. Traditionally, most global organizations used a country-by-country business structure. The primary reason for this structure, of course, was that this approach allowed for relatively simple reporting relationships and minimal international communications needs. The country manager communicated with headquarters, and everyone else communicated mostly in-country.

From a business or customer perspective, however, such nation-state-centered fiefdoms were often inefficient and ineffective. In many cases, the information employees needed to perform their daily tasks most effectively was not located within their country at all but in the heads—or privately maintained databases—of peers in some other part of the organization, as likely to be based halfway across the world as down the hall.

As communications technology has advanced, many companies—often painstakingly—have moved away from a country focus to a more global product line approach. This looser style of management requires extensive international communication for many country-based employees, something that would have been nearly impossible in the pre–e-mail era.

If we look ahead, we should see that, in addition to e-mail, text messaging systems can easily become the platform for far more advanced services. Lotus Notes, for example, applies a messaging foundation to task management, scheduling, workflow, and team collaboration, with all the benefits of asynchronous delivery and geographic independence. In fact, same-time or synchronous capabilities will be delivered in Release S, scheduled to ship in December 1998.

THE CHANGING NATURE OF BUSINESS

In the end, groupware and other network and collaborative software solutions have played an enormous role in enabling significant improvements in business processes and efficiencies. The greatest benefits have accrued in three critical areas: speed, efficiency, and innovation.

Speed

How many times over the past few years have you heard someone say that the *speed* of business is much faster than it used to be or, to use the more fashionable term, that *cycle times* are continually shrinking? I've heard this so much that I don't even pause to reflect anymore whether this proposition remains true. Why should today's businesses have to operate on ever faster cycles? And how do we know that they do? Surely business leaders of every generation feel that they are running faster than the leaders of the previous generation, and speed has always been an advantage. How sure are we that we can separate perception from reality?

There are, of course, a number of solid objective reasons why this sense of urgency seems to involve more than just our own selective perceptions. Around the world, *deregulation* has unarguably quickened the pace of change in once leisurely markets, such as banking, airlines, telecommunications, and many forms of health care. Similarly, *global competition* has increased the number of competitors in many markets, and increased competition is usually closely correlated with rapid rates of cyclical change. Just look at what happened when Japanese auto vendors started making big gains in the U.S. market! But perhaps the most pervasive reason that all industries are moving faster today has to do with *the imperatives of information technology* itself.

I can attest personally to the fact that product cycles in the IT industry are shorter and faster by a quantum measure than in just about every other industry. Very few software products can go more than a year, or at the most two, without significant upgrades. These frequent and often (we hope) dramatic improvements in product capability tend to encourage rapid customer adoption, lest others use the improved capabilities to get ahead.

Since information technology is deeply embedded in just about every business these days, rapid-fire technology cycles tend to accelerate non-technology business cycles as well. The effect only gets stronger as technology becomes more pervasive. Consider the role of IT as a key ingredient in any number of key competitive areas that have affected all of our daily lives:

- Financial services companies vying to be the first to roll out universal ATM access
- Telecommunications companies competing to offer personalized long-distance telephone discounts
- Auto companies striving to provide first dashboard, then dual, then side-impact airbags
- Computer hardware companies struggling to offer PCs using the latest Intel microprocessor at the lowest possible cost
- Airlines competing to offer ever new frequent flyer privileges and initiatives, from bank "affinity" cards to diners' and other discounts

In nearly every case, early market leadership was and will continue to be established by future-focused companies that invested aggressively in the burgeoning networked economy.

Speed is, of course, closely related to the wider issue of *responsiveness*. Businesses must continue to respond to changing opportunities, changing competition, changing technologies, and ever changing customer preferences. Moreover, as services compose a greater share of the economy and a greater part of just about all businesses, including manufacturing, rapid response times go straight to the heart of creating meaningful value and maintaining a competitive edge.

Efficiency

It's hard to think of a time when *efficiency* was not a mission-critical business factor. Businesses have always sought lower costs, and the most efficient firms have often been the most successful. But once again, today deregulation, globalization, and rapidly evolving information technology provide three extremely good reasons why quantum-leap improvements in operational efficiency have become more important than ever.

The essence of deregulation is, of course, to bring more competition to previously managed markets. Look at what happened to banks, airlines, and telecommunications firms that have been forced to compete instead of preside over cushy monopolies. All have gone through massive efforts to cut costs and improve service levels. As painful as much of this has been, in retrospect the United States was fortunate to go through many of these changes before most of its major economic rivals.

Globalization, I believe, has had at least as important an impact on the evolution of today's networked enterprises as deregulation. Today, most products and many services are essentially commodities that can be sourced from anywhere. Therefore, in the long term, only the most efficient firms will survive. This is true whether a business delivers television sets, personal computers, airline seats, telephone calls, groceries, or automobiles.

All of these industries are increasingly characterized by ever more intense price competition and battles for global market share in what IBM CEO Lou Gerstner likes to call the "the white knuckle business environment of the 1990s." As barriers to national markets fall, there are fewer places to hide. Fortunately, rapid advances in information technology have provided today's "white knuckle" global enterprises with huge improvements in operating efficiency and functionality. Historically, these great leaps of productivity have always been associated with the meaningful substitution of *machinery* for *labor*.

Today, although robotics and other manufacturing-related technologies remain important, the best analogy to the steam engine's replacement of manual labor during the last century would be the pervasive impact of information technology on nearly every aspect of commercial and industrial activity, from the acquisition of raw materials to the production of goods on the factory floor, to the maintenance of inventories of those goods, to the distribution and marketing of them down the value chain to the end user. The same efficiencies of scale, of course, have been provided to the "bit-based" service businesses—the purveyors of intellectual capital, such as research and entertainment—as to the "atom-based" enterprises—that is, those more traditional enterprises involved in the business of manufacturing concrete, physical products, as opposed to the bit-based, cyber-products of IT.

Innovation

The rapid introduction of new products and services remains on the top of just about any list of ways to maintain an organization's competitive advantage. Whether you're talking about minivans, direct-broadcast satellite TV, coffee kiosks, pharmaceuticals, exercise equipment, or no-load mutual funds, *innovation* is generally synonymous with profitability and industry leadership.

For an example of systems innovation, let's take a look at The Banker's Trust company in New York, where the paper chase had grown into a hydra-headed monster hobbling the workflow of many departments. Specifically, its domestic custody department—which manages the storage and keeps track of the ownership of securities—was drowning in reams of paper. On an average day, each of the twenty to thirty queries the department received was apt to trigger a cumbersome research process that often tied down a slew of administrators, generated thousands of pages of paper, and ate up hundreds of employee man-hours. Customers typically were forced to wait a week or more for answers to even the most routine questions.

After installing a network-based collaborative software system at the bank, same-day replies quickly qualified as a worst-case scenario. Most customers received answers within minutes. According to Global Assets Vice President Roger Porcella, the replacement of dumb terminals, a microfiche system, and reams of paper-based forms and reports with a "case files" system saved his department "thousands of research hours and eliminated the need to print 50,000 report pages a day."

THE CHANGING NATURE OF CORPORATIONS

Within a remarkably short period of time collaborative software solutions have redefined and redrawn the nature of traditional corporate boundaries. Subtle shifts in the status and relationships of the people within these rapidly evolving business organizations are occurring at every level of nearly every future-focused enterprise.

The greatest success of the network era has been the transformation of *data* into useful *information*, and *information* into even more useful *knowledge*. During this process, the impact of the ongoing IT revolution has moved steadily up an increasingly rejiggered corporate ladder. In many enterprises, knowledge workers have discovered that groupware provides more than merely a means to move beyond e-mail to what someone once disparagingly called "glorified e-mail."

Networking brings to the desktop a communications and computer experience that is simultaneously richer, deeper, and—in a word—more fun. An enormous amount of drudgery has been eliminated at the proverbial push of a button, even as the time, effort, and headaches saved have meant that most companies' ROI (return on investment) for installing these systems can be measured in the triple and even quadruple digits. On a more subtle level, long-delayed (and in some quarters, much feared) structural shifts also have been provided, with indispensable technological support.

The transition from the back to the front office was a first critical stage in this process. From the individual desktop PC to the network-empowered and enhanced PC was an equally critical second stage. Most importantly, the advent of the network-centric era paved the way for the development of the integrated enterprise.

This enterprise is the organizational structure—or one might say the relative *lack* of organizational structure—best suited to the challenges we face today.

CHAPTER 3

THE WEB:
FORGER OF
THE NEW IT ECONOMICS

PEOPLE EVEN REMOTELY FAMILIAR WITH THE HISTORY of the computer industry tend to be familiar with Moore's Law—defined by Intel cofounder Gordon Moore at the dawn of the digital era: Semiconductor density will double every eighteen to twenty-four months, thereby enabling each new generation of computers to provide double the processing power of their predecessors, even as product cycles shrink toward the blink of an eye. Those who don't know this law, no doubt benefit from it.

Remarkably, this law still holds true today and is expected by most technologists to remain relevant for at least another decade. The extent of the sway of Moore's Law remains the primary reason that quantum leaps in the advances of both value and efficiency in the information technology industry have given rise to a unique situation in our technological history. As some industry observers have noted wryly, if the automotive industry had paralleled those same advances in value and efficiency, the cars we drive today would cost about five dollars, and we'd be getting close to 250,000 miles to the gallon.

METCALFE'S LAW

The effects of Moore's Law on the growth of the IT industry and the spread of computing cannot, of course, be understated. But since the arrival of the Web and the Internet on the digital scene, a lesser known but potentially more profound and pervasive law is rapidly replacing Moore's Law in influence and preeminence in the network-centric, Web-based era.

Metcalfe's Law—named after Bob Metcalfe, inventor of Ethernet and founder of 3Com—states that *the cost of a network expands linearly with increases in network size, but the value of a network increases exponentially.*

The implications of this law are at least as profound as those of Moore's Law. According to Metcalfe's Law, as networks expand toward infinity, they become dramatically more useful and cost-effective. In practical terms, this means that Web sites, discussion databases, on-line services, and team rooms can attain the level of success and density (the *critical mass*) required to capture a market, even as the cost to service these networks decreases to virtually zero. Indeed, the importance of critical mass for the success of Internet sites is becoming increasingly clear, something the relatively new term "Internet portal" attempts to capture. In essence, the term refers to the emerging value of Internet sites as a form of brand. There are at least a dozen sites that fit this description today, including Netscape and, as a by-product of such emerging value, Amazon.com. Indeed, as the number of users connected to the Internet moves rapidly toward *one billion*—from an estimated 100-million-plus connected users today—such critical mass effects will become the Web's dominant dynamic. And the power of this Web dynamic will inevitably redefine the dynamics of the future.

UNDERSTANDING THE NETWORK-CENTRIC, WEB-BASED PARADIGM SHIFT

A new economics of the *network* has replaced the old economics of *silicon chips* as the principal driver not merely of the IT industry but of industry itself. In many ways, a basic Internet browser symbolizes much of the change taking place in this new era. All Internet browsers, regardless of make or brand, are designed to look *out* toward the network and out toward the world, in contrast to the way that Microsoft Windows once looked only *into* an individual PC.

More than anything else, this relentlessly *external* orientation provides the stable foundation of our network-centric, Web-based era, as the Web browser increasingly becomes the universal interface and conduit to new and existing digital applications. Perhaps even more critically, the browser, when and if used effectively, masks the identity of just about all other underlying hardware, rendering the inner workings of the Net effectively invisible.

For a time, distinctions in quality and user experience between browsers themselves were less than obvious. Even now, with two relevant products in the category—Netscape Navigator and Microsoft's Internet Explorer— the brand of the browser itself is still not a definer of the on-line experience.

As an indication of the shift toward a network-centric, Web-based paradigm, consider some changes in language alone. In the late 1980s, most IT discussion, on the part of both consumers and manufacturers, was about PC hardware, PC software, PC LANs, and PC/mainframe communications. Today, the dominant phrases begin with the use of "Internet" or "Web": Internet access, Internet pricing, Internet stocks, Web servers, Web sites, Web design, Web marketing, Web applications, Web commerce. Within only a few years, we've all undergone a seismic shift in IT industry mind share and perspective. And as the IT business has become ever more network dominated, businesses as a whole (indeed the world as a whole) have eagerly and compulsively followed suit. They've had little choice—the sheer depth of the paradigm shift has demanded it. Still, even the most network-savvy of enterprise thinkers must continue to ponder (and answer) the following four questions:

1. Why is there so much consumer and business interest in the Web?
2. How will the Web begin to change the nature of business communications?
3. What new economic dynamics are associated with these changes?
4. What new technologies will enable all of these changes to take place?

From Intel Hardware to Network Software

In the PC era, technology use tended to follow Intel's lead, and the introductions of the 286, 386, 486, and Pentium chips all became major industry events. I can tell you from firsthand contact and experience with everyone at Intel, from Andy Grove—the CEO—on down to many of his senior executives, that this is one company that has earned its place in the IT history books and that remains very much at the pointed end of the race onward. IBM also continues to innovate in this regard and like much of our industry enjoys a complex but productive and important relationship with Intel.

Nonetheless, in the new network era, although Intel chips will remain key hardware components, they will no longer be *the* critical technological enabler. Not only have scrappy new players such as National Semiconductor and Advanced Micro Devices arisen to challenge Intel's once impregnable dominance at the low end of the PC spectrum, but the PC market's rapid shift toward lower-end clients has fundamentally altered the strategic balance for the digital chip industry as a whole.

Consumer discussions of future Intel chips were pervasive during the PC era. But consider, if you will, how increasingly commonplace it has become for even relatively sophisticated users to not know (or care) what kind of microprocessor lies buried deep inside their machine. Even today's hot-button issue of *consumer bandwidth* (where a prevailing lack of communications capacity clearly limits the scope and quality of available services) is from a strictly business perspective hardly relevant or urgent, even though the issue is much bandied about in office corridors and in the media. For most business users, the real network issues are less about *bandwidth* and more about *network software*: applications, management, and reliability.

The World According to WORA and Java

Although the PC revolution enabled major advances in system interoperability, incompatible technologies remain a major and vexing feature of today's IT industry landscape. Fortunately, the Internet has improved interoperability by at least an order of magnitude. Today, most Internet surfers haven't the faintest idea (or for that matter the slightest concern) about what sort of servers run various Web sites. Nor do any of us generally need to worry about what sort of e-mail systems anyone else is using. This style of *transparent interoperability* (the fortunate legacy of Internet and Web universal standards) will prove critical to the rapid-fire development and deployment of many more complex electronic commerce and extranet initiatives.

The ability of software programs to run regardless of the underlying hardware platform is widely referred to as "Write Once Run Anywhere," or WORA. But the existence of a handy acronym by no means guarantees that the wonderful world of WORA is definitely, or even close, at hand. Although the ubiquity of the Web and the Net is by force of momentum clearly moving the IT industry in the right direction, long-term interoperability is still not assured.

For example, once Web applications begin to require access to both legacy (preexisting, mostly mainframe-based) databases and more complex application services serious incompatibilities could resurface in a number of key areas. For this reason, the Java programming language and the CORBA object model today provide our best hope for extending and ensuring interoperability to all manner of legacy systems, as well as to new "smart" devices such as TVs, phones, cars, and even chip-enabled household appliances.

Java is, in my opinion, the last great application renaissance in our industry, brought to you compliments of Sun Microsystems, whose chairman, Scott McNealy, and I have shared over the years more than a few burgers at various Hard Rock Cafes (his cuisine and venue of choice). Based on our discussions, I think it safe to say that Java has brought us nothing less than the last great standards debate of the Web enabled era— a debate that rages on as Java's success lessens Microsoft's grip on the centrality of Application Program Interfaces and Windows in the IT industry.

So what is Java? Apart from being an ancient kingdom in what is now Indonesia, or a slang term for a cup of coffee, Java is a programming language created in 1991 by Sun programmer James Gosling and his associates. Originally called Oak, after a tree that Gosling could see outside his office window, Java was born, oddly enough, as part of an effort to produce a consumer-oriented home control unit that would be able to run a "smart house" by performing tasks such as turning on the coffee machine in the morning and operating the home VCR. That device never saw the light of day, but as the Internet and the World Wide Web took off, Java jumped into the turbulent fray like a Mexican coffee bean.

From a technical standpoint, Java permits programmers to write applications in chunks of code called "objects." Though object-oriented programming has been a fixture on the digital scene since the early 1970s, Java was one of the first "object-oriented" programming languages to use chunks of code—commonly called "applets"—as a way to download a program in parts.

Java's main product differentiator is that applications or programs written in Java script can run on any sort of operating system or platform, including Windows, MAC, or UNIX. The key to all this is a device called the Java Virtual Machine (JVM), which sits on a user's computer and can order up bits of software either from the Net or from other computers to which it's linked on a network. It's a much more versatile method of running computers than the old style, in which all the computer code was specific to a particular chip.

Java is *the* programming language for our network-centric, Web-based era. It promises true interoperability on multiple levels and is uniquely suitable for transforming all sorts of mundane personal appliances into more sophisticated communications machines. A cell phone and pager system running on Java can use the Web as its main network, deriving much of its processing power for specific applications from the Web itself. One of Scott McNealy's favorite Java applications (as yet undeveloped) is a nifty little digital device called "The Java Ring." This ring would contain an embedded chip that would store your own authenticated user ID. One wave of the magic ring before any networked PC with Web access and you could gain secure access to ATMs, Web pages, personal e-mail, or other encrypted files.

The Digital Dial Tone, E-Commerce, and Virtual Communities

Up until the very recent past, most devices accessed network resources only when needed. But with the Internet, and with devices like the Java Ring on the horizon, we're rapidly moving into a world where network-connected devices are always on, always connected, always right there with a digital dial tone. This seemingly simple and commonplace (even banal) fact will have enormous implications on such potentially high-growth areas as "push" technology, collaborative computing, and real-time communications.

It won't be long before shutting off the network connection will become as unnecessary and as inefficient as constantly turning a PC on and off or, perhaps more tellingly, as silly as unplugging a telephone when not in use.

As the digital dial tone of the network-centric, Web-based era takes over, the historical emphasis upon improving *internal* efficiencies through *internal* automation systems will shift toward a more *external* focus. Future priorities for sales, marketing, service, order processing, and other key applications will increasingly involve direct connections to customers, suppliers, and other important parties. Current security issues will be overcome, and electronic commerce will emerge as one of the core applications of the Internet.

Electronic commerce offers radically new methods for marketing, selling, and delivering goods and services. The Web enables a company's technology systems to directly interface with any and all customers, regardless of time or location, potentially eliminating many face-to-face and telephone-based intermediaries. Examples within the IT industry include increasingly popular on-line software downloads, as well as the successful Web-based hardware sales of both Dell and Cisco. More importantly, this on-line business model is also spreading through many other sectors of the economy and impacting the sale of things such as books, automobiles, and travel and financial services.

One of the greatest benefits of the PC era was its empowerment of individuals and, eventually, of small groups of people within a single enterprise. PCs provided unprecedentedly powerful tools and capabilities at affordable prices. This trend will surely continue. However, the main contribution of the network era in this realm will be to eliminate *time, distance*, and *organizational barriers* between people. This erasure and removal of traditional corporate boundaries will inevitably lead to the establishment of countless *virtual communities:* groups, teams, and individuals with common interests, goals, and/or needs, both within and between organizations. Over time, the influence of these virtual communities in business, the arts, sciences, politics, religion, and other key societal domains will prove profound.

Taken together, the new network era's emphasis on *bandwidth, critical mass, system interoperability, direct customer connections, electronic commerce,* and the development of *virtual communities* will provide the underpinnings for an IT universe substantially different from its predecessor, which was defined by *microprocessors, LANs,* and *individual/*

group productivity. In combination, these new network imperatives mean substantial network change, whereas taken individually some are more noteworthy than others. As I noted earlier, for example, bandwidth by itself is almost irrelevant from a business perspective, but in conjunction with these other elements it is an important aspect of the IT future: Indeed, the sum of the parts is greater than the parts themselves.

THE NEW ECONOMICS

Today's robust U.S. economy and the Web's multifaceted IT paradigm shift have led many people to speculate about whether we are now entering a new and prolonged period of economic prosperity where the old rules and trade-offs are no longer operative. Indeed, the phrase "The Long Boom" (coined by corporate consultant Peter Schwartz) has entered the popular lexicon as a touchstone for the highly appealing notion that we are entering a period of sustained economic growth and global prosperity unlike anything the world has seen (or foreseen) to date.

Traditional economists frequently scoff at the notion that any new technology is going to cause an abrupt change in the old rules of capitalism, whereas those with Web fervor often take it as gospel that the Web can in fact change just about everything. Although I have no intention of taking a leap down the slippery slope of predicting the precise future of the global economy, I think it's important for all of us to recognize that the Internet is already causing some powerful and relatively rare economic dynamics that may well prove critical to business, regardless of whether the global economy is entering a period of prolonged acceleration.

The following, seemingly simple, example illustrates one reason some of the old pre-Web and pre-digital economic models seem ripe for revision: Take two competing companies, each with ten workers. Suppose a new technology enables both companies to make their products *twice* as capable but for the *same* cost. Now, classical and even neoclassical economists would say that no improvement in productivity and no economic growth has occurred. Why? Because the *same* ten people built the *same* type of product for the *same* cost—hence you cannot find any real productivity gain? In other words, classical economic models cannot account for the impact this kind of technological advance has on the economy.

But consider this same example from a strictly practical, strictly competitive business perspective. Ignore for the moment, the economic models and just look at the fact that the failure of *either* company to adopt this latest technology would be equivalent to *competitive suicide*. The lesson in this case is quite simple: Computers can be a matter of economic survival, even if traditional economic models prove incapable of measuring their effects on the economy. This fundamental difference in perspective is perhaps the main reason why technologists and economists often appear to be talking past one another.

THE THREE MASSES OF THE WEB

The advent of the Web promises quantum-level leaps in three major critical business areas: critical mass, mass customization, and mass communication.

Critical Mass

Since software and networks are the driving technological forces on the Web, it is not surprising that the source of the Web's economic power derives from the unique attributes of both technologies. Figure 3.1 shows the underlying economics of both software and networks. The key curves in the diagram lie at the very heart of the Internet's staggering power and momentum.

Software and information (and indeed anything that can be represented in terms of *bits*) have one essential aspect in common: *Whatever it costs to make the first copy, be it $1,000, $1 million, or $1 billion, the cost of the second copy is virtually nothing*. Whether you're talking about a CD-ROM, a tape, a floppy disk, or a simple Internet download, copies are potentially valuable commodities that cost almost nothing to produce. The average cost of any bit-based product falls exponentially with volume and eventually falls to naught.

Now in any business—whether it be "atom-" or "bit-" based—volume plays a critical if not decisive role in determining costs. Although many physical products have important economies of scale, the scale in question is rarely if ever exponential in nature. At some point, it inevitably levels off.

Network costs, however, do remain *relatively linear* with volume. The cost of adding one more person to a network does not fundamentally grow or shrink as the size of the network increases or decreases. As with telephones and facsimile machines, the value of a Web or Internet network

FIGURE 3.1   Software and Network Economics

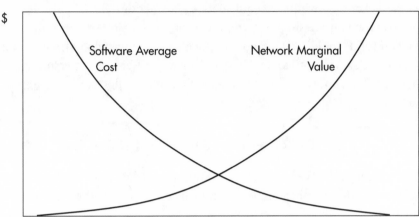

expands exponentially according to the growing number of users attached to it—Metcalfe's Law at work again. Consider, for example that a telephone system connected to ten homes is worth far more than ten times a system connected to only one home. At the same time that the *value* of networks goes up rapidly with *volume*, the average *costs* of the software and information on the network fall steadily (see Figure 3.1). This ever widening gap between *costs* and *value* symbolizes the unprecedented enormity of today's opportunity.

Why do I say *unprecedented?* Consider that in the past, the telephone industry enjoyed *network* economics but not *software economics*. In other words, the telephone industry and other bit-based businesses have always operated within an economy of scale that allowed for zero marginal *costs;* but until the Web arrived, these businesses were unable to exploit the marginal *value* of their markets because they could not attain the volume (critical mass) required for success. But with the Web, network economics and software economics have powerfully converged, and this combination has given rise to the Web's single most dominant dynamic: *critical mass.*

One can go even a step further and say that the *conceptual point* where the two curves in Figure 3.1 cross represents *the required critical mass for any Internet technology*. Once a product or service gets to the *right* of this point, a period of *increasing returns* begins. (Any point to the *left* obviously suffers from relatively *high costs* and relatively *low value*.) Internet scale economies can therefore generate virtually *infinite returns*, which means that the sheer size of an enterprise will tend to mean less in the cyberspace world than in the strictly physical, Newtonian world of the recent past, where economies of scale dictated that increased value and decreased cost required increased size.

As more and more businesses become predominantly cyber-based, these underlying economic issues are bound to exert critical effects on the direction and scope of such enterprises. This is why efforts to reach *critical mass* have defined the early years of Web competition. This phenomenon has been most noticeable on the IT vendor side of the industry—with companies going all out to establish clear leadership positions. But the importance of early leadership will steadily come to characterize widespread business use of the Web itself.

Consider one deceptively simple fact: Once your Web site is built, the marginal costs of serving additional users will tend to fall toward *zero*. This is utterly unlike any traditional physical sales, marketing, or customer service experience. To repeat (and repeat) my main point: These powerful effects of critical mass will reinforce a Web-based business dynamic in which the *strong* will only get *stronger.*

Mass Customization

Historically (and in particular before the modern use of IT), it was considered a truism that a trade-off always existed between *product volume* and *product customization*. It was generally assumed that customers would need to pay a premium, often a high one, for any customized features or services. Standard products were sold directly or through channels, and additional services were contracted for separately. This was the dominant model for most manufacturing and even most service industries.

But that model no longer holds true. Figure 3.2 depicts two curves that will look strikingly similar to those in Figure 3.1. This time, however, the diagram represents the changing relationship between *customization* and *volume*. Beginning with database technology, and steadily accelerating through the ever more capable Web, this relationship is being steadily

FIGURE 3.2   The Economics of Mass Customization

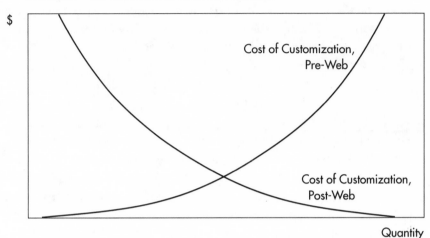

inverted. Database technology has drastically reduced the costs of customization in many industries. It costs *virtually nothing* to adapt travel itineraries to include flying preferences, hotel choices, car rental agreements, and other membership programs. Similarly, it costs Dell Computer practically nothing to configure a personal computer precisely to each customer's hardware and software specifications.

In fact, contrary to conventional business patterns, since much of this customization is *information based*, customization becomes easier and more efficient with rising volumes, as initial development and systemization efforts and costs become increasingly amortized over many more units. Similarly, essentially free customization provides the effect of *increasing demand for a given product,* since the products themselves meet user needs more directly. Consequently, individual customization actually becomes synergistic with mass market volumes—hence the phrase "mass customization." Let me provide an example.

The Levi Strauss Corporation some years ago partnered with Custom Clothing Technology (a start-up that it eventually acquired) to produce custom-fit clothes for women. A clerk at a Levi store would take several measurements, enter them into a networked database using a touch screen, and from there the data would be forwarded to CAD-cut, a computer-aided fabric-cutting operation. CAD-cut would in turn send the custom-cut pieces of denim to a Levi plant in Tennessee to be washed and stitched. Within two weeks, the customer would receive a customized pair of jeans for a $15 premium over the price of an off-the-rack pair of jeans.

Because of its oddity, this pilot program generated considerable interest at the time, but it could well become the norm—instead of the exception—for jeans buying in a network-centric, Web-based world, in which case the cost of customization could be amortized over the virtually infinite number of potential buyers for computer-custom-cut jeans, eliminating the $15 premium.

With *critical mass* we witnessed the blending of two unique sets of economic attributes: initial *network costs* and the costs of producing copies, or *product replication* costs. With *mass customization*, two formerly contradictory concepts—cutting costs and increasing customization—become fused into a powerful new business model. (Mass customization is, of course, closely tied with what is often called "one-to-one" marketing, but it relates to many other aspects of the business value chain as well.) In the end, mass customization is about boiling down routines and procedures into software-driven processes that can be amortized over a large number of transactions or customers.

Mass Communications

In the era before computers, information was almost always contained in some sort of limited physical package. This being so, there were often important trade-offs between the *amount* of information provided and the *costs* of physically distributing it. Figure 3.3, once again, looks very similar to Figure 3.2—and in fact to Figure 3.1. But this diagram helps, I hope, to schematize the relationship between communications *depth* and communications *breadth*. As with mass customization, you'll see a pattern where two attributes that have historically been at odds come together under the new Web-based paradigm.

One of the classical examples from the first wave of mass communications is television advertising. Particularly during the network era (and here I am, of course, speaking of television networks), television advertising tended to be both *broad* and *shallow*, whereas direct mail was often *narrow* but *deep*. Even with the rise of cable-based "narrow casting" and

FIGURE 3.3   The Economics of Mass Communications

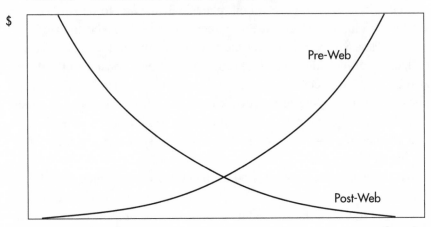

the growing numbers of special-interest print publications, this general pattern has tended to hold true, whether the product is newspapers, magazines, marketing materials, service manuals, or research and reference reports.

But with the Web, the marginal costs of both *storing* information and of *transmitting* it are effectively reduced to zero. So we now no longer need to think in terms of the *trade-offs* between *volume* and *depth* because, lo and behold, with the Web we can have *both*.

As was the case with mass customization, with the new combination of high volume, deep mass communications, there's a positive feedback cycle: *The more depth provided, the greater the volume of use. The more volume of use, the more depth required.* This positive feedback cycle becomes even more obvious—and powerful—when the *consumers* of information also become *producers* of information, as is the case with so many Web environments that incorporate community-created content.

The ability to provide both information depth and volume cost-effectively will transform the balance of power in many industries. Since information is so often directly related to power, the need to limit the volume of information provided has evolved into an important control mechanism, particularly in many inter- and intracompany dealings, as well as in most relationships with consumers. But as we move farther and farther into a cyber-based world where *most* information is available to *most* people, this traditional method of control is likely to significantly erode.

Consider, for example, the highly secretive and highly competitive world of *securities analysis*. In the past, a great deal of superb Wall Street research was reserved for the consumption of major customers, who paid a high premium to obtain it and who based the value of their relationships with securities firms largely on the quality—and the strictly controlled availability—of this research. In fact, the difference between success and failure in the world of finance often depended on the quality of such research, on its private provision as far "ahead of the curve" as possible, and on the skill with which a relatively small pool of consumers of such information put it to use.

Today, with the emergence of a large and ever growing number of on-line securities sites, we are soon likely to see even the best Wall Street analysis become widely and even freely available over the Web—provided either at no cost to the public at large or to certain types of active customers at a minimal cost in exchange for maintaining a valuable relationship. The need to limit availability of what was once proprietary knowledge will likely fade away. The automobile, insurance, and health care industries (to name a few) are the most likely to be significantly affected by this dynamic.

This capability to provide maximum depth *and* maximum volume will unalterably redefine the dynamics of information distribution as we know it today. Information providers (and increasingly, in the Information Age, every company has either become or is quickly becoming an information provider in some form) will no longer need to spend so much time worrying about printing and postage restrictions. Instead, content providers will be free to focus on providing *all* the information that their customers actually need.

UNDERSTANDING
THE TECHNOLOGY DRIVERS

Just about all of the technologies emerging on the Internet are designed to sit on top of today's already enormous investments in systems, servers, software, and networks. Table 3.1 provides a broad look at some of these new technologies.

TABLE 3.1   Representative Areas of Technology Innovation

Hardware	Software		Communications
Cameras/Sensors	Affinity Identification	Distributed Authoring	Cable Modems
Digital Versatile Disks	Agent Software	Encryption	DSL Adapters
Mobile Devices	Audio/Video	Java Applets	Smart Phones
Network Computers	Data Mining	Object Technology	Videoconferencing
Smart Cards	Digital Cash	Push Systems	Voice/Data Integration
Smart TVs	Digital Signatures	Real-Time Messaging	Wireless Data
	Directory Services	Search Engines	

The Future of Hardware

For the first time in the IT industry's history, *hardware* innovations will start taking a back seat to events in the more dynamic regions of *software* and *networks*. There will, of course, be important innovations in the area of hardware. But as time goes on, their implications will become increasingly predictable and probably will be confined to three major domains: mass-market PCs and devices that access the Web and/or cost less than $500, IT/consumer electronics convergence, and product mobility. Let's look first at low cost devices.

Low Cost Devices

In order to achieve a world with a billion or more users connected to the global Internet, end-user prices will need to come down dramatically, especially for low- and mid-market consumers. So-called "network computers," "Net PCs," Web TV, and Web-enabled cable set-top boxes are all part of efforts to get prices down into the sub-$500 level—ideally closer to $300 and eventually down to under $100. A second (and obviously related) aspect of low-cost access is the current effort to make systems easier to use and manage by *reducing complexity at the end-user level.*

As *network bandwidth* improves, these technologies should become increasingly viable and successful. Still, traditional PCs will remain the dominant platform for at least five years. In fact, in many ways products such as network computers and Net PCs are probably best understood more as *metaphors* than as *products*. They symbolize the current need for *low cost, ease of use*, and *ubiquity.*

That much of this three-part demand will need to be met through improvements in today's PC is important to IT vendors, but it is hardly a critical issue from the consumer perspective. In the long run, the primary role of low-cost devices will be to facilitate the formation of a critical mass of Web and Net users.

Technology Convergence

Digital cameras (both still and video), digital versatile disks (DVD), Web TV, and sound boards are all examples of the convergence between *computers* and *consumer electronics equipment*. Although this convergence has clearly become an important technology trend, its main impact will continue to be narrowly directed to the mass consumer sector. However, from a longer-term perspective, the coming full-scale integration *of sensors, cameras, and communications capabilities* into commonplace and everyday *things* will clearly transform the market for many traditional products.

As time goes on, information processing capabilities will be incorporated into an ever widening array of goods, from everyday household appliances to automobiles and entirely wired homes. However, major momentum in this direction is, I believe, at least three years away. Until then, human use of technology will remain our paramount concern.

Product Mobility

Personal digital assistants (PDAs), smart phones, and smart cards will clearly emerge as mission-critical products for an increasing army of mobile workers and consumers—the "lone eagles" of contemporary consumer and corporate lore. Indeed, possibly a decade or so hence, people will shake their heads at how people back in the Roaring Nineties used to lug around heavy laptops. Such a sight soon will seem as strange as spying someone today lugging a fax machine around an airport. Fully functional handheld devices will handle most communications needs.

But when access to a full computer and keyboard becomes necessary, smart cards will give users easy access to their "home" system resources, regardless of who owns the actual PC. In other words, people will likely share the next-to-invisible PCs of the future as easily and unthinkingly as we share each other's phones today. Of course, this development presupposes that network servers will *store* most relevant user information at remote locations, essentially recreating the user's familiar desktop-like experience no matter where the actual user happens to be. Such a development would obviously be a major advance in system utility, backup, and customer convenience. *Hardware innovation*, in short, should enable significant advances in *critical mass, ubiquity,* and *mobility*, all important extensions of today's current capabilities.

Networking: One Path Clear, the Other Cloudy

Less visible but still required and important developments will include ever faster desktop, server, and network switching equipment, which will remain an enormous customer investment area. From a vendor perspective, the outlook for networking technology is cloudy and could not be more polarized at the present time. Fortunately, from an end-user business perspective, the future becomes clear and relatively more straightforward: *Enormous increases in relatively inexpensive bandwidth will be there for those that need it.* Period. End of story.

Although fierce debates and controversies will no doubt continue to rage between contending technologies—*routers* versus *switches; gigabit Ethernet* versus *ATM (asynchronous transfer mode)*—from an end user's perspective, much of the basic technology involved will be transparent and largely invisible.

Businesses, whatever the dominant technology, will be able to obtain the capacity required for *advanced multimedia, videoconferencing,* and even *3-D applications*. Transmission costs should continue to fall rapidly. Such swiftly rising capacities and sharply lower costs will be badly needed in the Web-based business environment of the near future.

Best estimates are that *the volume of network traffic will double each year for the foreseeable future.* A stunning consequence of this exponential growth will be a fundamental shift in the nature of telecommunications traffic (see Figure 3.4).

Interestingly, the shape of these curves is largely identical to the economic inversions described earlier in this chapter. Consider that as recently as the late 1980s, over 90 percent of all communications traffic was voice, and the rest was data and fax. Today, the volumes of voice and data

FIGURE 3.4   Communications Industry Traffic Shifts, 1990–2000

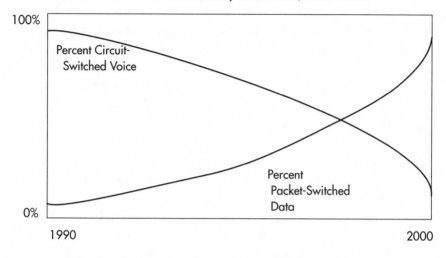

are believed to be roughly equal. By the end of the century, data will compose over 90 percent of all communications traffic and voice just 10 percent. And just a few years from that date, voice is expected to become a mere fraction of total telecommunications usage. This emerging reality is not intuitive and is hard for many nontechnologists to readily absorb. But the simple hard-core reality is this: *Computers can process and transmit far more information far faster than humans can.*

The implications for the communications industry of this shift from voice to data are and will continue to be profound. A telephone network designed to handle voice traffic is now being asked to handle mostly data. This shift is difficult because data transmission and voice transmission use such different technologies. Data travels in packets that are independently routed around the network and then reassembled at their final destination. Voice uses a dedicated point-to-point path. The essence of today's telecommunications challenge is the long-term need to manage voice services over a network that should be principally designed for data. Today, the opposite is the case. More than anything else, it is this revolution in underlying network technology that is behind the extraordinary turbulence in today's global telecommunications markets.

Enhanced business capabilities such as Internet telephony, Web/call center integration, and videoconferencing will be initially deployed in *intranet* and, increasingly, in *extranet* environments. In fact, one of the key benefits of these more private network environments is that customers will be able to increasingly distance themselves from the vagaries of the public Internet, purchasing separately whatever transmission capacity they'll need.

In contrast to the corporate market, the bandwidth outlook for consumer markets remains highly uncertain. It will likely vary dramatically from country to country. Of the three main contenders, two employ existing telephone wires:

1. ISDN (integrated services digital networks) is a proven technology but has relatively modest benefits over today's high-speed modems.
2. In contrast, so-called DSL technology (digital subscriber line) offers far greater capacity but remains substantially untested.
3. The principal alternative that does not use existing phone lines is the *cable modem*, at least in those countries that have deployed significant cable TV networks.

Investments in these technologies are picking up steam, but widespread deployment remains several years away, at a minimum.

In addition to ISDN, DSL, and cable, a variety of other consumer options are regularly floated:

- *Hardwired*: Utility companies continue to explore ways to take advantage of the wires that already run into every house. Indeed, a team in the United Kingdom has shown that the Internet can be distributed through ordinary *electrical power lines*.
- *Wireless*: These options include efforts to broadcast popular Web sites via satellite or to use the cellular phone type technology known as PCS.

Over the last year or so, progress in these satellite and wireless areas has exceeded expectations. They may soon become a viable alternative to the hardwired world. But as of today, there is virtually no significant Web-driven wireless usage.

Today, the hot-button competitive question seems to be, Which of these communications technologies is likely to prevail? But that issue will, I believe, be subsumed by the unavoidable reality that hardware solutions and systems are likely to vary greatly among and between (and even *within*) regions and nations.

It thus becomes extremely difficult to predict when consumers will attain the necessary bandwidth that compares to what business users already enjoy. Since bandwidth is the key industry enabler, this uncertainty is highly problematic and is one of the key reasons why the next three years or so will be so heavily dominated by business-to-business computing.

Software: The Final Frontier

Take a quick second look at the technologies listed in Table 3.1, which illustrates that software today is the most active segment of the IT industry. Arguably, software is the most important technology area today because only software is so central to all of the Web's driving economics—as shown in Figures 3.1, 3.2, and 3.3.

Software alone enables zero marginal costs, mass customization, the processing and management of mass communications, and the underlying potential for industry-wide transformation.

Perhaps the most challenging software issue is simply one of *adoption*. Historically, customers have generally adopted hardware more quickly than software. But today, the rate of software adoption will drive many of the most critical areas of Web evolution. Since developing and implementing new software remains expensive and complicated, not all software options will be pursued. There are, after all, only so many resources.

TECHNOLOGY DEPENDENCE AND COLLABORATION

From a broader perspective, the most interesting and important aspect of today's ongoing high-technology saga is how much of the future is moving steadily out of the traditional IT industry's hands. A business so accustomed to pioneering its own way suddenly finds that *if it is going to achieve its ends, it has to find a way to effectively work with others.* Now, that's a surprise.

This fact is perhaps most obvious in the bandwidth area, where— whether it be for business or consumer services—the computer industry is not about to lay down a new global communications grid, especially within the countless but critical local loops. The reality today, for better or for worse, is that the Internet itself consists of servers, routers, and software provided by the IT industry, but it runs across the telecommunications industry's wires. How these wires are installed, serviced, priced, and upgraded will determine much of the technology industry's future.

Nearly as obviously, as the computer industry reaches out to consumers, it will necessarily begin to rely on the support of more traditional entertainment and information services industries. Even with all of their billions, giants such as Intel and Microsoft would not want to pretend that they know all that much about developing highly engaging consumer experiences. In fact, when it comes to holding the hearts and minds of consumers, it tends to be better to leave things to the people who put on the Olympics, *Seinfeld,* or *Jurassic Park* than to those who devised Windows, or even Notes.

Computer industry influence and control over the content industries remains minimal; really only Microsoft is making a major effort, and its track record is distinctly mixed. Similarly, if a new broad base of consumers is going to be reached through new and inexpensive devices that leverage television and cable television resources, then close cooperation with these industries will prove essential.

In this regard, the early evidence in key areas such as high definition television and cable TV set-top boxes is not encouraging. Discussion between the leaders of these industries and many of today's top IT executives often has not proven productive and has been characterized by high levels of distrust. Progress has been disappointingly slow. There is, as a result, still no clear path toward true PC/TV integration. The lack of such integration is one of the few stumbling blocks in the path of the Web world today.

If the much touted transition to a world of electronic commerce is to be fully achieved, close collaboration with nearly all forms of government will be required. The Internet has suddenly found itself caught in the middle of complex issues of taxation, privacy, law enforcement, trade, intellectual property rights, and even pornography and gambling.

That these issues differ widely at a town, state, and country level only compounds the problem. Again, the history of IT industry and government collaboration is not particularly encouraging. The IT industry prefers to act now and solve problems later. Government, understandably, tends to lean toward a more deliberative approach.

Finally, the IT industry is as dependent as ever upon users' willingness to try and then adopt new products and services. In fact, many so-called electronic commerce projects will require higher levels of cooperation between customers and their IT suppliers than ever before. I can assure you that as more and more products and services are delivered directly on line, the boundary between a business responsibility and a computer vendor responsibility will become very blurry indeed. In fact, the boundary will in many cases simply be erased entirely.

Overall, today's consumers have never been hit so rapidly with so many technologies and applications. Thus it shouldn't be too surprising that consumers are hopelessly confused by the welter of competing digital-recording formats and by redundant technological fixes to problems that some people don't even recognize as requiring solutions. In the end, many new technologies will have to be adopted as much on faith as on proven return on investment (ROI).

At the end of the day, the issue boils down to this: Most businesses can't afford to wait and measure the feasibility of a technology investment by the success that their competitor experienced with it. If Moore's law also applies to the ROI for technology, not a single serious business can risk being behind the next wave.

CHAPTER 4

THE WEB/VIRTUAL OFFICE–BASED ERA

FROM NETWORK TO WEB: THREE STORIES OF MARKET-FACING ENTERPRISE

Aerotech and the Virtual Factory

Until about 1995, some fifty employees of the St. Louis–based McDonnell-Douglas Corporation were responsible for maintaining the value of all the information shared on the company network. A great deal of the information stored on that network existed simply to support a complex RFP (request for proposal) process, which demanded that highly complex design specifications be submitted to prospective subcontractors and subsystem component suppliers, enabling them to bid on specialized pieces of work.

All the people involved on both sides of this extraordinarily complex RFP process would travel to McDonnell-Douglas's headquarters in St. Louis and meet for days and sometimes weeks to review design and engineering specifications, before any contracts could be awarded.

After struggling for years to keep this cumbersome process under control, the group originally responsible for maintaining the network outsourced the use of its once proprietary intranet to a handful of external suppliers. After a few trial runs, this effort took off faster than one of the company's jets. In fact, the team grew so rapidly that McDonnell-Douglas was forced to set up a separate subsidiary called Aerotech to handle the volume of work coming in over the system. Today, several thousand supplier companies are constantly participating in this intranet-turned-extranet, which closely connects McDonnell-Douglas's employees to its suppliers, as well as to project managers in the Pentagon.

You could call this novel enterprise a form of "virtual factory" because Aerotech has succeeded in reducing the latency and the cycle time involved in the bidding process, which in turn has led to a dramatic reduction in subsystem costs—the key cost issue in manufacturing. McDonnell-Douglas has even transferred its computer-aided design specifications for all of its subcomponents to the computers at Aerotech, which secure them and download the numerical machine codes that actually drive the manufacturing and quality assurance systems. Aerotech's network is, in this sense, physically milling the component parts for complex weapons platforms like the McDonnell-Douglas F18 fighter plane and the Longbow helicopter.

Chrysler and SCORE

In 1989, after learning that over 70 percent of the parts in its automobiles were being provided by outside suppliers, a then struggling Chrysler Corporation began looking into ways to dramatically cut the costs of its outsourced components. Instead of simply requesting or (as had been the custom) demanding price cuts from its suppliers as its volume of orders increased, the Michigan-based multinational made a strategic decision to challenge its suppliers to identify opportunities for cost reductions on their own.

Why would Chrysler's hard-pressed suppliers have been willing to cut voluntarily the prices they offered Chrysler? The answer is that the company offered to share a significant portion of the savings with them. The resulting program, called SCORE (supplier cost reduction effort), is expected to save Chrysler—now Daimler-Chrysler—on the order of $2 billion annually by the year 2000.

In its initial paper-based incarnation, however, SCORE was an administrative nightmare. Suppliers would submit their cost-cutting ideas on hard copy via fax. Their proposals would then be manually input into a database that only Chrysler personnel could access. The paper proposals were often misplaced, and suppliers had no way of tracking or updating their ideas in response to input from their core customer. In its start-up phase, SCORE became a classic victim of its own success: As the program grew rapidly more popular, the volume of paperwork generated threatened to overwhelm with details, data, and sheer logistics a highly promising initiative. What was the solution?

In December 1994, Chrysler turned to the Southfield, Michigan, based Enterprise Consulting Group for help in cutting its flow of paper down to manageable size. Enterprise Consulting developed an on-line version of SCORE, based on a collaborative software solution, that seamlessly automated the entire process of submitting, tracking, and approving the suppliers' cost-cutting recommendations.

The result? Chrysler has improved its relationships with its core community—its suppliers—while saving itself substantial amounts of both time and money. The benefits of the new SCORE on-line system are twofold: It enhanced client relations at both ends of the value chain, and it increased efficiency—average processing time for proposals has been cut in half, from an average of 200 days to under 100, and the volume of proposals processed has nearly doubled, from 3,649 to 8,225 per model year.

Chrysler's second-generation, on-line SCORE system is a classic example of value chain innovation (VCI). VCI, involving everything from the production of "atom-based" products to the generation of "bit-based" ideas, extends the coordination of work beyond traditional company boundaries and redefines key client and customer relations all along the value chain.

QCS and On-Line Outsourcing

The Mountain View, California, based QCS (with regional offices in Nice and Hong Kong) was an outgrowth of founder Marcel van Heesewijk's mounting frustration with trading over the telephone and on paper while working as a supplier for various retail product lines in Asia. "We really were in the Middle Ages sometimes on the upstream side," van Heesewijk ruefully concluded. "People were determining on the backs of envelopes how many millions of dollars worth of containers of merchandise they would buy." By "upstream," van Heesewijk was referring to processes that link manufacturers with retailers, as opposed to "downstream" processes linking retailers directly to customers.

Clearly, a certain degree of innovation and automation was in order on the upstream side. A lack of automation stalled the flow of information between suppliers and retailers, leading to costly supply overruns, increasing the odds of purchasing errors, and significantly undercutting retailing profits.

QCS was established to help retail buyers collaborate with their worldwide supply chains by establishing and maintaining an electronic network that permits retail buyers, their suppliers, and an array of service providers to communicate, share complex data, and streamline the retail buying process.

Because it's so easy these days to establish a Web presence, one recent problem dogging the multi-trillion-dollar retailing industry is the difficulty of distinguishing between solid industry players and fly-by-night operations. By strictly controlling its membership, QCS has been able to prequalify suppliers, while offering both suppliers and service providers a select customer base.

QCS has also succeeded in helping retailers solve another major problem: the growth of nonperforming industry inventory. By helping retailing giants, such as Harrod's in the United Kingdom, maintain groupware-based catalogs, which contain all of the key performance information pertaining to a wide variety of inventory items, QCS's customers significantly depress the cost of moving nonperforming items around the world by eliminating or sharply reducing freight charges.

Not only has QCS been successful in meeting its own goals, it's also highly secure: The company offers private forums where members can negotiate with each other in an atmosphere of complete confidentiality—with total confidence that their security will not be breached. Such security offers no small value in a multi-trillion-dollar industry that has sometimes been subject to waste and cost overruns on a scale comparable to the defense procurement industry.

What do Aerotech, Chrysler's SCORE, and the Web start-up QCS have in common? All are prime examples of "market-facing enterprises"; all have learned to expand on lessons learned during wave two of the digital era—the network-centric era—to redefine and reconfigure themselves to compete in the age of the third wave: an era that is not only network-centric but Web-based.

THE IBM-LOTUS MERGER: CREATING AN MFE

In June 1995, when IBM CEO Lou Gerstner placed a call to Lotus CEO Jim Manzi to advise him—just hours before the news was due to hit the financial wires—that IBM would be making an unsolicited $3.2 billion tender offer for Lotus, many long-term Lotus employees greeted this news (which spread like wildfire through our headquarters on the Charles River in Cambridge, faster even than an e-mail message) with fear, shock, and not a little trepidation.

After all, for a young, comparatively freewheeling software company like Lotus, Big Blue was a symbol not only of everything we thought we weren't, but of just about everything that we didn't ever want to be: establishment, mainstream, bureaucratic, hierarchical, and—in a word—stodgy. Fortunately, the conventional stigmas applied to IBM proved totally false, but they certainly defined the skeptical sensations of the moment.

What the very few Lotus loyalists who packed their bags and fled the company in the wake of the merger failed to appreciate, however, was that Big Blue, under its newly installed CEO, was deeply involved in a profound process of reinventing and remaking itself along the lines of the new, more flexible, leaner, flatter, "enterprise-enabled" companies—of which Lotus, not at all coincidentally, happened to be a prime example. Of course, Lou Gerstner also had many executive empathizers in corporate America and beyond who grasped that this new model of the "integrated enterprise" was the wave of the future, arriving in the here and now.

As Gerstner himself would later put it, Lotus was to be "a principal hood ornament" on IBM's long-term strategy to transform itself into a market leader in the brave new world of electronic commerce, soon to become better known as "e-business." In this context, it's intriguing to note that the IBM-Lotus merger took place just as the Internet and the World Wide Web were reaching their critical mass and as the virtual and digital worlds had begun to display every sign of radically reshaping, reorienting and reconfiguring the ground on which we stood—at times, I admit, with knees trembling at the pace of cyberchange.

Fortunately for all of us at Lotus, as well as at IBM, the harsh stereotypes that depicted some corporate Darth Vader ravaging a peace-loving, idealistic, and visionary land of Lotus-eaters turned out to be greatly exaggerated. When IBM Senior Vice President John Thompson first visited Lotus headquarters, he turned up in slacks and a sports shirt, while the delegation from Lotus wore the traditional IBM garb: blue sports jackets, rep ties and khaki slacks. The cultural differences had obviously been somewhat exaggerated.

Some more subtle distinctions, however, were not quite so easy to determine. Just as dark suits were no longer the signature style of the new

Big Blue, neither were blue jeans and tee shirts the de rigueur uniform in our high-rise campus on the Charles. Yes, we all got a good laugh out of our sartorial mixed signals. But that minor epiphany crystallized for both sides the critical challenges facing us all, as it came down to actually managing the process of knitting two distinctly different companies and cultures into one global team.

The Task Force and the Team Room

A task force was quickly established, composed of some thirty-five senior representatives from both companies, who spent a good deal of highly compressed time working to make the merger into a marriage. Once Jim Manzi (who'd struggled fiercely to keep the company independent) had decided to depart, it would have been logical, not to mention traditional, for IBM to quickly put one of its own in charge of its new acquisition. But the "new" IBM was determined to no longer act like the "old" IBM. Within twenty-four hours of Jim's departure, IBM had named me and my colleague Mike Zisman—we'd run the Notes business together—corporate copresidents, thereby assuring the rank and file at Lotus that IBM meant it when it said that it had no desire or hidden agenda to make us over in its own image. Shortly thereafter, following the death of his wife, Mike Zisman scaled back his responsibilities in order to spend more time with his children, and I became CEO. (In spite of his "scaled-back" responsibilities, Mike never worked less than a sixty-hour week in my memory, and he remains my symbiotic co-spirit as Lotus executive vice president of strategy. We still finish one another's sentences.)

At the suggestion of several members of the joint task force, we formed a digital "team room." More than anything else in this immediate post-merger period, the success of this project underscored the fact that what IBM was attempting to do with the Lotus merger was to hasten its own transformation into a full-fledged market-facing enterprise. A digital "team room" is a safe and secure place in which a number of people can work without ever having to be in the same room. It's not a physical place or space but a virtual location that enables a select group of people to meet electronically while remaining in their separate offices, which might just as well be across the world as down the street or down the hall—it makes no difference. The team room is, in short, the ultimate manifestation of the Web-based or virtual office era.

A digital team room relies on a sophisticated collaborative software application to create a sense of electronic immediacy, intimacy, and privacy. It functions by steering and guiding secure electronic communications documents and e-mail messages from certain senders to selected recipients. The system establishes a mininetwork within a network that digitally replicates the experience of a group of people meeting in a room to hash out a solution to a problem.

One of the great intangible values of working in a digital as opposed to a physical space was that it permitted us to avoid the potentially heightened sensitivities of our people at that critical time. About the last thing we needed was to have IBM folks trooping en masse through our offices like an invading army on a recon detail.

IBM-Lotus Synergy

About the second-to-last thing we needed was to create a new meta-level of confusion in the already fragmented market for sophisticated business software. So the first substantive question faced by our task force of some thirty-five members was this: How do we eliminate redundant and/or duplicative products and services? To their credit, the IBM-based task force members proved both flexible and generous in cases where a Lotus product enjoyed a market share or brand loyalty greater than its IBM equivalent.

That said, it was not lost on those of us on the Lotus side of the fence that certain key components of IBM technology—such as their advanced continuous voice dictation system and their HTTP server—might be leveraged to improve the competitive position of our own collaborative products. The truth turned out to be not "might" but *did*—in many cases IBM technology saved us months if not years in market opportunity costs.

Another critical signal that IBM intended both to let Lotus be Lotus and to become a new IBM took place shortly after the merger, when Mike Zisman and I flew down to IBM world headquarters in Armonk, New York, to present a radical proposal for maintaining and potentially sharply boosting our market share in the face of an expected onslaught from Microsoft's Exchange—a long-awaited "messaging" product that had been so long in development that we'd occasionally grown complacent about it as a threat.

I must admit that at times we'd been inclined to dismiss it as a piece of "vaporware" (to the uninitiated, a software product talked about but not delivered—a phenomenon distressingly common in the intensely competitive IT industry). But with Exchange slated to be shipped any day, we faced vaporware no longer. To Lou Gerstner and John Thompson, head of IBM's software division, Mike and I proposed mounting a preemptive strike—a plan to cut by half the price of Notes, in an aggressive bid to grab and hold onto our dominant share of the groupware market.

With Microsoft having made strong inroads with its latest suite of products on both the spreadsheet and word processing fronts, this was no minor strategic issue. After about an hour's worth of discussion, Lou Gerstner looked us straight in the eye and said, "You guys are running the company, so you do what you need to do." John Thompson supported both our proposal and this radical decision in an equivalently rapid and decisive manner.

Nearly as noteworthy as IBM's immediate grant of permission to market our products aggressively was the speed with which this high-risk decision was settled. More than just about anything else, this convinced not only me but the rest of our team at Lotus that we were dealing with a new and vastly improved IBM and with a different kind of leadership, where empowerment was the normal management style. Before attending this critical meeting, some of our people had predicted that for any decision of this magnitude to be forthcoming, IBM would need a month or more to act. But we didn't have a month, or even weeks. Both Gerstner and Thompson recognized that this was a new business environment and that speed had to be of the essence.

Well aware that simply cutting prices was not going to be enough to hold back the tide, we mounted a coordinated marketing strategy to keep Microsoft from gaining a hammerlock on the wave of the IT future: the groupware and networking market. We sought and gained IBM's firm commitment to support us in boosting advertising and marketing costs by a significant 40 percent. We increased our demand generation and brand awareness spending not only in print but in a series of TV commercials that appeared in prime time—including during the Super Bowl—and featured a locally born (Worcester, Massachusetts) comedian, Denis Leary. These spots were deliberately engineered to be a bit rougher around the edges than any IBM marketing campaign would have been.

If there remained any doubt that synergy existed between IBM and Lotus, it didn't take long to erase it. In the midst of all this feverish activity to capture the lion's share of the networking and groupware market, we witnessed the global arrival of the Internet and its cousin, the World Wide Web. Forging a Web presence forced entire industries to start looking outward instead of inward. For the first time, they had to adopt a broader, wider focus—way beyond traditional corporate boundaries—and to reach out to customers, suppliers, and partners for actual input in running their businesses.

INTRANETS: A WEB TO *THE WEB*

I consider this change of focus a healthy development. In fact, that may be one of the world's largest understatements. It's just plain common sense that digitally integrating your customers into "touch-oriented" processes can have higher payoffs than merely automating your own organization. At the same time, coincidental with the Web's splashy arrival, the IT industry began talking up the concept of the "intranet" and making it a high-priority focus.

At first glance, a reasonable response to this development would have been, Hey, what gives? Wasn't an intranet, after all, a high-speed digital network linking users within a single company? Wasn't the increasing focus on "intranets" therefore a self-defeating attempt to turn back the clock to the good old days of internal proprietary knowledge, maintained on relational databases, supported by all the traditional and time-honored IT and MIS (management information systems) methods?

Well, yes and no. Certainly at first glance, this newfound exuberance about "intranets" seemed at best a paradox, and at worst a defensive response to the threats and challenge posed by the great unknowns of the Net and the Web. Looking externally, after all, is a route fraught with great insecurity, not to mention management headaches and undeniable implementation risks.

Although real dangers of reverting to an internal orientation at the expense of an increasingly present need to maintain a "market-facing" presence do exist in some circles, intranets will in the end perform a radically different function from their many internal predecessors. Intranets are, in fact, a necessary bridge to the world of external electronic commerce—a web, if you will, to the Web.

Not until both internal and external information become truly "interoperable"—fully compatible with rival systems—will large-scale, cross-company collaboration and transactions become feasible for most organizations. For that reason strong universal standards are needed. Without such standards, no two companies' efforts to move into the Web-based era could succeed, because no two systems could ever hope to be truly compatible or interoperable.

One great and important role provided by intranets is that the Internet standards they're based on are bound to provide a critical common denominator, enabling truly integrated enterprises around the world to establish compatible information formats. Once all Web-based formats become truly interoperable, the amount, speed, and sophistication of intercompany exchanges can increase by orders of magnitude. Like telephone and e-mail before it, this ease of communications will greatly enhance the quantity and quality of information exchange and greatly improve the return on investment in such systems. In sum: *You need to use Internet standards internally today, so that you can use them externally tomorrow.*

A major reason that intranets will provide a logical intermediate step between the old-style, inward facing business model and the new-style, outward facing enterprise is that in many cases internal and external information amount to pretty much the same thing. Is there any significant difference, after all, between *internal* and *external* customer records, product specifications, price lists, inventories, delivery dates, order entry, billing terms, receivables, and service requirements? Of course some proprietary information will forever remain "for internal use only." But the great bulk of necessary knowledge tends to be equally relevant inside and outside of the organization.

Intranets can and are playing a key catalytic role in integrating organizations to prepare for the third wave of computing: the Web-based era.

Consider the time, complexity, and expense traditionally associated with setting up an electronic data interchange (EDI) system—a classical extranet function. One hope for the future of e-commerce is that a common base of Internet and Web-based intranet technologies will help tomorrow's extranets avoid similar problems, which typically flow from a lack of true interoperability. Once the Web moves beyond today's mostly static publishing—which some have dubbed derisively, "brochureware"—

it will need to handle advanced messaging, automated workflow, more complex and interactive business forms, and all manner of real-time transaction processing.

To keep a reasonable pace with these growing demands, forward-looking and market-facing organizations, in addition to offering full and unstinting support for all mobile workers, will need to support highly distributed authoring—the capacity of many clients served by the same server to create Web pages; they also will need to support dynamic document-to-HTML translation—the ability to "translate" key documents into a protocol, enabling them to be posted as Web pages. Consequently, organizations will need to move away, as quickly as possible, from relying on specialized groups to build Web pages and toward enabling Web content to flow automatically out of everyday work activity.

FROM DATA TO INFORMATION TO KNOWLEDGE

Consider the following definitions:

- *Data* can be defined as simple unqualified *facts*. For instance, a company's accounting department might record a piece of data noting that Account A is delinquent by $5,000.
- *Information* tends to enrich *data* by giving it some context. For example, Account A has been delinquent for ten months and has been assigned to Frank.
- *Knowledge* is what information becomes when it is connected to *relevant know-how* or *know-why*, and thus supports or informs key decisions: as when company policy states, "Before declaring a delinquent account bad debt, you should first offer a payment plan. If this doesn't work, you need written permission from your supervisor to write off the debt" (*know-how*); or, "When it would cost more to collect them than we are owed, we declare delinquent accounts to be bad debt" (*know why*).
- *Work* is the product of putting some combination of *data, information*, and *knowledge* into *action*, as when an accountant actually requests and receives approval to write off the debt of Account A as unrecoverable.

These definitions are essentially refinements of the discussion in Chapter 2 regarding *structured data* versus *unstructured textual information*, with *work* typically being a variable mixture of the two. As one of my colleagues recently put it: "When you successfully combine *data, information*, and *knowledge*, the reward is often a *transaction*—a sale, an updated customer profile, or possibly a financial transfer."

Such transactions typically generate more *data*, making the process highly iterative. But, and it is always worth keeping this in mind, the end process is in some form *work*. Information, for its own sake, tends to have little value.

INSIDE THE ENTERPRISE FRAMEWORK

With these definitions as background, let's take a closer look at Table 4.1. Someday these terms (or their equivalents) may be as commonplace as e-mail, LANs, and databases are today. As you read along, try to map your own organization's activities and priorities to this more generic view. Also, keep in mind that the underlying business value tends to *increase* as one moves *upward* and to the *right*.

Layer 1: The Empowered Individual

With the nearly universal business use of today's personal productivity tools, the area in Table 4.1 corresponding to "the empowered individual" tends to be well understood. Certainly a basic set of word processing, spreadsheet, graphics, e-mail, on-line database, and Web access software is now the standard tool kit for most knowledge workers. The two main new frontiers are in the areas of *knowledge access* and, most importantly, *workflow integration*. Increasingly, enhancements to these two areas will present the greatest challenge to attaining that elusive goal: the construction of the integrated enterprise.

- *Knowledge access* consists of the specialized knowledge required for most individual jobs and includes expertise, procedures, tips, and other forms of on-line support.

TABLE 4.1   Enterprise Solutions Framework

	A. DATA	B. INFORMATION	C. KNOWLEDGE	D. WORK
4. Extended Enterprise	Customer and Supplier Transactions	Marketing Communications	Ecosystem Development	Market-Facing Systems
	On-line sales and other transactions	Connect to outside stakeholders	Operate alliances, markets, interest groups	Use cyberspace as principal business space
3. Integrated Enterprise	Enterprise Data Systems and Apps.	Enterprise-wide Communication	Enterprise Knowledge Management	Enterprise Process Innovation
	Build corporate database and applications	Encourage cross-functional communications	Leverage intellectual capital and best practices	Reengineer business processes
2. Automated Workgroup	Workgroup Data Systems and Apps.	Workgroup Communication	Workgroup Collaboration	Workgroup Process Innovation
	Establish departmental databases and applications	Encourage cross-functional communications	Enable collective discovery and decision-making	Improve conduct and control of workflow
1. Empowered Individual	Data Creation Access and Usage	Information Access and Authoring	Training, Education, and Expertise	Workflow Integration
	Enable user data collection, entry, and access	Enable creation, access, and distribution of information	Enable creation, access, and distribution of expertise	Assure integration into workflow systems
	A. DATA	**B. INFORMATION**	**C. KNOWLEDGE**	**D. WORK**
	Structured	Unstructured	Unstructured	Structured

- *Workflow integration* involves using advanced data, information, and knowledge tools to create more efficient and effective structured work processes.

For example, most employees use rule-based systems to guide their work, and they use specific tools and applications that are closely aligned with their actual work requirements. The goal of workflow integration is to provide enterprise-wide access to these rule-based systems, tools, and applications that may otherwise reside in individual, privately maintained databases, whether located inside employees' heads or on their PC hard drives. In too many organizations, individual work is still carried out as a series of isolated, ad hoc efforts. In the integrated enterprise, collective and collaborative work becomes the rule, rather than the exception.

Layer 2: Automated Workgroups

On layer 2 of Table 4.1, you'll find two main areas of important *new* activity: w*orkgroup collaboration* and w*orkgroup process innovation*. In the former, five major forms of group collaboration fall into area 2C:

1. *Team facilitation solutions* support workgroup formation, planning, administration, and communication, usually for a specific project. The best example of this would be a "war room" or a "team room" of the sort that we used to facilitate the early stages of the Lotus-IBM merger. In such a virtual "war room" or "team room" all of the relevant information and resources are maintained, centrally stored, and readily available.

Although some team rooms may be permanent, in practice they're usually set up and taken down at the beginning and end of specific projects. More often than not, they come into play when project participants work in different locations (or even different companies). Even when and if team room members are resident in a single location, this approach can often be more effective than using physical conference rooms, which are continually being set up and emptied and sometimes lack the requisite degree of security. Or, as in the case of the team room we established to manage the IBM-Lotus joint decision-making process, a digital room and an electronic meeting can often be far less obtrusive and noticeable than a real one. For reasons of security and privacy, a digital team room can be as secure as the command center of SAC.

2. *Electronic discussion solutions* provide a loosely structured *electronic forum* for workgroup discussions. Less formal than a team room, discussion groups are the in-house equivalent of an on-line chat service. Team rooms tend to be focused on a specific project; discussion groups tend to be long-running channels of communication in which specific topics are continuously and periodically explored. A subject is chosen, and the discussion proceeds, sometimes with, sometimes without a moderator.

Clearly, the main goals are to facilitate communications and share ideas, but also there's the potential embedded in the software solution to develop a shared history of information and process evolution.

The main challenge with discussion groups is to find the right balance between *focus* and *flexibility*. While some generate heated and valuable discussions, others wander aimlessly and inefficiently. Additionally, discussion groups, like team rooms, need to reach a certain critical mass to remain vital.

3. *Departmental reference systems solutions* enable the storage and access of *work documents* within a single department. These could be *manuals, reports, proposals, forms, case studies, account lists,* or *background reading.* Such systems provide an important repository of history and information—an organizational memory—that can be of enormous value, particularly in the area of training. To assure usage, many organizations are making such on-line depositories the *only* source for certain documents and information. If paper-based versions continue to be available, much of the value of these systems can be lost.

4. *Departmental calendaring/scheduling* solutions enable the maintenance and display of *schedules.* These are, of course, used much more by some companies than others; but as workers become more mobile, they often manage their own calendars instead of relying on secretarial support, and therefore calendar systems become increasingly important, especially in larger, physically distributed, and mobile organizations. Today, however, the bulk of scheduling in many organizations is now done via e-mail, which in and of itself has been a huge improvement over manual or telephone-based approaches.

5. *Document authoring solutions* automate the *group document* creation process. Over the last few years, many companies have developed staffs of technical specialists to maintain and update Web pages for both their internal and external applications. Using modern document creation tools, every employee is able to generate Web-ready materials directly, without any knowledge of HTML or other Web-related technologies.

Overall, each of the above workgroup solution categories is being adopted at a different rate by different companies. Indeed, perhaps more than any other area, the adoption of workgroup computing technologies is closely tied to issues of company culture and leadership. This is important since (as Table 4.1 implies) experience with advanced workgroup applications often provides the essential foundation and key catalytic ingredient for the development of more advanced enterprise systems, practices, and cultures.

2D: Workgroup Process Innovation

This category can be described best by means of a few brief examples, each of which can be viewed as a flow of work that spans traditional company lines. In his interesting recent book, *Cybercorp*, the consultant James Martin draws an important distinction between an *industry value chain* (which describes the way entire industries are organized) and a business *value stream*, which essentially explores individual organizations in terms of their various end-to-end processes. *Workflow computing*, for example, is explicitly aimed at *recognizing, defining*, and *automating* once manual and often ad hoc end-to-end activities. Typically, value streams consist of transactions, communications, and collaborative functions that cut across traditional sales, marketing, and customer support domains.

Consider the following examples:

- *Sales force automation solutions* enable redesigned sales force processes, incorporating account management, pricing, promotion, proposal development, and actual order taking tasks. The initiation of a new account, and all that it typically sets in motion, would be a good example of a value stream that should be automated as an integrated process, as opposed to a series of handoffs to various functional groups.
- *Customer service automation* solutions enable redesigned customer service processes, typically involving post-sales call center support; these applications often require close integration with other corporate data and knowledge systems. For instance, a service representative might take advantage of a customer service request to generate new sales based on knowledge of the account and relevant new company products and services.
- *Internal operations solutions* enable redesigned work processes in functional but often isolated departments such as information services, human resources, finance, and legal. As these services

ceaselessly migrate toward intranet environments, they often take special advantage of the document authoring capabilities described above, bypassing traditional production processes. Expense account processing is a good example of a common process that frequently cuts across many groups and is often inefficiently handled.

Layer 3: The Integrated Enterprise

Although the Web is a high-priority area of customer focus today, most organizations still have a great deal of work to do to improve their internal systems. Many corporate messaging systems are still being enhanced, and even the older legacy database systems—primarily mainframe based—often require frequent updating. Perhaps more importantly, the Web has actually brought new life and a whole new set of requirements to what were once thought of as relatively stable back- and front-office systems—systems, for instance, like enterprise data systems.

3A: Enterprise Data Systems

Enterprise data systems have been the traditional backbones of many corporations. Linking these older structured processes into emerging information and knowledge-flow systems will be one of the greatest technological challenges facing organizations in the upcoming years. At the departmental level, there are basically two main classes of activity:

1. *Enterprise databases*. Few corporations can operate without their online transaction systems running effectively. Indeed, the mission-critical requirements of corporate messaging systems today would do well to match the reliability, availability, and serviceability that these financial, inventory, and customer records systems have delivered for more than two decades.

2. *Enterprise applications*. Although not getting nearly as much media publicity, from a customer perspective this area has been almost as active as the Web itself. Companies such as SAP, PeopleSoft, Baan, J. D. Edwards, and others have brought advanced client/server and, increasingly, Internet technologies to what was once a highly proprietary legacy system

domain. As I will discuss in more detail below, these applications help bridge the boundaries between data systems and workflow processes in key areas such as finance, human resources, and manufacturing.

3B: Enterprise-Wide Communication

Corporate e-mail solutions enable the exchange of messages and information across the enterprise. Over time, these systems have expanded from simple text messages to all manner of forms, attachments, and media. Today, almost all medium-size and large organizations require a world-class communications system capable of 99.9 percent uptime, as well as rapid response and enhanced ease of use, and accompanied by management tools such as directories, remote support, security, authentication, and encryption. Although such systems are in place in most businesses, there is still a lot of work to be done, particularly in the areas of maintenance, management, and interoperability.

Corporate reference systems solutions and cross-functional scheduling and calendaring are enterprise versions of the same tasks described in the workgroup collaboration section. As a rule, the value and return on investment in many of these systems becomes even more compelling when information is provided on an enterprise-wide scale.

3C: Enterprise Knowledge Management

One could, of course, argue that enterprise knowledge management is the Holy Grail of the modern learning organization—in fact, I plan to do just that. Today's organizations are certainly attempting—with varying degrees of success—to create, organize, and distribute various types of both *know-how* and *know-why;* they are, in other words, involved in knowledge management.

Knowledge management (KM) captures information that otherwise resides in individual experience or *functional* "silos"— an IT industry term of art for privately maintained repositories of information that need to be rendered accessible to a broader class of employees so that the value can be more widely distributed. KM systems may also help systematize the process of *organizational learning*. On the next page, you'll find five major types of internal knowledge management systems. Later on, we'll take a look at how such systems need to reach out externally as well.

1. *Communities of practice solutions* enhance formal and informal knowledge sharing of "best practices"—the state of the art in business processes and protocols—among people with similar work responsibilities. Such a need has become increasingly commonplace in professional services firms, where individuals might be working on very similar projects but for different clients in different locations. Historically, there was no easy way for employees to even know that they were doing similar work, much less determine a way of effectively sharing their expertise.

2. *Knowledge-based decision solutions* enable the ongoing identification and extraction of knowledge and its automatic distribution to relevant employees. Such systems may include everything from distributing standard company policies and procedures to in-depth analyses of why particular projects have succeeded or failed.

3. *Competency development solutions* enable companies to leverage intellectual capital and deliver core business knowledge to individuals and groups such as engineers or other technical personnel having access to scientific information of common interest. Such systems are designed to assure that employees retain *automated access* to essential "need to know" information.

4. *Data warehouses*, *data marts*, and *data mining* solutions all apply advanced software to sift through a company's databases to try to find patterns, identify customer traits, and understand trends. These systems are often at the heart of efforts to achieve highly customized levels of sales, marketing, and service. In short, they seek to extract knowledge directly from data.

5. *Knowledge architecture solutions* enable the identification, categorization, and maintenance of key business information. This category is a bit abstract, but for internal knowledge sharing, as well as for many of the database and data warehousing applications described above, it's important to possess clear definitions of even commonly used terms. What precisely does one mean by customer, sales, or revenue? Some companies even have their own internal dictionaries to facilitate precise information and knowledge sharing.

3D: Enterprise Process Innovation

When companies coordinate work processes across departmental boundaries, they can often sharply reduce cycle times, remove conflicting goals and incentives, and eliminate redundancies. Usually these systems include transactions, communications, and knowledge management functions. Below are some typical examples:

- *Order management* solutions can greatly streamline the process of fulfilling customer orders and reconciling accounts.
- *Product development* solutions accelerate the introduction of new products, from initial research through commercialization and market launch.
- *Purchasing* solutions shorten cycle times and provide more control over the enterprise-wide purchasing process.

Cultural Note: Using information technology to change existing systems and processes can be an extremely difficult task, comprising an array of business, cultural, and technical challenges. Although the systems described above can deliver improved efficiencies, more rapid information reporting, and better control over everyday operations, a serious risk still remains that project goals will not be fully met, that costs will exceed even the most padded budget, and that the organization will turn inward as it becomes too focused on working within the system, at the expense of responding to external market signals. Getting an organization to transform itself around structured software processes is rarely a simple matter.

Layer 4: The Extended Enterprise

The extended enterprise is of course a focus of enormous current excitement, with relatively new terms such as *extranets* and *electronic commerce* now circulating freely and widely. Just about everyone agrees that this will be the next great frontier in computing. As we shall see, its impact on just about all major industries and business activities will be both highly diverse and generally profound.

Despite these revolutionary prospects, however, it is important to see how these new developments arose from a context of existing systems, services, and applications. Unless there is close integration between external and internal activities, the real potential for electronic commerce will likely remain elusive. Thus both the extranet and intranet perspectives (see Table 4.2) of the enterprise are crucial to its success. But the integration of these two perspectives is often neither simple nor straightforward.

TABLE 4.2   Enterprise Solutions Framework: An Intranet and Extranet Perspective

4. Extended Enterprise	Customer and Supplier Transactions	Marketing Communications	Ecosystem Development	Market-Facing Systems
		E X T R A N E T		
3. Integrated Enterprise	Enterprise Data Systems and Apps.	Enterprise-wide Communication	Enterprise Knowledge Management	Enterprise Process Innovation
2. Automated Workgroup	Workgroup Data Systems and Apps.	Workgroup Communication	Workgroup Collaboration	Workgroup Process Innovation
		I N T R A N E T		
1. Empowered Individual	Data Creation Access and Usage	Information Access and Authoring	Training, Education, and Expertise	Workflow Integration
	A. DATA	B. INFORMATION	C. KNOWLEDGE	D. WORK

4A: Customer and Supplier Transactions

The ability to buy and sell directly over the Web is, of course, an indispensable component of genuine electronic commerce. In order to accomplish this goal, a company's Web site needs to be able to process effectively Internet-generated transactions, something most Web sites today are not set up to do. Overall, there are basically two types of Web-based transactions.

1. *Electronic data interchange systems* (EDI) have been around for nearly two decades. Such systems generally offer fast and accurate information exchange between different companies' computers, but they have historically been highly proprietary, making them both inflexible and expensive. Consequently, they have been mostly used between relatively large organizations that have regular, repeated dealings. EDI is rarely used by small businesses, and not at all by consumers.

2. *Interactive Web-based solutions* enable on-line transactions, usually between a company's Web site and various customers, suppliers, and so on. These systems can be either private, through some sort of restricted password system, or open to the general public. A new generation of transaction-enabled Web servers is making these systems increasingly reliable, scaleable, and affordable. In addition, many businesses need to tie these Web-based transactions back into their legacy operational and customer

records systems. Only new companies tend to have the luxury (and challenge) of conducting business entirely with modern Web technologies.

4B: Marketing and Communications

Electronic publishing solutions enable distribution of documents for public viewing. This area composes the great bulk of today's Web activity. Well over 90 percent of what is on the Web today consists of static published information about organizations, products, services, and such. Although there is, of course, great value in being able to reach so many people so quickly and inexpensively, the static nature of the experience is, as I noted above, sometimes disparagingly, and somewhat fairly, known as brochureware.

Interenterprise e-mail solutions enable the internal and external exchange of messages and attachments. Historically, most e-mail was within a single organization, but now the flows are, in some organizations, becoming roughly equal inside and outside the enterprise. There is little doubt that, over time, external communication via e-mail will become as simple and as commonplace as communication via telephone today. It is an extraordinarily powerful new tool for developing and maintaining customer intimacy, although, as most of us have experienced, unless used properly, e-mail exchanges can all too easily burst into flames. Fortunately, many employees have by now had enough experience with their internal e-mail culture to know how to use it smoothly externally.

Push technology systems can help overcome some of the problems of today's static systems by providing information directly to users based upon predefined areas of interest. The trick is to be able to anticipate customer needs sufficiently well that the pushed information is in fact relevant to the recipient. Otherwise, the result is often indistinguishable from bothersome spam. Push technology to date has not lived up to the heavy hype it received in late 1996 and early 1997, but it nonetheless is an important new technology that is steadily maturing.

Both *push* and *publishing* systems increasingly need to distinguish between public and private communications. Obviously, some information—product literature, press releases, annual reports—is best distributed as widely as possible, while other information—price lists, account information, proprietary research—tends to be for restricted use only.

Close security, password, user authentication, and digital signature technologies are needed for these more exclusive systems. These tools for restricting access are becoming common to a rising percentage of Web sites.

4C: Ecosystem Development

The term "ecosystem" refers to the web of partners, suppliers, and customers whose success is important to your own organization's success. Typical ecosystem examples include:

- *Electronic market solutions* enable communities of suppliers to organize around customers and compete for their business. For example, as I noted at the beginning of the chapter, QCS provides a secure network that connects clothing retailers and suppliers to create a more efficient retail sourcing and buying process.
- *Alliance operation* solutions enable communities of organizations to collaborate for competitive advantage. These are used extensively within the IT industry, with its many new and ever changing alliances. In an era of complex "co-opetition," these arrangements must be managed securely and clearly. But they also often need to be set up and shut down quickly and inexpensively. Before the Web, this was not generally feasible.
- *Communities of interest* solutions enable groups of people with common interests to carry out joint discovery and decision-making. For example, scientists trying to find a treatment for a rare disease obviously can benefit by easily sharing ideas and information. In fact, the need for knowledge workers to interact with others in their specific areas characterizes almost every form of professional development, including lawyers, insurers, engineers, accountants, and so on.
- *Interactive distributed* learning solutions enable the delivery of electronic libraries and collaborative training to dispersed individuals and groups. The Web is particularly useful for organizations that need to quickly train customers on their latest products and services. These systems are usually both cheaper and more effective than printed manuals. Similarly, they are much less expensive and much more permanent than face-to-face training initiatives.

4D: Market-Facing Systems

Market-facing systems can be defined most simply as follows: *Market-facing systems are systems that enable a customer's market experience to be defined entirely on line.* Like the workflow and reengineering applications shown below them in Table 4.1, market-facing systems are not so much about any particular technology as they are about pulling together various services to actually conduct business electronically.

Typical market-facing systems encompass marketing, sales, order processing, and customer support functions, as you can see in the following examples:

- *Customer self-service* solutions allow consumers or business customers to meet their needs directly on line. Such systems can consist of sales, marketing, or service functions, often all three. This is the most visible and highly publicized area and is typified by offerings from Amazon.com and Federal Express, as well as all manner of on-line financial and travel services.

- *Customer integration* solutions enable businesses to integrate so closely with their customers as to preclude serious competition. For instance, Shell Oil computers can directly monitor its customers' oil inventory levels and automatically issue replenishment requests when inventories reach certain customer-designated levels. This eliminates a great deal of order/delivery paperwork and has the effect of locking in customers, or at least making it more difficult for them to switch distributors.

- *Channel integration solutions* enable businesses to work with their channels in order to create and share distribution process efficiencies. For example, an automobile company might set up a network for its regional dealers that facilitates the location of particular car configurations. Such systems can be a two-edged sword, in that they could enable manufacturers to bypass the channel altogether. However, more often than not, they tend to redefine the value delivered by the channel, as we shall see.

- *Supply chain integration solutions* enable businesses to manage their supply base and capture efficiencies more effectively. For example, companies can post bids, specify delivery requirements, and monitor supplier satisfaction. Although not getting anywhere near the publicity of consumer Web transactions, over the next few years these business-to-business systems will actually be the single biggest area of electronic commerce activity.

WHAT SHELL CHEMICAL LEARNED FROM YOUR LOCAL WATER COMPANY

Let me close this chapter as I started it—with a corporate anecdote that illustrates the nature of business in a market-facing, Web-based world.

The Shell Chemical Company's newly installed supplier managed inventory system (SMI) permits Shell to assume full responsibility for managing the fuel inventories of its key customers. The strategic vision was initiated by Shell marketing director Ken Valentine, who one day decided that there was no reason why Shell shouldn't function, from an administrative point of view, just like your local water company.

"When you get up in the morning," Valentine would later recall, "you don't have to call the water company and order thirty fresh gallons of water for your shower. You never have to go read a meter—they know how much you're using." Nor do you have to pay your local water company every time you turn on the faucet—in fact, in many cities, water company payments are automatically deducted from the customer's checking account.

Using SMI, Shell is now able to let its customers and suppliers share and provide key information, permitting Shell to proactively anticipate customer requirements and—of more importance for this $4.5 billion global commodity chemical producer—to forecast its own production needs more accurately.

CHAPTER 5

THE MARKET-FACING ENTERPRISE

INSTEAD OF STROLLING—OR DASHING—into a typical brick-and-mortar branch office to make a deposit or withdrawal, customers of Atlanta Internet, a Web-based bank, log onto the Net from any PC anywhere and begin banking to beat the band. At any time of the day or night, at home, at work, or from an airport pay phone, they can pay bills, make deposits, transfer funds, or even view images of their canceled checks, all for monthly fees considerably lower than traditional banks, whose overhead costs, generated by the need to maintain a physical branch network, must be covered by fees and other revenue.

Although just about every traditional bank today is moving aggressively ahead with some form of on-line banking service—roughly 4.5 million Americans did some banking on line in 1998, up sharply from some 200,000 in 1995—pure Internet banks like Atlanta Internet, Security First Network Bank (the first cyberspace bank to go public in May 1996), and CompuBank (a Houston-based start-up) are still relative rarities on the financial scene.

But virtual banks are proliferating: According to the *Wall Street Journal*, over the past year the U.S. comptroller of currency has received at least a dozen inquiries from companies interested in operating Internet-based banks. On-line stock trading sites, such as e.Schwab, are also on the rise and flourishing, as are travel sites like Travelocity, and millions of customers are discovering that they prefer the interactivity and sense of control that can be gained from handling their own stock trading, banking, and travel needs. Of course, none of this would be possible or feasible without the aid of skillfully constructed Web sites that expertly guide customers through the transactional experience with the dexterity (or simulation thereof) of a skilled travel agent, stock broker, or bank teller. In each case, customers are experiencing the benefits—not to mention the novelty—of interacting with true market-facing systems.

WEB-BASED MARKET-FACING SYSTEMS

So what do I mean by this ominous-sounding term? It's really quite simple. In Chapter 4, I defined market-facing systems as systems that enable a customer's market experience to be defined entirely on line. Another way to define the term is to say that in a market-facing system computers both *define* and *manage* an overall business environment.

Such environments are today typically provided over the Web. But the MFS concept itself is entirely independent of information technology. Any system where a computer is a direct source of sales, marketing, customer service, or other business value can accurately be labeled a market-facing system. It's simply that with the advent of the Web and the Net, the competitive need—and the capacity—for many organizations to communicate with customers by means of an MFS has drastically increased.

The Travelocity Web site (*www.Travelocity.com*) provides business travelers with instantaneous access to the Sabre global airline ticket distribution system, the same system used by some 33,000 travel agencies worldwide to purchase airline tickets and book hotel and rental car reservations. Travelocity provides total access to more than 420 airlines, 39,000 hotels, and fifty rental car agencies around the world. An affiliated site called BTS (both owned and managed by AMR, the parent holding company of American Airlines) provides similar as well as enhanced services to corporate customers.

Among the vanguard of companies that moved quickly to establish a MFS to their competitive advantage was Federal Express, which put up a Web server in November 1994 to provide public access to the company's internal package-tracking database. The company, which moves about 2.5 million packages around the world every day, was surprised to find that a staggeringly high number of customers *actually preferred* tracking their own packages on the company's Web site, as opposed to speaking in person to a customer service representative on the phone. FedEx was also pleasantly surprised to find that its interactive Web site saved up to $2 million a year in customer service costs.

Today, with the ability of computers to directly manage business activities that cut clear across almost all major enterprise functions, the most profound effect of this development will be the wholesale transformation of many traditional organizations into fully integrated "market-facing enterprises" (MFE).

One of the first and best-known market-facing enterprises—so much so that it has become a virtual symbol of the field—is the highly successful bookselling site—and "virtual company"—Amazon.com. This company spawned an entirely new product category and compelled off-line competitors such as the Barnes and Noble book retailing chain to create Barnesandnoble.com. Today, both sites are vying with sites put up by other national and regional book stores and chains for the attention of millions of electronic book buyers. In fact, Barnes and Noble's rapid response to the Amazon threat propelled it into the ranks of the truly powerful MFEs.

The rapid development and establishment of MFEs in recent months across nearly every segment of the economy, from automobile and PC sales to health care to financial services, has left even the most avid Webtopians gasping for breath.

According to Daniel Nissan, president and CEO of the New York–based, on-line grocery service Netgrocer, "the problem with most on-line grocery delivery systems is that they actually go to the trouble of delivering groceries." Unlike more established competitors like Peapod, Streamline, and Shoplink, Netgrocer relies on outsourcing all delivery services to the FedEx Corporation, which saves Nissan the need (and the costs) of managing his own fleet of delivery trucks. The reliance on their own delivery services limits Netgrocer's competitors to rolling out their services only in selected local and regional markets. On the other hand, by dispatching all packages via FedEx, Netgrocer has been able to fulfill orders from anywhere in the continental United States from its sprawling North Brunswick, New Jersey, warehouse.

With orders currently increasing by 50 percent per month, Mr. Nissan—a Tel Aviv native and, before founding Netgrocer, an executive at Vocaltech, an Internet telephone company—is convinced that he has discovered a business model for on-line grocery delivery that will enable him to cut costs and overhead in comparison to his competitors. Indeed, according to a profile of Mr. Nissan and his company recently featured in the *New York Times*, Peapod—apparently in response to Netgrocer's national threat, has recently announced that it will introduce its own national express mail service later this year.

The value chain innovation (VCI) being practiced by Netgrocer—and countered competitively by Peapod—is a marvelous example of the current breakdown of traditional methods of production, distribution, and delivery for many goods and services industries. As more and more industries adapt to the radical impact of the Web on their businesses, value chain innovation has become something of a rallying cry for today's fully integrated enterprises.

The ongoing need to continually innovate and restructure the value chain in this new Web-based world is perhaps best illustrated by an example from the pre-Internet period of the financial services world: The introduction of ATMs drastically reduced bank transaction costs and, for a period, provided banks that aggressively deployed them with a competitive edge over regional rivals. Once virtually every bank in every major city was tied into the ATM network, however, ATMs became a core segment requirement rather than a point of product and service differentiation. Market-facing systems will no doubt eventually reach a similar point of saturation. Already since 1996, providing content and basic business process information over the Internet has become the expected norm, as opposed to the novel exception.

The Web's ability to quickly and inexpensively publish current, customized messages to specific audiences and then to accurately measure their responses is already making it the preferred means of distributing corporate information. Increasingly, businesses, and eventually consumers, will come to rely almost totally on the Web to learn about *your* organization.

Your ability to master the appropriate techniques, etiquette, protocols, and practices will define much about how your organization is seen by the world. This will become increasingly important as Web sites become more interactive and more directly linked to key business processes. The bottom line is that for many businesses, your customers will spend more time at your Web site than they will either in your offices or with your actual employees. Thus perhaps it is now more accurate to speak of customer "self-service."

Market-facing systems essentially allow you to put your customer to work for you. Happily and most importantly, many customers appear quite eager to do this, and as more and more customers find their way on line, the number of satisfied on-line, Web-enabled customers is expected to grow exponentially—in accordance, as you may recall, with Metcalfe's Law.

The Federal Express package tracking service is an obvious example of customer self-service. Increasingly customers will want to tie directly into *your* computer systems to answer such everyday questions as:

- What is the status of my account?
- When will my order arrive?
- How can I change my account profile?

Even more broadly, the widespread deployment of Web-based market-facing systems will allow companies to deal directly with millions (or even hundreds of millions) of customers a year, all the while providing a consistent and highly customized experience. By the year 2000, *customer service applications* will be among the Web's most active areas of innovation.

EXTRANETS AND VALUE CHAIN INNOVATION

Although they haven't received anywhere near the publicity of popular on-line *consumer* services, *business-to-business* Web-based systems are likely to dominate electronic commerce over the next few years. *Extranets* can significantly cut costs and provide enhanced value in many important areas, including product sourcing, inventory management, design collaboration, channel management, customer feedback, and time-to-market. In fact, it has become clear by now that extranets will be one of the principle drivers of improved business efficiencies over the next decade.

The Wal-Mart Way

One of the earliest efforts at value chain innovation using an electronic data interchange system deployed on an extranet was pioneered by Wal-Mart, when it created an automatic product replenishment system in partnership with Procter and Gamble. The stores' cash registers were electronically linked to Procter and Gamble's computerized inventory system, so that when consumers bought Procter and Gamble products at Wal-Mart, the system automatically triggered a purchase order and transfer payment between the two companies. By intimately linking these two companies' workflows, this system reduced inventory levels and logistical costs dramatically—it also added to Procter and Gamble the not-negligible value of speedier payments for its products.

As an extension of Wal-Mart's VCI, certain products can actually be delivered *directly* on line. These include many forms of "bit-based" businesses such as financial services, insurance, publishing, software, entertainment, health care, legal advice, training, education, and many government services. In addition, even the distribution of "atom-based" products such as PCs, cars, and other physical devices can be transformed by the ability of MFSs to introduce new levels of customization, choice, and convenience.

Value Chain Shifts

The combination of order of magnitude increases in communications capability and order of magnitude decreases in costs will inevitably lead to shifts in the way value is created and delivered. This will have direct implications for the organization of industries and their underlying value chains. Historically, the boundaries between organizations have often been derived from the underlying patterns of information exchange, as well as production and distribution economies of scale. As these underpinnings change, so will the underpinnings of many, indeed nearly all, industries.

Taken together, the strategic agenda outlined above clearly has little to do with building flashy, cool-looking, Web sites. What's really going on here is that the Web is challenging every company to integrate this powerful new technology into their fundamental business processes in ways that add new value. The real enterprise leaders of the coming decade will be those who expose both their information assets and their core business processes appropriately, not only to their own workforces but to their customers, suppliers, and key market allies.

Clearly, not every company that builds an extranet system will succeed. As inventive and powerful as these systems can be, long-term competitive

advantage is not guaranteed, as other companies will adapt their own businesses to pursue the same opportunities. But investing in IT is no longer
about staff productivity, it's now about attracting, satisfying, and retaining
customers. In other words, it's about survival. Information technology
may not *ensure* success, but success without information technology is
becoming increasingly rare.

THE THREE STAGES OF
ENTERPRISE DEVELOPMENT

The three stages of enterprise development, from basic (dark background)
through intermediate (gray background) to advanced (white background),
are illustrated in Table 5.1. The diagram should be read from the lower left
to the upper right as illustrative of an enterprise evolutionary process,
from the most elementary level—the empowered individual (lower left)—
to the market-facing system in the upper right-hand corner.

The Basic Stage

During the late 1980s and the early 1990s, basic systems—from data creation access and usage through workgroup data systems and applications
on to enterprise data systems—provided an important competitive edge to
some enterprises. Now, however, virtually every organization of even
modest size and complexity has (or should have) an enterprise-wide data
and messaging system, as well as technology-enabled workgroups and individuals. Some sort of home page and associated Web publishing environment has also become a bottom-line requirement. However, as noted
above, the great majority of such sites merely provide static HTML
pages—so-called brochureware—with little true interactivity.

The Intermediate Stage

By 1998, a reasonably enabled technology company should have moved
beyond these basic systems and services to include more advanced workgroup, workflow, and reengineering activities, and perhaps even some
forms of enterprise process innovation. The increasingly broad-based use
of enterprise software products from companies such as SAP, PeopleSoft,

TABLE 5.1   Stages of Enterprise Development

4. Extended Enterprise	Customer and Supplier Transactions	Marketing Communications	Ecosystem Development	Market-Facing Systems
3. Integrated Enterprise	Enterprise Data Systems and Apps.	Enterprise-wide Communication	Enterprise Knowledge Management	Enterprise Process Innovation
2. Automated Workgroup	Workgroup Data Systems and Apps.	Workgroup Communication	Workgroup Collaboration	Workgroup Process Innovation
1. Empowered Individual	Data Creation Access and Usage	Information Access and Authoring	Training, Education, and Expertise	Workflow Integration
	A. DATA	B. INFORMATION	C. KNOWLEDGE	D. WORK

☐ Advanced   ▨ Intermediate   ▨ Basic

Baan, and Oracle is evidence that these one-time leading edge applications are now moving steadily into the mainstream. Some level of intranet usage is also a common aspect of this group.

According to Advanced Manufacturing Research, a Boston-based market research firm, the market for various forms of supply chain software is expected to reach $2.4 billion in 1998, up from $1.6 billion in 1996. By the year 2002, this market is expected to swell to $12 billion. With many companies already using so-called enterprise resource planning programs—which coordinate the relationship of raw materials procurement to, for example, certain administrative functions—some more forward-looking enterprises, in order to produce and distribute customized products while keeping inventory costs to a minimum, are seeking to create flexible pricing programs and to balance conflicting demands from suppliers and customers. As one observer recently put it, "Enterprise resource programs tell producers what they have; supply chain programs show them what can be done with it."

In addition, most medium to large organizations have also taken at least a few steps toward establishing various electronic communities, either through extranets, push technology, or other collaborative approaches. Although these organizations must continue to work on their intranet infrastructures, in many cases they are also beginning to address the cultural and managerial changes associated with increasingly virtual office systems and their effects on workflow, team work, training, and education.

The Advanced Stage

The most fully integrated and leading edge IT users are pursuing competitive advantage in three primary areas:

1. *Externally*, by using the Web to introduce important value chain innovation on either the supply or demand side via what we have labeled market-facing systems
2. *Internally,* by taking formal steps to begin to leverage and manage their knowledge management assets
3. *Innovatively,* by continually seeking greater efficiencies through large-scale process innovation, as well as through real-time transaction links to customers, suppliers, partners, and other relevant parties

Advanced IT users can be found in nearly every industry, as both market-facing systems and knowledge management technology become ever more relevant and useful to just about every industry sector.

GAINING A COMPETITIVE ADVANTAGE

So what's to be gained by being the first kid on your block to take advantage of market-facing systems? One answer can be found in the history of the other great communications revolution of this century—that of telephony. Strange as it may sound to us today, prior to the widespread use of telecommunications business interaction consisted mostly of face-to-face meetings and written, paper, correspondence.

The widespread use of the telephone not only made business processes more efficient, but also fundamentally altered the nature of communications itself. Whereas previously people might not have made the effort to pay a visit next door or across town, much less to another part of the country, the telephone unshackled them, encouraging and enabling a new range of communications and standard business procedures.

Short conversations between employees, partners, suppliers, and customers became economical in collapsed time. Not surprisingly, relationships between those once disparate parties changed dramatically. In some cases, stronger ties were forged, even in the absence of face-to-face interaction. At other times, business was conducted virtually anonymously. In all cases, business and customer expectations grew more demanding with regards to how long it should take to accomplish a particular task.

I have no doubt that the implementation of MFS will follow a similar pattern. Just as the telephone eliminated the need for many face-to-face meetings, so will the Internet displace, or at least seriously decrease, a great deal of telephone usage. Many inquiries and orders handled today by the telephone will eventually be managed over the Internet, at considerably lower cost. Recent research from the consultancy Booz-Allen and Hamilton indicates that a typical bank transaction that costs $1 to process would cost as little as $.01 on the Web. The same research also showed that the processing of a typical airline ticket costs $8 from a ticket agent versus just $1 on the Web.

In this sense, there is really nothing revolutionary going on, only the ability to handle existing work in new and compelling ways. Customers value the ability to interact with their suppliers, to be able to customize an order, to ask questions, to get timely and accurate service at a reduced cost, and to have their feedback institutionalized as part of a company's planning cycle.

As simple as all of this may sound, however, it's important to grasp that market-facing systems go beyond improving current modes of communication. They transform the content of customer conversations: how they get started, how they flow, and in many cases how they are resolved. It's in these changing customer dialogs that the essence and source of the lasting competitive advantage can be found. As with the telephone, someday we will wonder what business was like before market-facing systems became commonplace.

ASSESSING NON–COST VALUES

As illustrated by the aforementioned examples, technology-based market-facing systems can provide compelling cost savings by effectively *dis-*

placing more labor-intensive sales and distribution processes. It's certainly safe to say that wherever and whenever these changes are possible, market movements will follow. It has also become apparent that, like it or not, *cost savings* are today by far the most important driver of changing customer buying preferences.

Non–Cost Values: The Most and Least Affected Industries

Yet surely the *potential for cost savings* is not the sole arbiter of the rate of Web-based business evolution. Customers value improved service and other forms of value that the Web can help enable. How should we factor these values into the business equation? Let's explore this question by compiling two simple lists: a list of industries that, from a *consumer perspective,* appear to have been *most affected* by the Web, and a list of those that seem to have been the *least affected:*

The Most Affected Industries

- Books
- Stock trading
- PCs
- Automobiles
- Travel

The Least Affected Industries

- Food
- Consumer durables
- Clothing
- Local services
- Banking and insurance

What are we to make of this pattern? Certainly, we can say that those industries most affected by the Web share a strong *cost saving* component. But do they have anything else in common? Possibly.

The Six Cs

Consider the "six Cs":

1. Choice
2. Customization
3. Consistency
4. Convenience
5. Community
6. Change

The industries in the first list share many of these six noncost features, whereas those in the second list share relatively few.

Choice

All five of the items in the first list exist in great variety with virtually limitless consumer choice. Obviously, there are literally hundreds of thousands of books in print, tens of thousands of stocks and mutual funds to choose from, many thousands of different PC configurations and automobile options, and virtually limitless travel options. Volumes have grown sufficiently great that no one physical location can hold all of the available products. The list of industries in the second list also tends to enjoy a significant degree of consumer choice, but in the case of *durables, local services*, and *banking/insurance*, the options are usually significantly more constrained.

Overall, most of what is demanded in these industries can be contained within traditional retail outlet spaces.

Customization

The first list can also accommodate high degrees of product customization. Most people have their own particular set of reading interests, just as they have their own financial portfolio. Similarly, the Web enables on-line PC sellers to configure a system precisely to each customer's particular preferences. An on-line automobile service could clearly do the same. Obviously, many travel arrangements are highly customized. In contrast, many types of food, consumer durables, clothing, and financial services tend to come in standard versions, with customization very much the exception, and often coming at considerable cost.

Consistency

Consistency is an often overlooked value. But consider the fact that there is virtually no qualitative differentiation between any one version of a particular book, share of stock, PC, automobile, or airline seat. In contrast, there is obviously much more variation in food, clothing, and local services. This very high product consistency helps to eliminate the doubt often inherent in buying products sight unseen, on-line grocery services like Peapod and Netgrocer notwithstanding.

Convenience

The extent to which the Web enables a significant increase in *consumer convenience* is also an important factor. The ability to trade stocks immediately twenty-four hours a day is an important new capability, as is the ability to browse through reader comments in an on-line bookstore. Automatic on-line pricing and configuration systems for PCs and cars provide highly useful information in a totally nonpressurized environment. Although much of this convenience is potentially relevant to the second list as well, in reality it is often not effectively available: Going to the ATM for cash is still a common practice; arranging for grocery deliveries can be awkward; and clothes ordered by phone may not fit, and such phone orders may thus result in complex return/exchange situations. In short, while theoretical convenience exists almost everywhere, practical realities differ widely.

Community

Here, the main issue is whether the product in question tends *to generate strong community activity* and *affinity*. Consider the strong identification many people have with books, music, PCs, cars, and travel. Although there is clearly some of this potential with food, clothing, and other areas, the level of interest does seem distinctly lower. How much community interest is there in ovens or refrigerators?

Change

Finally, the *rate of change* is an extremely important factor in shaping the Web's appeal. Stock prices change every minute; books rapidly go out of print or out of stock. PC hardware and software technologies change constantly, as do airline fares. In contrast, customer tastes in food are quite stable, and clothing fashions vary yearly, at most. Similarly, how much have televisions, stereos, and refrigerators changed over the last ten years? How about the basic functions of your bank accounts and insurance policies? The Web's ability to incorporate change twenty-four hours a day is simply more important in some realms than in others.

MARKET-FACING SYSTEMS
IN PERSPECTIVE

The emergence of market-facing systems and their organizational analog, the market-facing enterprise, will have any number of important business implications in the years to come. At this stage, I would emphasize five major areas of impact.

1. *Huge changes in IT economies of scale.* In the back-office era, systems were managed by specialists and served relatively small groups of users. IT customer populations were usually measured in the thousands or even less. In the front-office era, the target market was the white collar workforce, usually measured in the tens of millions. With market-facing systems, the target market—mostly if not entirely on-line consumers—is measured in the hundreds of millions today and may be measured in the billions a decade from now. No wonder scaleability—the ability of a system to grow according to the scale of the size of the network—has become such an industry buzzword.

2. *Convergence of business and technology rates of change.* As critical business systems become increasingly and fundamentally *based upon information technology*, the rate of business change and the rate of technology change are rapidly converging. In other words, to maintain a state-of-the-art Web site, nearly all businesses will have to move at speeds closer to that of the full-throttle IT industry. One could argue that perhaps the pace of technology change will slow, but given today's fierce IT industry competition, this is doubtful. More likely, large gaps between technology

availability and usage will develop, creating new areas of potential competitive advantage.

3. *Conversion to market-facing systems.* You are already (or will soon become) part of a market-facing system. To most of the public and even to most of your customer base, your Web site will emerge as the single largest part of your organization's everyday image. In many industries, far more people will know you through electronic systems than through face-to-face dealings. The Web is much more than the vehicle of your public relations campaign: It's the engine of your marketing, sales, service, and community activity, and it's all there, in full public view, twenty-four hours a day, all around the world.

4. *CEOs required.* Too many organizations have spent too much time trying to decide who should be responsible for their Web site—marketing, sales, the IT organization, communications, and so on. The truth is that *no one group* is ideal. Eventually, just about all critical company functions will be replicated in cyberspace. In this sense, the only true point of accountability is with top management, which should view a Web site in the same way it views its more physical operations, keeping close watch on a wide array of vital signs. Only through top executive leadership can an objective, balanced strategy be maintained. Inevitably, without strong CEO leadership, the site will be distorted by the functional biases of one group or another, or perhaps worse, will get bogged down in committee-style procedures.

5. *The importance of Web sites.* An advanced, appealing, and highly interactive Web site is a key component in demonstrating the technological competence and commitment of the organization to the public at large. Just as almost every business today has its own form of competitive analysis to measure differences in various functional areas, so will companies spend a lot of time comparing and contrasting their own ability to generate effective market-facing systems. Such systems will become an increasingly critical competitive front.

SORTING THROUGH
THE NEAR-TERM REALITY

Many critical business functions, and indeed entire industries, have the potential to be greatly transformed by the power of market-facing systems and to become true market-facing enterprises. But just because so many things *can* be transformed doesn't necessarily mean that they *will be*. Many of these changes will take a decade or more to play out. From a macroperspective, it's important to stress the essential difference between two main trends: the rate of evolution for *Web functionality*, and the relative impact of the Web on major *economic and societal sectors*.

Consider first the evolution of Web functionality: In just a few years, we have advanced from simple Web publishing—brochureware—to various forms of customer service and, more recently, to far more robust sales transaction systems. The collaborative technology base that will enable the vault to the next phase is also now in place.

One example of this evolution took place in my own company, as we moved to create a Lotus Web site, which currently contains around 130,000 pages of information. This vast store of information, all available to anyone with Web access, is maintained by some fifty "authors" scattered around offices all over the country, all of whom, supported by a half dozen full-time Web professionals, are fully capable of authoring HTML pages. This ongoing effort is fully collaborative and is a fine example of distributed authoring. In the process of overseeing the creation of the Lotus Web site, I've learned a little something, so trust me when I speak of the path that leads to a market-facing enterprise.

Note, however, that what has happened at Lotus is the exception and not the rule. As noted earlier, concepts often move much more quickly than markets, and thus the great majority of the Web is still in the first stage of Web functionality: the static publishing phase. Thus in spite of the evolution in Web functionality, the relative impact of the Web on major societal and economic factors is minimal, though this is changing. Figure 5.1 plots the current and projected pervasiveness of Web-based market-facing systems within various sectors. Let me conclude this chapter with a brief, sector-by-sector look at the near-term reality.

Business to Business

As noted before, *business extranet applications* will evolve more quickly than any other market segment. Businesses are quickly putting their intranet infrastructures in place; most target users have PCs or other access devices; and unlike consumers, they often have access to high levels of communications bandwidth. Thus, the potential for wholesale transforma-

FIGURE 5.1   The Pervasiveness of the Market-Facing Systems

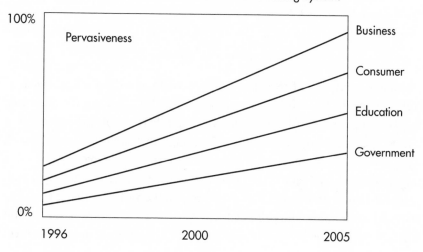

tion is clearly there. Nevertheless, some industries will be affected much more profoundly than others.

Business to Consumers

Although consumer use of the Web continues to build, total transformation will not be possible until much higher levels of consumer Web access and utilization are achieved. Today, only about 40 percent of U.S. households have a PC, and only about half of those are connected to the Internet. Nearly universal Web access, even in the United States, is simply not possible for at least another four or five years, quite possibly longer. This puts a ceiling on certain developments, especially in many countries outside of the United States.

As long as businesses need to serve both on-line and non-on-line customers, redundancies and complexities will be unavoidable. Indeed, juggling existing and new business models is inherently difficult and is likely to be the greatest challenge that many established companies face. More pointedly, the ability to focus entirely on a new business model is often the key to a start-up's eventual success against wealthier, more established players. For Barnes and Noble to match Amazon's on-line capabilities is one thing; but to do it in an environment where over 90 percent of its business, and all of its profits, come from a nationwide chain of retail stores is quite another.

Education to Consumers

Despite a good deal of recent progress through admirable efforts such as Net Day and Tech Corps, the fact remains that K–12 education all around the world remains substantially unwired, and there is still little clear commitment to changing this situation. Although this topic is generally outside of the scope of this book, I think it is fair to say that over the next five years, the most likely areas of innovation will be in higher education, both adult education and, perhaps most interestingly, in the ability of on-line learning to do something about today's stunningly high college tuition levels. For most businesses, the possibilities of on-line, university-level training are particularly relevant to efforts to promote knowledge management, lifelong learning, and the oft-labeled "learning organization."

Government to Consumers

Although a great deal more could be done in this potentially powerful service arena, government initiatives will be hampered by the same lack of universal consumer usage discussed above. Until pervasive service is established, most governments will be reluctant to offer important new sources of value, lest they be accused of favoring the so-called information "haves" over the "have-nots." Governments will, however, continue to put much of their emphasis on static Web publishing and the access to simple electronic forms; even widespread citizen/government e-mail usage is proving difficult. Whereas businesses will be rewarded for providing enhanced services to early Web adopters, governments might well be criticized. This is unfortunate but probably very difficult to overcome in the current climate.

Still, once again the overriding message is here and clear: Market-facing systems are real, and they are already providing tremendous competitive advantage to organizations (MFEs) ready and willing to take advantage of them. The story is familiar: Lead, follow, or get out of the way—and options two and three carry a hefty price.

CHAPTER 6

KNOWLEDGE MANAGEMENT: THE SUSTAINABLE COMPETITIVE EDGE

In today's economy, the most important resource is no longer labor, capital or land; it is knowledge.

—Peter Drucker

In a time of drastic change, the learners will inherit the future.

—Eric Hoffer

AFTER GRADUATING FROM THE NATION'S oldest military college—Norwich University in Northfield, Vermont—and before entering corporate life, I served as an officer in the U.S. Marine Corps and later in the U.S. Marine Corps Reserve. It's not widely known, but every year more than 100,000 volunteer service people serve in the Marine Corps, whether on reserve duty for three days each month or to attend an annual two-week training exercise. In addition to the skills maintenance and preparation for emergency service that civilians generally associate with military reserve service, reservists perform actual tasks—from the maintenance of military locations to complex occupational tasks like combat flight training to mission-critical administrative functions.

Every few days the personnel at many of the marine posts around the country and the world turn over nearly completely, with volunteers moving in and out to spell and relieve each other as they arrive and/or return to their civilian responsibilities. Nonetheless, much of the work in which they are engaged cannot be completed in a few days. In fact, a single project may span several weeks and thus may involve personnel who have never met but who need to engage in information sharing.

According to Major General Thomas Wilkerson, the remarkable commander of a remarkable organization, the U.S. Marine Corps Reserves—and a man whom I consider a close friend—most reservists typically serve no more than three years, resulting in a fairly rapid turnover by civilian standards. Reservists reporting to duty and picking up incomplete projects from other reservists need the information already acquired by those who have recently preceded them.

I can recall arriving at a marine air base squadron in South Carolina only to be given a large box of records that needed what today we would call "knowledge management" so that a substantive administrative effort that had been started could be completed. This kind of midstream work was and can be very frustrating. But I'm happy to say that today things are different for reservists.

We at Lotus were fortunate to be asked to work with General Wilkerson in the deployment of several collaborative network solutions to bridge these gaping knowledge gaps. Today, when marine reservists report for duty, they are greeted with e-mail from General Wilkerson, as well as with on-line photography of the people with whom they will be working. Included in this digital package is background and contextual information regarding the projects on which they will be working. Archiving and key word retrieval help everyone involved to quickly assimilate the knowledge and records associated with peers they may never meet in person.

Now every leader and every volunteer and officer at every Marine Corps command in the land and abroad can know what others know at posts all over the world. This leaves individuals more prepared for that emergency call—which can come at any time—than ever before. Today's Marine Corps reservists can enjoy the kind of community that fosters the ready availability and transfer of knowledge that was previously, and at best, only tacit. Today, when reservists achieve goals that engender commendation, their good work can be disseminated rapidly enough to remote superiors that reservists can be recognized with a medal or certificate in the company of those with whom they served when they achieved the objective for which they are recognized.

Context, community, and continuity are well supported in this and all scenarios of good knowledge management. In this case, and with this particular organization, the stakes certainly couldn't be any higher. In the military, whether it be active duty or reserve, readiness is a matter of life and death. Most days, collaboration in the Marine Corps Reserves is about attaining heightened levels of knowledge and professionalism in what remains a most remarkable organization. For an organization with so much cherished history behind it, the Marine Corps is one of the most modern, advanced, forward-looking IT organizations in the world.

So if your view of this organization is bayonets and gunpowder, guess again—in the ongoing war of competitive readiness, IT has become the ultimate weapon. Perhaps most notably, the Marine Corps Reserves, an organization where command and control have historically been accompanied by the maintenance of strong and highly traditional hierarchical management structures, is today about as collaborative an organization as you will find anywhere on the planet.

MANAGING RELATIONSHIPS/ MANAGING KNOWLEDGE

The Chase Manhattan Corporation is one of the largest banking organizations in the United States, with more than $300 billion in assets and quarterly net income approaching $1 billion. The bank's Middle Market Banking Group is the dominant player in its market—serving organizations with annual sales ranging from $3 million to $500 million. The Group's mandate is to provide a wide range of financial products and services, including cash management, international trade, leasing, financing, investment banking, and credit. The group employs some 650 "relationship managers" (RMs), each of whom manages anywhere from thirty to sixty banking relationships in this "middle market." A "relationship" is defined either as a company or as a person who owns one or more companies. The RM's main responsibility is maintaining current relationships and cultivating new ones.

For Chase's relationship managers, spending time with customers has always been the number one priority. But back in 1993, these skilled executives were spending as much as *a third* of their time trapped at their desks, mired in low-level administrative activities, like tracking down routine customer information from legacy systems and funneling it into tables and spreadsheets. The senior executives in the group, seeking to maximize the amount of time that the RMs could spend with their customers, concluded that the Group needed a relationship management system (RMS) that would help them to better understand their own relationships with their customers.

One problem that the Group encountered in attempting to organize its disparate systems was that the information that it did have was poorly organized and was categorized according to product and transaction, not by relationship. This made it nearly impossible to track the productivity and profitability of a banking relationship that a senior manager may have been attempting to assess. It was next to impossible, for example, for the bank to know whether it was making money on a loan to a customer but losing money on other aspects of the same relationship. The group as a whole couldn't tell—and certainly couldn't assess the matter jointly— whether any one relationship was a profit or a loss leader.

Chase's new RMS provided just the level of granularity required to regulate and manage this complex web of relationships. Accessed through a desktop icon, the system extracts timely information about each relationship from the bank's legacy databases and composes a customized picture of the entire relationship that can be displayed on a single PC screen. The RMS sits on top of the bank's legacy systems and, rather than supplanting them, makes them more productive.

Interestingly, much of the same data had been available to the RMs in hard copy form, distributed monthly in twelve-inch-thick paper reports. But not only was the information often not timely, it was unwieldy and cumbersome to use. To manipulate data, RMs had to manually input it into spreadsheets, which were hard to measure against comparable reports.

Today, Chase's RMs simply scan entire customer portfolios on screen and tailor the information displayed so that the system can focus in on potential trouble spots. Most importantly, senior managers can easily access the same system, which means that they don't have to schedule a separate meeting with an RM to obtain customer balances, active loans, and other required information.

The RMS is a perfect case of mere *data* being turned into *information,* of that *information* being turned into *knowledge,* and of that knowledge being more appropriately distributed—rendered accessible—throughout an organization. That's a great example of knowledge management. Collaboration, I like to say, is the DNA of knowledge management. *True knowledge management is the ability to take information stored passively inside people's heads and render it public, actionable, useful, and explicit.*

Experience has taught us that true knowledge management is as much about *people* and *culture* as it is about technology, which is why I so much appreciate an observation made by Fortune editor Tom Stewart: "Technology without people won't work, but people without technology won't scale."

Knowledge management is, I believe, the next great step on the collaborative IT evolutionary scale: from *groupware*—and its document-centric, messaging-reliant applications—to the sort of same-time, real-time, asynchronous, collaborative communication that the market-facing enterprise will need not merely to survive but to thrive.

Knowledge management is much more than a simple shift in branding or terminology; it is a series of important breakthroughs in various new information technologies, which break down into three basic areas:

1. Creation
2. Discovery and search
3. Distribution

These three basic technologies are combined in all full-fledged KM systems with continual advances in distribution, workflow, and replication, in both synchronous and asynchronous modes.

Additionally, knowledge management is not just another case of vendor hype or the makings of another competitive food fight. Business and government leaders all around the world see the knowledge management era coming. In December 1997, in the midst of the greatest economic and currency crisis the Asian region had seen in decades, I met with Deputy Prime Minister Anwar Ibrahim of Malaysia, whom I have come to respect enormously.

Despite all that was going on in his part of the world, this charismatic leader was focused on one thing: how to create a knowledge-based economy rather than one based on palm oil and other natural resources. While the world was wondering whether the *ringgit* would rise or fall that day, he was talking to me about knowledge management. Even at the height of the crisis, Deputy Prime Minister Ibrahim recognized a wave of the future when he saw one.

A NATIONAL AND CORPORATE PRIORITY

In a September 1997 *Harvard Business Review* article, Peter Drucker outlined the demographic reasons why knowledge management has become such a critical social goal in the developed world, and not merely a corporate luxury. Most of today's advanced economies are experiencing sharply lower birth rates, which over time will no doubt result in often precipitate population declines.

Knowledge management, Drucker believes, may provide the key to enhanced productivity for fewer and older workers. As Drucker so precisely puts it, with "the underpopulation of the developed countries an accomplished fact," the predictable consequence is that the ratio of older to younger workers will steadily rise, with serious implications for long-term economic growth. In an environment marked by population decline, shrinking societies must continue to improve their productivity or face growing impoverishment. More specifically, shrinking societies will have to rely heavily on older workers to maintain any sort of competitive edge.

In today's rapidly changing world, maintaining the competitive edge of fewer, older workers will require continual learning and training. Drucker's basic message is that knowledge management will be absolutely essential for the improvement, and perhaps even for the maintenance, of our current living standards. I do not want to mince words. I see knowledge management not as an abstraction or a luxury or just another set of lofty, high-minded words. Intellectual capital has in recent years become the central currency of our times.

The industrial economies of *product* and *scale* that have long driven business competition are being suddenly supplanted by the knowledge-based economies of *service* and *expertise*. Mobilizing a new class of resources requires *an integrated system of knowledge management* that can maximize the use of enterprise information and expertise, while facilitating and even institutionalizing ongoing organizational learning.

Today, many forward-thinking companies are in the early stages of developing KM systems and strategies, believing that they will soon become a key competitive requirement. In a recent study, the Meta group forecasted that by the year 2000, global companies will be spending over $50 billion per year to manage their internal knowledge resources. Similarly, a recent survey conducted in the United Kingdom showed that over 60 percent of large enterprises can claim that they possess a unique body of knowledge that gives them a competitive edge.

But beyond the numbers, both CEOs and CIOs have increasingly come to recognize that in the coming decade knowledge will be king. And the benefits to those who master its core principles will be tremendous.

SEVEN REASONS WHY KNOWLEDGE MANAGEMENT IS SO IMPORTANT NOW

Why is knowledge management suddenly so important? This really is a very good question. After all, hasn't knowledge management *always* been important? Well, in a manner of speaking, yes. Certainly, in the eons of history before computers, *knowledge* was recognized as being more important than mere *data* or raw, unprocessed *information*. Expertise, experience, insight, and even intuition have always been critical aspects of business success. In fact, it would be a rank injustice to the collective intelligence of the agricultural and industrial eras to suggest otherwise.

Certainly, conventional wisdom has long dictated that know-how and know-why are the keys to both business and personal success. Similarly, there is no denying that knowledge has always been inseparable from innovation, creativity, judgment, and effectiveness. To use a bit of a cliché, knowledge has always been closely associated with power. This is one reason why people have always tended to hoard it so secretively.

What's different today is not so much that knowledge is more important than it used to be. What's changed is the scope, form, scale, and pace of knowledge development. In most medium to large organizations, knowledge has grown well past the stage where it can be successfully managed within the minds of individuals. When Tom Stewart of *Fortune* says "technology without people won't work, but people without technology won't scale" what he means is that today's more structured, technology-enabled knowledge management systems are quickly becoming the only way for large organizations to cope with today's knowledge requirements.

Why is this the case? I can think of seven good reasons.

1. *Globalization.* Operating in multiple parts of the world provides substantial competitive advantage to those organizations capable of effectively leveraging shared experiences and resources. For reasons of time, volume, and distance, this type of sharing is often impossible without

modern technology systems. Put simply, global businesses tend to be much larger than national ones, and size puts significant pressures on face-to-face, telephone, and even e-mail communications.

2. *Speed.* A combination of globalization, deregulation, and increasing reliance on ever changing technologies is forcing businesses to operate on ever shorter market cycles, and therefore plans must be made, changed, and abandoned more quickly than ever. Effective high-speed corporate maneuvering requires rapid, on-demand access to many forms of information and knowledge. There is nothing like watching a company deal with an emergency situation to see how effective its internal information and communications systems really are. Do they hold up, or do people resort to manual, often seat-of-the-pants methods?

3. *Service orientation.* As just about every business becomes more customer and service oriented, individual and group access to up-to-date customer information is increasingly critical, as is the need for continual on-the-job training. Customers expect immediate responses even to complex problems; this can happen only if all the necessary information and relevant know-how is available on line and internalized into employee behavior.

4. *Worker dispersion.* Workers are increasingly more mobile and geographically dispersed. According to recent research, by the year 2000 there likely will be more than *50 million* mobile workers. This makes traditional, face-to-face, intracompany knowledge sharing increasingly ineffective. High worker turnover is another aspect of the need to improve overall employee training, education, and knowledge access. All around the world, concepts of lifetime employment are changing. Among the big four accounting and consulting firms, at any given point in time it is estimated that as much as fifty percent of the workforce is either in its first or last year of employment. In this sort of environment, systems for capturing and reusing employee knowledge are often indispensable.

5. *Closer business relationships.* As companies engage in closer working relationships with their customers, suppliers, and even their competitors, they are exposed to many more sources of potential learning. Too many companies today still see knowledge management as primarily an internal activity when in fact there is often a great deal to be learned even from companies well outside of your industry. More broadly, the World Wide Web itself can be an extraordinarily powerful source of new knowledge which must be integrated with each organization's everyday learning processes.

6. *Technology.* The convergence of advanced messaging systems, groupware, and the Web provide the technical foundation needed to support enterprise-wide knowledge management. In other words, the opportunity for sophisticated and highly focused KM is really just now arriving, as intranets emerge as a common organizational platform. During 1998, companies like Lotus will be adding additional *distance learning* and *same-time capabilities* to their products to further strengthen this foundation. In fact, same-time capabilities are critical. In knowledge management terms, responsiveness has much to do with the seamless capability of moving from asynchronous to synchronous modes. And remember that KM has much to do with responsiveness. To this end, in fact, both Lotus and Microsoft have made multiple acquisitions in the same-time space in 1998. Lack of tools will no longer provide an excuse for inaction.

7. *Competition.* Market-facing systems and market-facing enterprises provide a powerful new means for crystallizing the intellectual capital of organizations into forms that enable systemic business advantage. Increasingly, almost everything a business knows and is able to do will be embedded in its outward-facing systems. However, any market-facing system that remains static can be copied and matched easily by competitors. Constant improvement is often the key to sustained market advantage, and therefore organizations need to continually renew and channel their expertise into their everyday operations. As one industry executive put it, "Our goal is to learn every day how to do things a little better and smarter."

For these and probably many other reasons, organizations have come to recognize that knowledge is often their main economic resource and that the knowledge worker is their most essential corporate asset. Employees must learn as they work, and it is imperative that the organization both supports that learning and harvests its value for reuse by others.

ACTION JACKSON:
PUTTING "KNOWLEDGE" IN CONTEXT

The terms "knowledge" and "management" are both used so frequently that there is a natural tendency to assume that we all have a common understanding of what the term "knowledge management" really means. Unfortunately, this is not so. If you asked a dozen companies what they mean by knowledge management, you might well get a dozen different answers.

In Chapter 4, I used the example of an accounting firm with a delinquent account to define four key terms. As a way of working toward an understanding of knowledge management, let me review these definitions:

Data can be defined as simple unqualified *facts*. *Information* tends to enrich *data* by giving it some context. *Knowledge* is what information becomes when it is connected to *relevant know-how* or *know-why*, and thus supports or informs key decisions. *Work* is the product of putting some combination of *data, information*, and *knowledge* into *action*.

Knowledge, in other words, is more than the random or even organized accumulation of bits of information. *Knowledge is the resource that enables one to convert information into decisions and actions. Knowledge needs to be actionable.* There, I've said it, and I'll probably need to say it again.

Time and time again staff members at Lotus and elsewhere have handed me requests for additional information regarding a pending management issue. My standard response rarely varies: Will we decide differently after having absorbed this additional information? The number of times the answer to this question turns up "No" boggles the imagination. Yet how many times knowingly or unknowingly is information rehashed in this way? What a staggering waste of time, and talent!

At the risk of repeating myself: Knowledge is information that is first absorbed into and then filtered through the beliefs, experiences, capabilities, and judgments of the learner and then interpreted by that learner and turned into productive use and action.

To use a musical analogy: *Information is the score that in the hands of the knowledgeable musician can be turned into a jazz improvisation.* Actually, jazz is not my favorite genre, but the analogy makes the point; choose any metaphor that works for you, including a prolonged lick by The Grateful Dead's late and lamented Jerry Garcia or a spreadsheet in the hands of a skilled financial analyst. A spreadsheet, now isn't that a much more pleasing analogy?

EXPLICIT AND TACIT KNOWLEDGE

Combining *information* with *know-how* (and *know-why*) and converting it into productive use is a process of toggling between two kinds of knowledge: explicit knowledge and tacit knowledge. (These terms were first popularized in the important book by Nonaka and Takeuchi, *The Knowledge Creating Company*.) *Tacit* knowledge resides with the individual in the form of know-how—habits, patterns, behaviors, insights, and the like. In other words, it's *known* but usually *unspoken*. Sometimes "tacit" knowledge is referred to as "people" knowledge, since it often exists within the minds, rolodexes, and networks of managers and employees. *Explicit* knowledge, by contrast, can be expressed through reports, analyses, manuals, directions, practices, e-mails, software codes, and so on. *Effective knowledge management systems enable tacit and explicit knowledge to feed off of one another in an iterative manner.*

For example, one employee, in describing to another employee how to write a business plan, makes her knowledge explicit and available. That explicit knowledge then gets rendered tacit through the new employee's action and application: That new employee, in actually writing a business plan and asking for feedback, internalizes the knowledge and archives it as new understanding and new behavior.

The need to link knowledge to action suggests that knowledge management and collaboration should be closely integrated processes. In other words, a knowledge management system must support the continuous process of transforming personal knowledge (the tacit) into organizational knowledge (the explicit) and then driving this newly explicit knowledge throughout the organization. This explicit knowledge must then be internalized again into personal, tacit behavior at the individual employee level. In order to do this, information management, which is concerned with storing and processing explicit information, must be combined with collaboration, which is concerned with tacit activity and learning.

THE CREATION, APPLICATION, AND DISTRIBUTION OF KNOWLEDGE

Knowledge management as an organizational competency is built on a foundation of groupware, messaging, and database technology. Knowledge management systems integrate *structured* and *unstructured* information with *collaborative work processes*. The ultimate goal is not merely to *find* or *discover* information, but to *enhance an organization's agility, responsiveness, and creativity*. As you can see in figure 6.1, this enhancement involves a three-prong effort as knowledge is created, distributed, and applied.

Figure 6.1   The Three Aspects of Knowledge Management

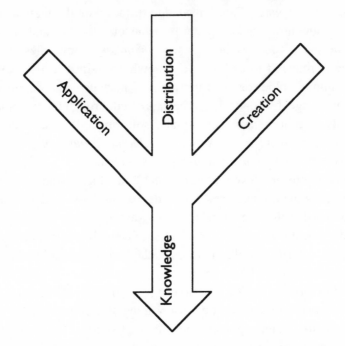

Typically, IT organizations tend to focus first and foremost on *knowledge distribution*, perhaps because this is the most technology-dependent part of the process. The emphasis on distribution tends to rely on sophisticated search and storage technology and is aimed at getting the right information to the right people. For example, documents—located in e-mail, company databases, intranets, or Web sites—can be tagged so that knowledge workers can search for them and distribute them with ease throughout the organization. With today's technology, distribution has become the easy part.

Creation and application are the more critical and difficult parts of the triad, requiring much more than just fancy software technology. Recently, researchers at Xerox Parc studied thirty-five organizations to assess their internal learning systems. They concluded that organizational learning, another name for the creation and application of knowledge, is fundamentally social. In most companies, the primary social units are departments, specialized teams, and various communities of practice. Within these workgroups, people interact, learn, and practice new behavior. Workgroups are constantly receiving new information, thinking, producing, testing, and evaluating. This is the cycle of modern applied learning. The role of technology is to extend this cycle in real-time, asynchronous, and highly distributed ways.

AREAS OF KNOWLEDGE MANAGEMENT

Consider the following five broad areas of knowledge management and ask yourself which are most relevant to your own organization.

1. *Distributed learning applications.* DLAs use a variety of technologies to deliver training and education, ideally enabling close integration with day-to-day work responsibilities. Most organizations need to provide regular, formal learning experiences to assure that workers remain current with the required skills and knowledge. While many individuals are motivated to learn for both personal and professional development reasons, the logistics of attending classroom education are increasingly difficult and expensive to manage.

In response, corporations, higher education institutions, and training businesses are setting up virtual, distributed learning systems. Through technology they hope to

- increase the speed, flexibility, and reach of training and education;
- reduce the high costs associated with classroom training;
- leverage instructors' expertise across a broader population of participants; and
- institutionalize team learning to enhance group performance and productivity.

These systems can be as simple as the top-down, electronic publishing of relevant materials or as complex as highly interactive on-line courseware. In short, distributed learning systems seek to provide explicit knowledge, and then make it tacit through practice and experience.

2. *Communities of practice applications.* CPAs enable individuals who engage in similar types of work to capture, share, and leverage their collective knowledge. More often than not, these people don't actually have

any formal need to work together, and therefore participation is usually based primarily on a sense of mutual benefit. Today, such systems are most commonly found in professional service areas such as accounting, consulting, science/engineering, and computer services, but their functionality can be applied equally well to sales, customer service, maintenance, financial reporting, and many other areas.

Communities of practice are relevant to just about any company that has people developing the same type of know-how but working on different projects or in different physical locations. CPAs are also becoming increasingly common between enterprises. In short, communities of practice applications are generally about making tacit information explicit and then distributing this information to the relevant individuals.

3. *Data warehousing/data mart/data mining applications.* These are designed to derive knowledge from information already captured in existing customer records, databases, and other systems. In most cases, this information has been captured through transaction processing operations. The trick is to use this information to discern trends, understand customer demographics, and refine marketing strategies.

Today, data warehouse systems are generally complex and expensive and are therefore used mainly by large banks, by retailers, and by travel and telecommunications firms. Indeed, market estimates suggest that today fewer than 10 percent of large and medium organizations are taking real advantage of these systems. However, as more and more business is conducted on the Web, the ability to understand specific customer interactions will be increasingly required. It can be an important differentiator. Warehouse systems are essentially about *information creation:* They try to discover knowledge from existing sets of information.

4. *Expert systems/rule-based applications (RBAs).* Expert systems and RBAs are designed to incorporate *explicit company knowledge into actual business processes.* Expert systems frequently fall into the realm of advanced software that can, for example, help a customer service representative sort through complex airline fare systems or manage a customer's on-line troubleshooting experience.

At a more mundane level, however, rule-based systems can be as simple as the telephone prompting systems that allow customers to automatically step through routine inquiries. In fact, the early evidence here suggests that relatively simple rule-based systems are often easier to install and extract value from than more highly publicized expert systems, which have made little reduction in the need for experts such as doctors, lawyers, tax advisers, and scientists. Expert systems are essentially about embedding explicit knowledge into computer software programs.

5. *External information integration*. Historically, the field of knowledge management has been principally viewed in terms of ways to identify and leverage internal knowledge sources. However, with the arrival of the World Wide Web, corporate learning processes must make every effort to take advantage of this powerful new resource. Over time, the value of external sources of knowledge will likely equal or even exceed internal ones, especially as extranets and other technologies accelerate interfirm collaboration.

Integrating knowledge drawn from the Web raises new issues of awareness, quality control, distribution, and process integration. In response, some companies are even hiring knowledge finders, aggregators, and editors to assure that important sources of intelligence are not overlooked. Indeed, this has become an important new role for traditional market researchers, librarians, and competitive analysts. If anything, the Web is increasing the need for these information intermediaries, who some thought might soon become obsolete in the digital era.

SIX DIFFICULTIES OF IMPLEMENTING KNOWLEDGE MANAGEMENT

The important applications described above could easily make one think that developing advanced knowledge management systems is a no-brainer. What company wouldn't want to take advantage of these benefits? Yet it is clear that knowledge management has been a difficult area for many businesses. In fact, a recent study by Booz-Allen suggests that as many as one third of KM projects are basically failures. How many of the above areas of knowledge management activity is your organization actually involved with? What has been the success rate?

The difficulty of successful knowledge management is not new. Over the years, knowledge management has had a number of different labels—*executive information systems, decision support systems, information warehouses,* and others. Yet as often as not, such systems, worthwhile as they may have been, have not yet had the transformative effect many have hoped for.

There are six main reasons why effective knowledge management often has proved difficult to implement. If you are planning any new initiatives in this area, you might want to make sure you have considered the following:

1. *Company size.* The size of an organization and its geographic distribution can make informal, person-to-person knowledge exchange difficult. Although this actually increases the need for knowledge management systems, it also poses serious manageability issues. If your organization has 1,000 sales people scattered all around the world with various levels of experience, how easy is it to tailor a KM system to meet each of their needs?

2. *Information volume.* The sheer volume of information that is available in printed or electronic format can be a major barrier. If a system is overloaded with irrelevant information, employees won't bother to seek out the nuggets they need. So-called "push" systems can actually make this problem worse unless information is sufficiently and effectively targeted. Some companies have addressed this issue by assigning moderators, editors, or other types of filters. However, to be effective these intermediaries must be extremely sensitive to the needs of their audiences: Lotus case studies show that users have mixed views about whether specialized discussion groups should be moderated or not.

3. *Lack of incentive.* As noted earlier, if knowledge really *is* power, what is the motivation for people to share it? Many companies have struggled with how to provide meaningful incentives so that individuals will contribute to knowledge management systems. These companies recognize that there is often a strong cultural tendency to hoard knowledge or to share knowledge only on a "need-to-know" basis. Clearly, specific carrots and sticks can occasionally help, but more often strong top management leadership and a real commitment to cultural change is required. Experience strongly suggests that establishing and successfully demonstrating clear knowledge management benefits usually precedes serious cultural change. However, this raises fundamental chicken-and-egg-type problems.

4. *Lack of metrics and short-term horizons.* Knowledge management systems have real costs in terms of software, development, and management. But how does one measure the benefits? Are there specific organizational objectives that reward and encourage the sharing and reuse of knowledge? Additionally, although there is little doubt that the value of successful knowledge management systems builds over time, many orga-

nizations understandably prefer to evaluate ever changing IT investments based on short-term priorities. What if the payoff from knowledge management is necessarily several years away, whereas the IT agenda is dominated by short-term goals?

5. *Lack of know-how and experience.* Few people have a lot of practice in documenting their ideas and knowledge. In fact, many employees are uncomfortable writing down the things that they think they know; it often feels awkward, unproductive, and tedious. Additionally, many individuals agonize over trying to write things in the most polished and impressive manner. This can be wasteful. In short, getting knowledge into the system is often a painful process of extraction. This is where the "creation" element of the three critical prongs of knowledge management comes in. If you don't make it easy to create and capture knowledge, you can forget about discovering and distributing it.

6. *Rapid obsolescence.* The rapid pace of business change can quickly make certain forms of knowledge obsolete. To retain relevance, many knowledge databases require a considerable amount of updating and review. Often it isn't clear who is responsible for doing this. If a knowledge base becomes seen as dated, usage and value will drop off rapidly.

Taken together, any one—not to mention all six—of these obstacles can be daunting. But companies can address them by sticking to the fundamentals:

- Explicitly link knowledge management with strategic business imperatives; in other words, give the KM process a crystal clear focus and purpose.
- Combine state-of-the-art groupware and messaging technology, which to be fair has really only become available in its best forms over the last two years, beginning in early 1996.
- Identify and address the many behavioral, cultural, and organizational issues that can either block or enable the effective proliferation of knowledge management solutions.
- Show sustained top management commitment and responsibility.

As numerous studies have shown, these cultural, social, and leadership issues are often far more important to the learning process than any technical virtuosity.

KEEPING FOCUSED ON
THE CHALLENGE AHEAD

Perhaps the most important message of this book so far has been that just as e-mail, voice mail, LANs, relational databases, and client/server architectures played a decisive role in shaping enterprise competition during the late 1980s and early 1990s, so will market-facing systems and enterprise knowledge management systems give rise to a new form of organization: the market-facing enterprise.

Today's business climate is characterized by chronic and often radical change. Therefore, predictability becomes impractical. Regardless of the industry, an organization's ability to anticipate and respond to change rests on being able to bring current, targeted information to the right constellation of learners in an environment that supports innovation and action. If this environment is *global, distributed,* and *asynchronous,* then knowledge management, enabled by traditional and emerging collaborative technologies, is the most direct means of enabling an active response to the changes of the day.

Eric Hoffer will be proved right: In a time of drastic change—and believe me, you and I are living in one—the learners will inherit the future. Knowledge management systems, and the collaborative computing technologies that support them, will prove to be key elements in the success of all organizations in the emerging era of the virtual office.

CHAPTER 7

CONVERGING AND TRANSFORMING INDUSTRIES

The future is already here. It's just not evenly distributed.
—**cyber author William Gibson**

FANNIE MAE, THE LARGEST SOURCE of residential mortgage funds in the United States, recently joined forces with Finet Holdings Company, a mortgage lender based in Walnut Creek, California, to offer on-line mortgage preapprovals and applications. By linking Fannie Mae's computers with Finet's computers on the Internet, Fannie Mae can provide a mortgage approval directly to the customer.

Prospective borrowers need only send thirty "data points" of information—name, address, mortgage amount, and twenty-seven other key variables—to Finet's Web site at *www.iqualify.com* to get the process started. The information is then transmitted to Fannie Mae's computer network, which processes the information, orders electronic credit reports, and reports back to the customer via e-mail, often in under four minutes, according to a recent piece in the *New York Times*.

Dan Rawitch, CEO of Finet Holdings Company, maintains that his company can move quickly to act on the on-line mortgage application and cut a check within forty-eight hours of Fannie Mae's approval. Customers are not required to go through Finet—they can also approach other lenders with their Fannie Mae approvals from the Web site. The fee for an on-line mortgage application is $39—and can, of course, be paid by credit card.

The above example provides merely a taste of *some* of the impact technology has had on *one* of our service economy's key sectors: financial services. But it also provides a splendid example of what I've come to call "the myth of disintermediation."

REINTERMEDIATION AND DISINTERMEDIATION: FACT AND FICTION

"Disintermediation" is a fancy, newfangled term (as you are no doubt well aware) for the *elimination of traditional intermediaries*, be they retail stores, direct mail operations, or 800-number-style telephone support operations. With market-facing systems the selling of products directly to consumers and businesses has become a powerful (and in some cases powerfully destabilizing) force in many industries—hence PCs from Dell, books from Barnes and Noble or Amazon.com, on-line stock trading from e.Schwab, and on-line travel services from Microsoft's Expedia and AMR's Travelocity.

In spite of this kind of undeniable displacement of traditional intermediaries, disintermediation as such is a myth, and I offer the story of the relationship between Fannie Mae and the Finet Holdings Company as proof: Although the *mortgage* itself may be funded by Fannie Mae, the on-line *credit-approval* service is provided by an intermediary—Finet—and the *fee* for the service is being paid through the good offices of yet another intermediary, a credit card company, which in turn is likely to be owned (at least in part) by a bank.

Not surprisingly, scenarios like this have sparked an interest in so-called *reintermediation*. Historically, whenever transportation and communications infrastructures have markedly *improved*, industry value chains have tended to *lengthen*, with products and services becoming increasingly specialized. This has led many to suggest that the Web will also create whole new classes of intermediaries: market-facing enterprises whose primary presence is on the Web and who will provide portals that allow on-line users to access producers of goods and services.

Everyone agrees that the stakes are high. And contrary to popular and conventional wisdom (and to what you tend to hear or read in the media), I believe that reintermediation is likely to prove widespread.

Examples of Reintermediation

Let me offer some prominent examples of reintermediation:

- *Yahoo!* which is presently the leading gateway to the Web, has struck a deal with the insurance aggregator InsWeb. According to Forrester Research, InsWeb provides access to mutual fund information, on-line trading, loans, tax preparation, and insurance.
- *Quicken*, a subsidiary of software giant Intuit—which Microsoft attempted to acquire before antitrust issues intervened—has set up a Web-based service offering instant information on loan and mortgage rates, along with a wide range of other financial services, thus leveraging the substantial base of users already loyal to Quicken financial software.
- *Bankrate.com*, an advertiser-supported company, provides information on prevailing loan and other rates from banks and other financial institutions around the country.
- *Carpoint*, a Web site from Microsoft, reportedly sells $200 million worth of cars per month.
- *GoTo.com* is a new search site that lets merchants, content providers, and Web publishers bid for placement in search results. For example, Sears might bid a penny to have its URL (universal resource locator) pop up every time a site visitor queries "tools." Or Black & Decker might compete—according to Forrester Research—and up the ante by paying two cents to ensure that its links shows up first on the search engine. "We've created a stock market for attention," claims GoTo.com CEO, Bill Gross. "We think that some bidding wars will break out in the most competitive areas, like cars, travel and consumer electronics."

In none of the above cases has true disintermediation occurred—only the much more prevalent trend of reintermediation. To better grasp why this is the prevalent trend, let's begin by listing those products and services sold directly and those sold indirectly.

Direct-Sale and Indirect-Sale Products and Services

(Mostly) Direct-Sale Products and Services

- *Utilities:* Consumers have historically bought their telephone service and other utilities directly from a service provider.
- *Financial services:* Most consumers deal directly with their banks or brokerages.

- *Periodicals:* Most newspapers and magazines are sold and provided directly through subscriptions, although certainly newsstand sales are important.
- *Education:* Tuition fees are paid most often directly to schools, unless gathered through taxation.
- *Local services:* Repairs, construction, hairdressers, restaurants, gardening, and other such services are nearly always contracted for directly.
- *Cars:* Automobile dealers tend to specialize in the sales and services of a particular manufacturer's cars. Admittedly, this example is something of a special case. Since car dealers are not legally owned by their manufacturers, they could be viewed as an *indirect channel*. However, the special bond created by regional franchise exclusivity makes most dealers operate in a virtually direct manner. In many ways, car dealers are really an example of a hybrid direct/indirect approach.

(Mostly) Indirect-Sale Products and Services

- *Consumer durables:* Refrigerators, TVs, stereos, and PCs are still mostly bought in stores.
- *Food:* Major brands and fresh produce are almost always sold through stores.
- *Clothing:* Clothes are overwhelmingly sold through department stores, although a few manufacturers have their own stores and catalogs, such as L. L. Bean, Lands End, and Ann Taylor.
- *Books:* Virtually no mainstream publisher sells its own books.
- *Travel:* Although you can book airline tickets directly, most people and businesses still use travel agent intermediaries.

What can we learn from these brief lists of products and services? For one thing, the first list consists mainly of sometimes atom-based, but more often *bit-based services* rather than products. The second list, by contrast, comprises almost entirely *atom-based products* purchased periodically and on a discretionary basis. Finally, the list of products sold *directly* tends to have a strong *local* component, whereas most of the products sold *indirectly* (through intermediaries) are typically sold across broad geographic areas, with little localization.

Technology Displacement

Now let's look at these same products and services in terms of their potential for *disintermediation.*

Financial services tend to be the most commonly cited area of disintermediation. However, since banks and brokerages still conduct most of their business directly with customers, how can they be further disintermediated? In this case, the issue is primarily one of terminology. When people speak of "disintermediation" with regard to businesses *already* selling directly, what they are really referring to is a process I would prefer to call "technology displacement."

Businesses that traditionally have used a direct-sales and direct-service approach will continue to do so, but if a business moves from providing *direct sales* either in person or on the phone to a sales and service environment that occurs *directly on line,* then a technology shift has occurred—most often because a market-facing system has been implemented.

For example, retail brokerage houses will continue to deal directly with customers, but the means of communication is gradually shifting from telephone and mail toward Web-based, on-line environments like e.Trade. Customers will continue to conduct their business directly with the same (single) organization, only the method of interaction will be different. Has any true disintermediation occurred in this case? No—this is a prime example of *technology displacement*, from mail and phone lines to on-line communication.

Disintermediation/Reintermediation: What Exactly Is the Difference?

Look again at the list of indirect-sale products and services. These products and services obviously possess the greatest potential for true disintermediation, which I would define as follows: *Disintermediation removes at least one product distribution layer from an industry's value chain.*

A customer could use the Web, for instance, to buy directly from a manufacturer, bypassing traditional channel intermediaries. But when we look at what is actually taking place today on the Web, it is *reintermediation* and not *disintermediation* that seems to be at work. Let me offer a few specific examples.

Books

The resounding success of Amazon.com represents an important expansion in publishing distribution channels. Still, Amazon employs a traditional channel model—that of the book retailer, and its rival Web site, Barnesandnoble.com—along with other retail-based bookselling Web sites—is a *retailer* who has devised a new value chain. This isn't true disintermediation at all. It's not as if a retailing enterprise had been supplanted by a wholesaling activity. It's not as if full-service book publishers like Random House have begun to sell their books directly—or even that a major book distributor like Bookazine has decided to go on line to sell books directly (and at substantial discounts) to the public.

That would be *true* disintermediation. What the success of Amazon.com and Barnesandnoble.com demonstrates is that a new *channel* has arisen that will compete with and no doubt coexist with existing channels. This is a genuine *technology* shift, but not an actual *value chain* shift. From a value chain perspective, there remain distinct *producers*, distinct *distributors*, and distinct *resellers and retailers*. This remains true for now and, I would strongly maintain, for the foreseeable future.

Travel

Much the same pattern holds true for travel services. Whether you make reservations through an on-line service such as Microsoft's Expedia or Sabre's Travelocity or you use the telephone to work with a local travel agent, you are still dealing with a *travel intermediary*, as opposed to going directly to a hotel or an airline. Expedia may be a very different type of company from the typical travel office, but it is still performing much the same intermediary function. Again, competition may be changing rapidly, but no real value chain shift has occurred.

PCs

Perhaps the closest example of true disintermediation can be found in today's personal computer business. Companies like Dell, Gateway, and IBM have shown the power of selling PCs directly over the Web, bypassing traditional stores and other resellers. However, even this case is not so clear-cut. The PC business has a long history of selling products directly.

Over the years, this has been done in person, through the mail, and then heavily via telephone. The Web is replacing these older approaches and is steadily gaining share, although I wouldn't want to overstate this point because Web-based PC selling remains a minority of the go-to-market volume. To the extent that it's happening, however, it's for one very simple and sound reason: Web-based PC sales are enormously cost-effective.

In Sum

Not much, as yet, appears to be happening on the Web in terms of selling food, clothes, or most consumer durables, although according to a recent report released by *CyberDialogue* on on-line commerce, consumers spent $3.3 billion purchasing goods and services on line in 1997.

Still, it's certainly safe to say that disintermediation, as I have defined it, has been somewhat overhyped. What has been occurring is a combination of *technology replacement* and *competitive reintermediation*. Despite some of the hype, my generation's parents are not likely to suddenly abandon their retail rituals and purchase all their music CDs over the Web because they *can*. Once again, the social instruments that retail experiences have become are an integral part of value chain shifts and go-to-market behavior, whereas the impacts of technology are more incidental.

Of course, calling a change "reintermediation" or "technology displacement" does little to minimize or undermine the power of market-facing systems or market-facing enterprises. It certainly doesn't diminish the degree to which e.Schwab has terrified the traditional brokerage firms or the amount of turbulence generated within the once stable world of retail bookselling by the advent of Amazon.com. These industries, as well as most others, are undergoing profound and accelerating change due to the rise of the Web. The point is simply that the major changes under way are not, for the most part, easily characterized as the elimination of traditional intermediaries.

DIRECT-COST SAVINGS AND
THE WEB REVOLUTION

A truism in the early days of the Web stated that its greatest impact would be on bit-based business, only to be followed in the rather distant future by the eventual transformation of basic atom-based industries. Surprisingly, in the four years since the Web has been a significant presence on the industrial and commercial scene, precisely the opposite pattern has prevailed.

Although most major bit-based businesses—including telephony, print publishing, entertainment, and on-line and Web-based newspapers and magazines—have been only marginally impacted by the Web to date, atom-based businesses have undergone radical change.

Indeed, an increasing number of atom-based industries are on the verge of revolution. Amazon.com clearly created panic at Borders and at Barnes and Noble, which made haste to follow suit with its own Web site. Similarly, Dell's highly successful Web-based sales site has energized PC resellers. More recently, the automobile dealer business, with its bizarrely secretive sales and pricing culture, has shown signs of imminent transformation, as customers flock to the Web to attain more accurate vehicle information. Indeed, to the surprise of many, these atom-based Web success stories have become the signature examples of what consumer electronic commerce really means. *Why?*

The explanation is really quite simple: The *cost savings* gained by atom-based businesses through bypassing traditional product channels are proving to be more compelling than any enhanced services that characterize most on-line, bit-based offerings. In the case of books, PCs, and cars, consumers benefit directly from the real costs that are being squeezed out of the distribution system. Sure, there may also be any number of other highly attractive *nonprice benefits,* such as convenience, customization, and choice. But in most cases, these are of distinctly secondary importance.

In many bit-based businesses, especially those supported by advertising, there are few if any consumer costs to be squeezed out by removing a link from the value chain (my definition of true disintermediation). Thus such Web-based, bit-based businesses need to compete mostly on convenience and functionality. With a still immature Web, such enhanced services are possible, but often risky. The result is that very few bit-based businesses have been truly revolutionized.

What, you may ask, about on-line stock trading services like e.Schwab? Aren't these services compelling symbols of a bit-based revolution? The answer is only partially. In the case of most on-line stock trading sites, the Web is being used essentially as a way to replace telephone calls. In effect, this eliminates a human customer services agent and thereby lowers dealer commissions, resulting in lower transactional costs that are passed on to the consumer. But has a link been removed from the value chain? Clearly not. Instead, this is another prime example of the far more prevalent trend of technology displacement.

All of this adds up to one simple fact: Most early consumer e-commerce excitement is found in areas where buyers can save money. Perhaps this shouldn't be surprising, but with our tendency to extol the Web's capacity for new levels of *information* and *service*, the critical role of *basic cost cutting* should never be underestimated. The central role of lower prices has profound implications for near-term Web evolution.

Businesses primarily supported by *advertising*—publishing, TV, sports, and so on—will find it more difficult to save consumers money. Such businesses just happen to be in one of our most bit-based sectors. Perhaps less apparent, industries such as insurance and banking won't truly take off on the Web until they offer a more tangible customer value proposition, something they have thus far almost totally failed to do. Indeed, banks, with their recent efforts to charge for ATM use, appear to be heading in the opposite direction. The obvious exception, of course, are the various on-line banks featured above, but these represent a minuscule presence in the mammoth financial services sector.

As companies examine their own consumer Web strategies, they should keep in mind a single and simple question: What can *we* do on line that saves our customers money? If the answer is, "Not much," then the Web will probably not revolutionize your core business anytime soon. The Web will still be very likely to redefine your marketing and customer support strategies, but in the end it is the actual sales process that is the lifeblood of most organizations.

In any business where the Web can enable *direct cost savings*, existing market leaders had better get cracking. If today's participants don't pursue alternative business approaches, new players surely will—as the on-line grocery enterprises mentioned in Chapter 5 can certainly attest. Business history strongly suggests that, more often than not, newcomers often get there first. Which is why major changes in technology often do lead to major shifts in competitive leadership. This rule of "first come, first serve" will likely prove at least as true on the Web, where economies of scale are more powerful than in previous business eras.

THE FUTURE IS HERE, BUT . . .

Looking ahead into the uncertain future, most of us are tempted to ask ourselves two questions:

1. What effect, if any, will the Internet have on the shape and structure of my industry?
2. How different will the world look when we finally get to the other side?

In order to gain a clearer perspective on the events transpiring today, consider the hundred year period that directly preceded the emergence of the Information Age—a period that ran roughly from 1870 to 1970. During this period, which can in retrospect be characterized as the peak of the Industrial Era, major advances in transportation and communications enabled a system of multinational corporations, large bureaucracies, and highly structured school systems to steadily transform a predominantly rural and agrarian society. Mass production was the moving spirit of the times, a fact that is perhaps most evident in the generic names of some of our most important corporations in the United States: *General* Motors, *General* Electric, *General* Mills, *U.S.* Steel, *Standard* Oil.

Now, several decades into the dawn of the Information Age, it's clear that at least part of this older structure is gradually—and sometimes rapidly—giving way to something new and different. Companies are becoming far more focused, specialized, and interdependent in a way that the vertically integrated giants of the industrial era never were. And in virtually all economic sectors, consumer choice has expanded dramatically.

Still, although it's possible to sense the seismic changes now underway, at this stage of technological evolution we are nowhere near the point where the full influence of a wide range of long-term effects can be clearly observed. In my opinion, the era of technology-driven industrial transformation will not really have arrived until a fully wired, nearly universal service, high bandwidth infrastructure is largely in place. Only when today's substantial technical and individual access restraints have been removed will the full potential of today's technologies begin to be more fully defined and exploited.

To make the same point in another way, let me borrow an astute observation from the writer William Gibson (who coined the term "cyberspace" and described a precursor to today's World Wide Web called the Matrix in his 1984 novel *Neuromancer*): "The future is already here. It's just not evenly distributed." I take this to mean that much of what is going on today in start-ups and pilot projects may be representative of what will become commonplace five and ten years from now. Of course, many of today's new initiatives will fail; and in retrospect, others will certainly look foolish.

Consequently, the task facing nearly all of today's business leaders will be to sift through what is going on within their particular industries and make what one hopes will be sound judgments about what will and what will not exert substantial and transformative industry-redefining power on their individual sectors.

SEVEN AREAS OF INDUSTRY TRANSFORMATION

Industry transformation will take a number of distinctively different forms and is likely to occur in the following seven areas:

1. *On-line delivery products and services.* Products and services consisting principally of bits—such as banking, insurance, video, audio, and publishing in its various forms—clearly possess the greatest potential to be completely delivered on line. There isn't much any of these businesses do that at least in theory could not be delivered over a network and managed by software. That the on-line delivery of such products and services has yet to occur on a large scale should not be misinterpreted to imply that these changes won't happen in time. Although in the short term atom-based businesses have been the most affected by the Web, in the long term bit-based businesses will evolve at a more rapid rate than their atom-based counterparts.

2. *Industry convergence.* As is the case with health care, sometimes the only way to use technology efficiently is to restructure the information processing procedures inherent in the existing value chain. Financial services, media, and electronics industries are also showing powerful patterns of convergence, as regulatory barriers fall and as businesses come to share a common digital foundation.

3. *Value chain extraction (VCE).* As information processing transforms specific work efficiencies, certain key functions will move from one industry to another. For example:

- Banks might provide home billing systems as a convenience to retailers.
- Insurance companies could potentially manage much of a company's internal benefits.
- Manufacturers might monitor their customers' inventory levels (as Shell Chemical does now with SMI.)

As industries tend to extract value from *each other*, the net long-term effect should be a significant restructuring of current value propositions in industries across the board.

4. *Value chain insertion (VCI)*. In many businesses on-line processing will become a distinct layer of the business itself. Perhaps the clearest examples of this growing trend are

- ISPs (Internet service providers) or other service companies that design and host Web sites and effectively become an integral part of their customers' value creation activity.
- Computer companies that develop pure technology tasks, such as *smart cards, electronic cash,* and *customer verification,* and thus make themselves a central part of their customer's operations.
- The Internet itself, as it becomes a primary part of just about every industry's value chain.

Not surprisingly, exerting maximum influence and control over emerging electronic infrastructures has become a key competitive strategy in most if not all industries.

5. *Changing industry concentration*. Much of what the Web is doing today and will be doing in the future can be characterized as the transformation of business tasks into processes manageable by software. Software markets tend to have nearly infinite economies of scale and therefore tend to be highly concentrated. This suggests that a more pervasive deployment of market-facing systems might push certain industries toward increased concentration.

Indeed, this transformation appears to have taken place already in sectors such as financial services, media, and the software industry itself. On the other hand, the Web greatly reduces some barriers to entry in some industries, and this fact alone could lead to the entry of new and different players.

6. *Product transformation.* In the case of products themselves—whether they be cars, refrigerators, or furnaces—the trend will be the transformation of *products* into *services.* As microprocessors, sensors, and wireless communications become standard components of a widening array of consumer goods, existing relationships between product and service providers is bound to change dramatically. In the age of "smart products"—particularly smart products connected to software-managed networks via the Internet—the age-old distinction between products and services is likely to erode.

Consider a "smart house" wired with appliances that can be accessed and managed by a service firm directly over the Net—the appliances themselves—*products*—will be simply extensions of the *service.* A company like General Electric, which already possesses a massive software-managed services arm, will see the connections between its products and services grow stronger as the distinction between them grows gradually fuzzier.

7. *A changing geographical mix.* For a variety of reasons, businesses that retain a strong *regional and national orientation*—financial services, retail stores, telecommunications, health care, media, and education—will see opportunities to expand beyond their local, regional, and national boundaries. Since issues of distance and physical geography mean nothing on the Web, sustainable regional and national differences will have to be grounded in real variations in regional and national demand.

Facing these seven areas of transformation, business leaders today will have to confront the following strategic questions:

- Are my industry's value chain channels *appearing, disappearing, or changing?*
- Is my industry *colliding*—or about to collide—with a previously separate business?
- Is my industry now *outsourcing* part of its traditional value chain, or is its value chain *lengthening* because of added functions extracted from others?
- Is my business becoming more or less concentrated, or more or less geographically dispersed?

THE IMPACT OF TRANSFORMATION: FOUR CASE STUDIES

To provide a sense of how these transformations will play across some of the world's greatest industries, I've chosen four industries as examples: financial services, health care, retail, and manufacturing. Each industry will provide a mini–case study of one or more of the types of industry-wide transformations listed above.

In all the cases explored, the assumption will be that universal citizen and business access to a high bandwidth infrastructure has been achieved. So the question becomes, In the high bandwidth infrastructure world of the future, what type of transformation can we logically expect in this industry? In short, *If we could build a truly wired world, what would we do with it?* The same question may also be phrased differently: What will happen when a full-blown Internet begins to make its mark on your business?

Financial Services: Cutting Costs and Creating Value

Nowhere has the influence of new technology been greater than within the financial services sector. From the earliest days of punch-card data processing, banking, brokerage, and insurance firms have been among the leading users of computer technology, consistently spending a greater share of their revenues on IT than any other major sector.

Today, financial institutions are facing a fundamental redefinition of their industry, including new products, new distribution channels, and new competition. Leading bank executives are fully aware that virtually everything a financial service does today could, at least in theory, be conducted over networks and managed by software. They know that the era of bricks and mortar is rapidly fading away.

Although the insurance industry innovation has lagged behind the banking and brokerage businesses, all three sectors face many similar issues, particularly as cross-sector mergers and acquisitions make it clear that these businesses are converging into an increasingly interrelated marketplace. This convergence should not be surprising since all three businesses are essentially financial intermediaries that seek to match savings with varying levels and types of risk. Consider the most basic functions of each of the three poles of the financial services tripod:

1. *Banks* have traditionally provided the lowest risk and lowest return investment—matching government-insured savings deposits with various commercial loans.
2. *Brokerage houses* have traditionally provided a higher risk and return ratio—often for individual investors seeking direct equity ownership.
3. *Insurance companies* also manage risk, but from a different perspective: They basically mediate against various types of individual and/or business loss through the pooling of dedicated investment resources.

One feature distinguishing the financial services sector as a whole from nearly every other industry—with the exception of health care—is the high degree of government regulation to which it is subjected, virtually regardless of place or time. The reasons for this are not hard to locate in business history.

Sound banking is fundamental to the stability and prosperity of any country. Banks tend as a consequence to be subject to the heaviest regulation and enjoy the greatest protection of any industry. Virtually all national governments try, not always successfully, to require prudent operations and to create favorable market conditions for their banks.

To a lesser degree, public confidence in the brokerage and insurance businesses is also supported through regulations that exert serious constraints and that also protect existing firms within the sector. To cite just the most obvious example, banks, brokerage houses, and insurance companies all manage large sums of other people's money. Consequently, it becomes the task of government regulators to ensure, wherever possible, that that money is not stolen or squandered by the enterprises to which it has been entrusted. Since the issues of trust and security remain unchanged by the impact of technology, it is highly unlikely that the emergence of the Internet will eliminate these traditional government oversight functions, even in an era of deregulation; it is also unlikely that such a scenario would in any way be desirable.

Given the unique character of financial services, two critical issues appear to govern the impact of new information technology on the industry: *lower costs* and *new opportunities*.

Lower Costs

Technology is changing today's cost structures in the financial services industry in three basic ways:

1. *Low-cost voice and data communication* permits companies to locate the production side of their business separately from the point of delivery. Traditionally, this has enabled credit card servicing centers in places such as Oklahoma and Nebraska to serve the entire U.S. market; but as banks become more national and international in nature, centralized production is emerging in an increasingly wide span of areas. The Internet can only accelerate this process.

2. The development of *automated, remote delivery channels* such as ATMs and the Internet permits banks, insurance companies, and brokerage firms to cut customer service delivery costs dramatically. Indeed, given the potential savings in this area, knowing when and where an individual, in-person approach is still justified for either consumer or business services is one of the billion dollar questions within the industry. Various estimates show that on-line service delivery costs are often only about 10 percent as much as those involving a human customer support representative. Thus far, such cost savings have really only affected the brokerage business, but banks and insurance companies will need to find ways to exploit these fundamentally lower cost structures.

3. *Embedded expertise* is fundamentally a case of using automated knowledge management to cut the cost of decision-making. Embedding expertise in software (e.g., sophisticated credit scoring, price adjusting, portfolio analysis tools, and customer what-if scenarios) allows financial service companies to offer a high level of expertise to more and more customers, while simultaneously reducing the cost of delivering such traditionally high-end services to its premium customer base. The Web will dramatically expand the power and reach of any and all such services.

New Opportunities

Necessary as all three forms of cost reduction are—and are likely to become in the near future—the key to future market leadership is going to be found in entirely new types of business activity. New opportunities will most likely appear in five basic areas:

1. New products and services
2. Convergence opportunities
3. Value chain innovation
4. Infrastructure ownership and management
5. Global expansion

New products and services

These include new automated payment systems such as ATM/debit cards, smart cards, electronic benefits transfer for government distributions, consumer bill paying, Internet payment methods (possibly even electronic cash), and a range of commercial and retail electronic fund transfer mechanisms. The support and leadership of the banking industry will likely prove critical in most of these areas.

Additionally, technology will enable *previously impossible* or formerly *unfeasible* services. Three previously impossible, formerly unfeasible services come to mind immediately:

1. Allowing small firms to make a market in public stock
2. Enabling individual savers to check the daily valuation of their investments
3. Offering less creditworthy borrowers access to funds (albeit at a compensatory high rate of interest)

All three services can now be provided at relatively marginal costs because new technology is making entirely new classes of service available for new categories of customers.

Convergence opportunities

"Convergence" is typically the term used within the financial industry to describe the increasing product, regulatory, and holding company overlap between traditionally distinct *bank, brokerage*, and *insurance* institutions.

The underlying dynamic driving financial services convergence is that integrated financial service companies can leverage established customer relationships, existing sales channels, and new, low-cost delivery systems across a wider product base, taking better advantage of existing customer relationships and product interdependencies.

This capability is of special interest to financial companies maintaining extensive branch and/or agency structures. To justify the high degree of investment they need to support these branch networks, these companies need the branches to create as much business volume as possible. This opportunity of increased volume has been the principal driver behind the wave of megamergers currently sweeping the financial services sector all over the world.

Amidst the transformations underway, certain firms will find that whole new areas might become more attractive than some of their established markets and might be ripe for cross-sector "picking." For example, a *brokerage firm* like Merrill Lynch may be more successful than a commercial bank in winning and serving the small business lending market for affluent, independent professionals such as doctors and lawyers. Conversely, a *bank* might do better than a brokerage firm in marketing mutual funds and annuities to conservative, older, midlevel investors. And an *insurance firm* might be better positioned to sell and service 401K or other company retirement benefits to midsized companies than either banks or brokerages.

Of course, diversification will not be the all-purpose solution to the impact of technology on the sector as a whole. Niche firms such as specialized mortgage or credit card companies that use direct mail, telephone, and increasingly, electronic means of access are more likely to maintain an efficient, narrow (and some would argue, more competitive) market focus. Indeed, it appears that both broad-based providers and low-cost specialists are likely to remain viable in the coming high bandwidth digital universe.

From a consumer perspective, this situation is ideal: The competition between the convergence-driven diversification of some companies and the niche marketing of others will continue to drive heightened efficiency and innovation.

Value Chain Innovation

The goal of value chain innovation is to make it attractive for companies or individuals to outsource practices they have traditionally performed for themselves. For example, a bank might take over major portions of its clients' payables and receivables, payroll, tax accounting and filing, credit card payments, collections, direct deposit, EDI payments, and retirement fund management.

At a retail level, banks—typically through their credit card business—have interposed in individual consumer payments and record keeping. Here, they can provide consumers with an important brand-recognized guarantee—for facilitating problems with defective or undelivered goods. Previously, consumers often relied upon a retailer's name and reputation (e.g., Sears, Roebuck and Company). This guarantee function will prove particularly useful on the Internet, where consumer reliance on trusted "name" brands and sound, solid companies is likely to command a premium.

In both the business and consumer sectors of their market, financial industry firms will grow and prosper by *extracting value previously resident within nonfinancial companies*. The net effect of this extraction will be a great increase in customer intimacy and collaboration. Many businesses will be willing to outsource these financial functions because they do not consider financial services to be one of their core competencies. On the other hand, if banks do not continue to improve their own efficiencies, their customers might well extract value from them, by increasingly managing their own financial needs.

Infrastructure Ownership and Management

One of the banks' prime historical roles has been their operation of the world's underlying payment systems. Banks dole out cash, clear checks, transfer funds, and run both our ATM and credit card systems. It barely registers on even informed consumers' radar screens that the world's largest credit organizations like MasterCard and Visa are collectively owned by the same group of banks, in much the same way as the NASDAQ exchange is controlled by the National Association of Securities Dealers. Much of the bank and brokerage industry's future will depend on its ability to extend these historical franchises into smart cards, Internet transactions, and other forms of electronic payments.

This critical infrastructure issue is leading to some very complex yet highly strategic partnerships and alliances between financial services and

IT firms. For example, IBM and more than a dozen of the nation's largest banks, through their Integrion joint venture, are attempting to develop an electronic commerce infrastructure. Meanwhile Microsoft is working closely with credit card giant First Data Corporation toward similar ends. And Hewlett-Packard and EDS (Electronic Data Services) are developing various retail credit card processing systems.

Further complicating the picture is that virtually every nation (or in the case of Europe, region) will be working toward developing its own Internet payment systems. Already on the Internet today, there are efforts to bring together various types of financial information so that consumers could, for instance, shop for the best mortgage rates or get an integrated picture of their savings, investment, and insurance situation.

Recent examples include Insuremart.com, Insurequote.com, and InsWeb.com (with more popping up all the time). Should these new initiatives be successful in introducing a retail-like layer of value, the effects on how banks compete and position themselves could be profound. Banks have always dealt directly with their own customers, but the Internet could potentially introduce a whole new set of financial intermediaries.

Global Expansion

Over the last decade, the brokerage business has become truly international, with investors willing to seek the highest return almost regardless of location. In contrast, the insurance business is predominately national in nature. Banking is somewhere it the middle, with banks developing multinational capabilities to serve their multinational customers. In fact, the needs of global corporate customers continue to drive the formation of larger and larger worldwide providers.

Still, it is not yet clear that these gargantuan economies of scale are relevant to other than a few, high-end commercial markets. Retail banking remains highly national in nature, and significant cross-border retail services have yet to be convincingly demonstrated. Coupled with the strong nationalist element inherent in this sector, the overall issue of financial industry globalization remains a matter of considerable debate.

Nevertheless, many financial service firms continue to expand geographically. Economies of scale and business diversification are two often cited reasons for this expansion. Perhaps a more compelling reason is that as deregulation has spread, protected national markets have often created inefficient local firms that might be easy targets for more aggressive global competitors. With the recent turmoil in Asia and the coming monetary integration of Europe, a new wave of global financial services alliances may well develop, just as they have during the deregulation of the telecommunications and airline industries.

Regardless of whether a set of truly international competitors emerges, it is already clear that the global use of technology within the financial services sector is becoming increasingly uniform. Consider these three examples:

1. *Increasing reliance on packaged software*. The U.S. financial services business has long been the most aggressive in taking this approach, establishing an important hothouse for software and service firms. As the global financial services industry begins to leverage third-party resources more extensively, companies that have grown up using packaged products will have advantages over those accustomed to more costly, in-house systems. Internally developed software will remain important but only in the areas where adequate packages do not exist. Packaged software will eventually dominate Internet-based financial services systems.

2. *Emerging market modernization*. As a new free-market spirit is infused into developing countries all around the world, local banks are rapidly expanding and modernizing. With the installation of state-of-the-art hardware and software systems, these countries can potentially leapfrog several generations of technology. Indeed, the United States is now essentially exporting banking systems and software on a nearly franchised level to a number of countries. As the recent problems in Asia drive home the need for banking reform, this technological change should accelerate.

3. *The Internet*. Although each nation's use of the Internet will certainly vary, both the underlying communications technologies and specific financial industry concerns—such as transaction processing, security, authentication, and encryption—will likely evolve similarly in most parts of the world. This will, eventually, have a powerful homogenizing effect, and the overall impact on the financial services industry promises to be massive. Radically lower operating costs, new delivery channels, new and converging products, outsourcing opportunities, emerging new payment infrastructures, new retail intermediaries, and a largely green field of in-

ternational expansion all combine for an exciting and tumultuous future, one that is linked inextricably to technology evolution and utilization.

Health Care: Restructuring Around Information Management

On the surface, the health care industry appears less concerned with global competition than most other major economic sectors. Because the industry is primarily a service business, and because each nation has strong local issues and structures, health care today is mostly dealt with at a national level, regardless of whether it is publicly or privately managed. Of course, health care products such as pharmaceuticals and medical equipment are sold all around the world and thus are important exceptions. However, although often of critical importance, these products account for only a small share of the world's total health care spending.

Nevertheless, the sheer size of the health care industry makes it critical to the world economy. Accounting for anywhere from 7 to 15 percent of a modern GDP, it is often the single largest national expense and therefore represents a huge business and consumer cost. Those countries that can provide both high-quality and low-cost health care will effectively be providing a platform on which more direct business advantages can be based. As people live and work longer, this will become an increasingly important economic and social factor.

Despite its vast size and commensurate importance, health care has historically been relatively slow in its adoption of IT. Health care has often been viewed as at least a quasi-public industry and therefore has not been subject to open competition. Additionally, the unique importance of societal health has tended to make the industry relatively immune to traditional cost-cutting pressures. Finally, systems of insurance and public subsidies have often masked the real costs to consumers. For these and other reasons, the impetus required for significant change didn't hit the industry until the last decade, when the imperatives to better control costs became too great to ignore.

Even so, many if not all health care organizations are still at the basic level of IT operation. Relatively few have reached the intermediate process-automation-driven level, and arguably none could be generally viewed as advanced MFEs.

More specifically, health care's unique mix of consumer, hospital, doctor, business, government, and other interests has always made it an extraordinarily paper-intensive and bureaucratic industry. This very same ecosystem diversity has made it difficult to use computers to tackle the problem in a meaningful way. System incompatibilities, concerns regarding privacy and confidentiality, cultural resistance within the health care community, and the above described lack of financial pressure have limited usage mostly to various intraorganizational applications.

All of this is, to put it mildly, unfortunate. Few industries are as dependent on the flow of information and knowledge. Virtually every aspect of the health care business requires expertise, accurate record keeping, communications, and quality control. This, along with rapidly changing technologies, rules, and procedures, should make IT central to effective health care operations. Although certainly not a pure bit-based industry, there is an almost unique need to integrate information management and patient care systems.

Although ecosystem development is generally characterized as a product of relationships between suppliers, channels, and customers, it is equally relevant to the health care industry's unique web—pun intended—of extended enterprise connections. Health care is a fascinating example of how Internet standards can help solve previously intractable information handling problems. The health care industry also provides a real-world example of why purely technological solutions are unlikely. Significant cultural, collaborative, and organizational change will also be required for meaningful health care modernization.

Figure 7.1 shows some of the major parties involved in processing health care information. It is clear that even a typical hospital visit will trigger many of these groups to request access to various aspects of a patient's treatment, condition, cost, and status. Historically, patient information has been gathered and dispensed through an immense hodgepodge of mostly incompatible computer and manual systems. This has often resulted in extraordinary levels of data redundancy, re-keying, and manual distribution. From a technology perspective, the question on the table today is the following: *Can the increasingly universal acceptance of Internet standards make a qualitative difference in solving this long-standing problem?* I think so. To begin to see why, let's look at six of the key attributes of a successful extended enterprise and apply them to health care.

FIGURE 7.1   Diverse Needs for Health Care Information

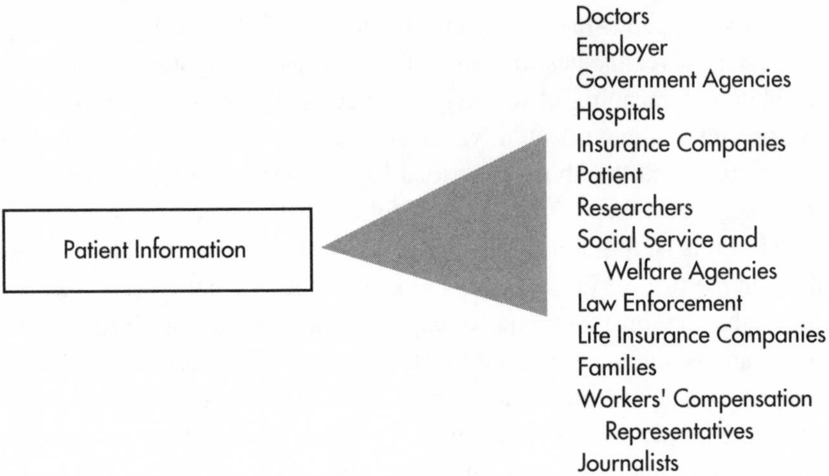

Doctors
Employer
Government Agencies
Hospitals
Insurance Companies
Patient
Researchers
Social Service and
    Welfare Agencies
Law Enforcement
Life Insurance Companies
Families
Workers' Compensation
    Representatives
Journalists

Patient Information

1. *Communication*. Simple electronic mail between various parties offers enormous benefits unavailable to physical methods of communication, particularly when e-mail is expanded to include the ability to easily attach relevant forms and records. Most U.S. health organizations of any modest size either already do or will soon have some access to the Internet. However, use is very limited, and little patient information is distributed this way. Similarly, physicians have shown much more interest in using the Net for research and collaboration with colleagues than for direct communications with patients or other parties. How many of you have ever sent, let alone received, an e-mail from your doctor? In short, in terms of electronic interenterprise communication, the health care industry is clearly lagging.

2. *Coordination*. A great deal of health care staff time is spent scheduling various visits, tests, treatments, and so on. Schedules are often handled by a series of phone calls, often without the use of even voice mail. Neither cross-enterprise scheduling software nor workflow software, which could keep track of patient case information through various stages of treatment or referral, is used with any frequency. Suffice to say that the health care industry is almost totally dependent on expensive clerical staff for even the most mundane scheduling processes.

3. *Reallocation of work.* As discussed in the financial services section, when enterprises begin to work closely together, it will sometimes be more efficient to reassign work from one organization to another. For instance, an insurance company might provide the Internet software and content that an employer needs to train and manage a health care benefits program; it might even maintain, update, and remotely operate such a system, which could appear simply as an icon on an employee's desktop PC. A similar system could easily be operated by insurers for health care providers. All of these applications should be relatively straightforward, but their initiation does require a certain level of sales, service, and marketing energy, traits the health care industry is only beginning to appreciate and reward. Historically, health care incentives have tended to be much more like those in government and education than those typically found in the private sector. What other business would call its customers "patients"?

4. *Privacy/security.* Clearly, medical record data requires the highest levels of information security and privacy. In any extended enterprise environment, the security challenge is substantially greater than when confined within a single organization, particularly in light of the previously described range of people who might request access to health care information. Without complete confidence in this area, serious interenterprise deployments will simply not occur, a point that brings us to the currently destructive policies of the U.S. government in this regard. Network users must have confidence that their communications, whether personal letters, financial transactions, or sensitive business information, are secure and private. Access to products with powerful encryption capabilities are critical to providing such confidence, yet the U.S. government prohibits our industry from exporting anything other than kindergarten levels of encryption. And time, to put it mildly, is not on our side. Internet commerce is doubling every *one hundred days.* More than 10 million people in North America have purchased a product over the Internet, and another 40 million have obtained product and pricing information before making a conventional purchase.

Despite what policy pundits might believe, this particular genie—strong encryption—can never be put back in the bottle. Full-strength encryption products are available at the touch of a button all over the world, including in the United States. So bad people intent on doing bad things won't be deterred by U.S. policy. At the same time, government stonewalling on this issue could retard the growth of e-commerce to a tragic degree because we can't export what's needed to compete.

In health care today, paper documents often rely on various codes, specialized employee knowledge, sequencing, and even ambiguity to ensure that the essential details will be understood only by those who are authorized to know. Given the legitimate, even if often highly exaggerated, fears regarding Internet security, the confidentiality issue will loom large for the foreseeable future. In fact, although it gets the lion's share of media coverage, customer record security within the financial services world is actually a much simpler problem; critical financial data is usually centrally stored, with much more limited and predictable patterns of distribution.

5. *Interenterprise deployment.* Historically, the patient (customer) would be in one enterprise, the health care provider in another, and the insurance company in yet another. Since all groups often need to use a system for it to be effective, a major aspect of deployment involves gaining the necessary commitment from all required parties. This basic chicken-and-egg dilemma is particularly troublesome in health care, where normal patterns of business leadership and market evolution are often not fully developed. Indeed, many health projects have had a poor record of acceptance, especially among physicians, who understandably are reluctant to change practices if there is even the slightest potential of adversely affecting patient care.

6. *Adaptability.* As if all of the above challenges weren't enough, any health care system needs to be able to change *rapidly* and *constantly.* Medical treatments, insurance policies, and government reporting requirements will all continue to change regularly. Developing a formal process of change management across diverse organizational elements is difficult for any industry. Imagine if the rules and methods of buying stocks were constantly changing. Given the costs of many health care information systems, long life cycles are highly desirable; this will continue to necessitate adaptable systems and services.

When all six issues are taken together, the extreme difficulty of the task becomes clear. Using technology to transform the health care business is neither a simple nor straightforward task. In fact, in the early 1990s, many informed observers concluded that there was neither sufficient incentive nor leadership to overcome the immense inertia within the system. This conclusion led many to believe that a solution could be found only by substantially changing the system. Here, there have generally been two main options: nationalized health care systems like those used in many countries around the world, or "managed care" systems that essentially integrate health care provision and related insurance obligations.

These issues, of course, rose to the fore during the first term of the Clinton administration. Since America has always been reluctant to even consider any sort of nationalized approach, the managed care option has become the main agent of change. The raging debate over various health care approaches is driven by factors almost entirely removed from technology concerns. Nevertheless, the current direction of U.S. health care management does have important and generally positive technology implications. In fact, information technology may well have become a more important catalyst for change than is commonly or even consciously realized.

Most broadly, the widespread adoption of managed care systems in the United States is likely to enable the health care industry to go through the typical business pattern of first building a robust intranet and then using this as a foundation for more advanced, external interactions on extranets and on the Web. For example, managed care organizations certainly have a strong incentive to develop and deploy efficient record and workflow systems, particularly as these companies begin to compete for business and actually develop a sales, marketing, and customer service mentality. These same systems could well become robust enough to provide direct links to patients, employers, governments, and other privileged parties.

From a consumer perspective, the desire to pursue better health care electronically should never be underestimated. Patients (or should we say customers) will be eager to go on line to learn about their particular ailments, treatments, and concerns. Additionally, the Web's privacy and relative anonymity will make it a powerful platform for inter-patient information exchange.

At the end of the day, there is little doubt that the Internet will play a major role in developing more informed and less passive health care consumers. This could prove the necessary counterbalance to the potential for excessive power devolving to managed care entities.

Retail: The Outlook for Intermediaries

Of all the potential areas of business transformation, few have received as much attention as the area of on-line retailing. Will we all someday be buying various goods from home over computer-based networks? If not, what role will electronic communication play in our everyday shopping experience?

These are questions that affect almost everyone. With estimates of on-line sales of retail goods ranging from $3.3 billion in 1997 (*CyberDialogue*) to $2.4 billion (Forrester Research), the retail end of the Internet and Web transformation has become a thing of the present, not just of the future. Still, according to some estimates (Forrester) only 20 percent of wired adults made a purchase of retail goods in 1997. As Forrester observes, "Winning retailers will have to focus on growing market share by converting lookers to buyers."

Retail stores have long since become a defining aspect of the American economic and social landscape. Even a small downward trend in store utilization could have a major impact on such widely disparate areas as commercial real estate development and prices and wholesale prices for consumer goods.

To some, it seems only natural that the sudden availability of virtually limitless acres of cyberspace should put huge pressures on today's limited and expensive physical space. For people nonplussed by shopping malls and other forms of retail proliferation, any shift toward a more cyber-spaced approach will likely be seen as important cultural progress.

On the other hand, unlike Web banking, bill paying, or just plain surfing, shopping often has a very strong social element that even the most robust on-line systems will probably never match. Today's cyber stores are unique, in that the only way one would ever know if any one else is there is by the slowness of the site. On-line attempts to simulate the presence of other shoppers have a very long way to go. Nonetheless, in an increasingly busy two-worker life style, many families are looking to maximize convenience, and this might open the door for certain types of on-line ordering.

Amidst these various possibilities, I believe that the real retail power of the Internet will emerge from its ability to create new stores, not from its ability to eliminate existing ones. Let's see why.

Table 7.1 presents a top-line view of the likelihood of various types of goods being successfully sold over the Internet. In these ratings, no distinction has been made between a retail store that stocks its own inventory and a retail store that serves primarily as a showroom, with actual order

TABLE 7.1 Consumer Goods Purchases: A "Seven C" Analysis

	Community	Customer Costs Savings	Consumer Choice	Need for Customization	Product Consistency	Potential Convergence	Rate of Change
Electronics							
Television	L	M	H	L	H	M	L
Stereos	H	M	H	L	H	L	M
PCs	H	H	H	H	H	H	H
Video games	H	H	M	L	H	M	M
Phones	L	M	H	L	H	L	L
Durables							
Ovens	M	M	M	L	H	L	L
Refrigerators	L	M	M	L	H	L	L
Dishes	L	M	H	L	H	L	L
Pots/pans	M	M	M	L	H	L	L
Automobiles	H	H	H	H	H	H	H
Groceries							
Produce	M	L	M	L	L	M	H
Meats	M	L	M	L	L	M	L
Dry goods	M	L	H	L	H	H	L
Supplies	M	L	H	L	H	H	L
Clothing	H	M	H	H	L	L	M
Hobbies							
Sports equipment	H	H	H	M	H	H	M
Recreation equipment	H	H	M	L	H	M	M
Tools	H	H	H	L	H	M	L
Entertainment							
CDs	H	M	H	L	H	H	H
Books	H	H	H	L	H	H	H
Newspapers	H	L	L	M	M	L	M
Magazines	H	L	H	M	M	L	M
Videos	H	H	H	L	H	H	M
Decorative							
Furniture	L	H	H	H	M	L	M
Personal							
Health aids	H	H	L	H	H	M	H
Beauty products	H	H	L	H	H	M	H
Sex/hygiene	H		L	H	H		H

Key: H=High; M=Medium; L=Low

fulfillment taking place from centralized warehouses. After all, both of these approaches are still retail stores, since consumers are going to a physical location and actually seeing and touching goods before purchase. How these orders are fulfilled is almost entirely a separate question.

Taken together, the list in Table 7.1 comprises the great majority of today's consumer retail spending. I have lumped individual line items into nine broad categories, each of which is rated either high (H), medium (M), or low (L) in seven different areas (the six "Cs" I discussed in Chapter 5 plus a seventh: cost savings).

1. *Electronics.* Looking at the ratings across this category, the one thing that jumps out most is the strong need for PC customization. PC buyers have a huge array of hardware, software, and networking options, and having everything preinstalled and tested on a machine before delivery is a highly appealing service. Not surprisingly, PCs are currently really the only electronic product category with a very active on-line sales presence.

The rate of change evaluation also argues strongly for PCs remaining a special case. Because new models will continue to represent an important part of the business for the foreseeable future, personal computers and video games are the most likely products to be sold on line. The rapid introduction of new machines tends to make the in-store stocking of inventory less efficient. In contrast, for items that change slowly, high-volume, in-store distribution can be quite cost-effective.

Unless there are substantial cost savings, most people will want to *see* a television or *listen* to a stereo before buying one. PCs, stereos, and video games are also natural areas for the development of on-line communities, whereas TVs and phones are not. However, with the arrival of high definition TV and the eventual convergence of PCs and TVs, some of the PC-type values may well spill over into the TV realm. Overall, the high levels of product consistency suggest on-line sales potential, but only if significant cost savings or other value can be delivered. Right now, it looks like such savings and value will remain in the PC category, with stereos and video games having reasonable potential.

2. *Consumer durables.* This category will almost certainly be among the *least* active retail segments on the Web. Both consumer purchases and product changes are relatively infrequent, and therefore there is little consumer product knowledge, and almost no community building (except perhaps among cooking aficionados who want to keep up with the latest

materials and techniques). The only real opportunity would appear to be in the area of *cost savings*, which could be significant. Interestingly, the ratings across all areas are virtually identical, suggesting that what happens to one product will likely happen to the others.

3. *Automobiles*. This category is big enough to justify being treated separately. Like personal computers, automobiles score "high" in every category, suggesting very strong transformation potential. Potential areas of cost savings include reduced inventories, lower dealer commissions, and more efficient customization. High community building potential and regular product changes also add potency to the mix, as does the general lack of consumer goodwill toward many of today's automobile dealers, at least in the United States.

Even here, change will not happen overnight. Major car manufacturers will be reluctant to compete with their long-established dealer channels, especially since they will continue to depend on them for service and support. Perhaps the most likely path will follow what has already happened in many parts of the personal computer business. Many leading PC makers work cooperatively with their channels to get as close to an on-line ordering model as possible. The net effect on both the PC and car businesses is that the retail channel will have to either provide more value or receive lower product commissions. It's a net plus for consumers.

4. *Groceries*. Here, we see a markedly split pattern, as shown by the product consistency and rate of change evaluations. Given the widely varying quality of meats and produce, buying these products on line is not an easy or natural process. What do you do if you receive some meat you don't really like the looks of? On the other hand, various dry goods, paper products, and all manner of household supplies have the requisite product consistency and potentially high convenience. Innovative grocers like Netgrocer and Peapod have already found ways to exploit this opportunity. Possibilities for established grocery chains include offering highly consistent goods on line that can then be picked up either at the grocery store or perhaps at a drive through window. The actual store would then tend to specialize in more perishable items. This could shrink floor space, shorten checkout lines, and improve customer convenience.

Community building remains an almost totally untapped area for today's supermarkets, with nutritional information, new product requests, and perhaps most importantly, frequent buyer programs all having real potential to build customer loyalty. In addition, supermarket Web sites could easily provide hot links to various food company sites for more detailed information. Push technology could also be of great value in notifying customers when particular items of interest are either available or on sale.

Overall, since grocery stores already run on very low margins and since on-line delivery requires a certain amount of extra handling, the potential cost savings are likely to prove minimal. Thus, the challenge for on-line grocers is to demonstrate the convenience of on-line buying and the power of community building to maintain customer loyalty in what has become a highly competitive business.

5. *Clothing*. Retail apparel stores will be with us for a long time. Although it is certainly true that some items, such as men's white dress shirts and undershirts, could be as easily ordered on line as through a catalog, most consumers still want to touch and try on most moderate to expensive clothing before purchase. It's hard to imagine a day when computers can accurately reflect or project the look and feel of an actual garment. Returns and exchanges are another major problem with on-line delivery. In addition, clothes shopping, perhaps more than any other category, is for many people often a social experience.

Recognizing these barriers, many clothing retailers are in the process of using technology to make in-store retail shopping a more entertaining and educational experience. They may also engage in community building efforts much like those described for groceries above. But overall, the retail clothing store appears to be here to stay.

6. *Hobbies*. This should be one of the more active categories. Hobbyists usually want very specific goods, equipment, and tools that are not widely available, and they often know exactly what the retail prices are. Hobbyists also, almost by definition, are ideal target markets for community building services. Perhaps more importantly, specialty stores often have high channel markups, limited geographic availability, and high product consistency, all prime sources of on-line delivery value. On the other hand, many people clearly enjoy going to a store dedicated to one of their personal areas of interest. This, and the fact that many of these goods do not change rapidly, will certainly keep specialty stores around. But, overall, this should prove to be an active and innovative category.

7a. *Entertainment (retail)*. As pure bit-based businesses in this category, the long-term transformation potential is very high. Take a look at today's reality: All those "H" ratings in Table 7.1 indicate that books and CDs have already become natural Web markets. Nevertheless, the appeal of being in a good book or music store will continue to keep stores viable. This raises a very interesting question: What happens when on-line ordering is more efficient but the in-store shopping experience is both more valuable and pleasant?

Clearly, stores would not survive if they were used only for browsing purposes, and later people were actually making lower-cost purchases on the Web. A logical economic solution might be to charge money for the value of the in-store experience, but all retail logic argues against this. Perhaps the solution lies in some sort of store/Web community model, where purchasing at the store generates credits in a way that makes it roughly equivalent to buying it on-line. Another possibility would be that for many books sold in relatively low volumes, stores would only keep a "demonstration copy." No one really knows how these trade-offs will shake out, but it seems clear that there will be some interesting business model experimentation, especially as the major retail chains get seriously involved in the on-line business

7b. *Entertainment (advertiser supported)*. Advertising-based entertainment such as newspapers and magazines show generally lower ratings. Barring significant increases in paper prices, current costs are already quite low. Perhaps more importantly, in many cases, the on-line Web experience is actually less convenient than a typical newspaper or magazine; it is, among other things, less portable, disposable, readable, and comfortable. This tends to suggest that the on-line versions will tend to be used in different ways—customization, search, interaction, archiving, and so on. On the other hand, it almost goes without saying that books, CDs, newspapers, magazines, videos, and just about every other form of entertainment have high community building potential.

8. *Decorative*. Like apparel, there is a very important touch/feel aspect to these businesses that should continue to make stores compelling. People still want to sit on a chair, touch a rug, or take a piece of art home to see how it looks on a wall. There is also much less community building, with the possible exception of arts and crafts. Overall, this will be among the least active retail areas.

9. *Personal*. As indicated by the large number of "H" ratings, this may well prove to be the most active of all retail areas on the Web. Put simply,

in those areas where the in-store shopping experience is a distinct negative, the Web's privacy and anonymity may make the Web the most appealing way to acquire various goods. Jo Tucker, director at Interactive Media in Retail Group (IMRG) in the United Kingdom, offers an intriguing example of how things work in this category: "The most unusual thing selling on-line in the U.K. is from a large-sized women's clothing store. It turns out that the sales came from transvestites."

Indeed, this may be the only highly active retail product category driven primarily by personal preference. In addition, there is also a real opportunity for cost savings, as well as for educational and community building activity. Interestingly, whether the category is health, cosmetics, or sex/hygiene products, the ratings are basically the same.

What does this brief look at retail spending add up to? Taken together, the ratings of the nine product categories indicate that the strongest drivers of change appear to be a potential for *cost savings,* customer *convenience,* and various forms of *community-related value.*

It also appears that issues of *mass customization* are most relevant for computers, automobiles, and information/entertainment, while *product inconsistency* is the main concern dogging the development of a major on-line presence for food and clothing.

The only category to get consistently high marks is *community building.* Here, using both push and pull technologies, retailers will work closely with manufacturers to increase the amount of information available to consumers. They will also find new ways to reward customer loyalty and to more effectively target their wares. In other words, the Web will greatly increase both the range and extent of customer services that the traditional retail channel will offer. One could even argue that customer service should be an eighth C, but customer service is a critical aspect to all businesses and thus receives an "H" rating almost by definition. What has changed is that the ability to deliver new levels of service is going up in just about every retail category.

Overall, it would appear that the Web will somewhat reduce the amount of required retail space, although not nearly to the extent some have suggested. The real challenge for today's retailers is to match the best of the physical experiences with the best of cyber experiences, trying to find new paths to competitive advantage in today's crowded and highly competitive markets. It will be the successful development of these hybrid models that will help define tomorrow's retail leaders.

This "seven C" analysis of retail spending leads to the conclusion that Internet-driven retail change will be much more evolutionary than revolutionary. Still, it seems intuitive that some more powerful forces will eventually be unleashed by the Web, particularly once the technical problems of achieving a high bandwidth infrastructure have been solved.

Probably the one force most frequently mentioned as a potentially powerful catalytic force is that of *software agents*. These are computer programs that go out on the Internet to represent the interests of consumers—checking availability, finding the lowest prices, notifying us about sales, and so on. Although there remain some significant barriers to the widespread use of such agents—standards, increased network and site traffic, merchant support—the potential seems real enough. In fact, agents may well emerge as a natural extension of today's search engine technology. Agents are, in this sense, the ultimate refinement of "pull" technology.

However, even here the changes will be largely evolutionary. Much of what agent software is designed to do can be handled equally well by push-type systems. Perhaps more importantly, agent technology does little to solve many of the problems identified in the analysis above. In many retail sectors, there will still be issues of product consistency, customization, returns, and so on. Agent-based systems will clearly work best in those areas where high product consistency is a feasible and attainable goal.

Manufacturing: A New Capacity for Change

The manufacturing industry is an example of an industry where most of the themes covered in this book come together into a powerful wave of internal and external change. In the case of manufacturing, IT will clearly contribute in eight central areas:

1. Market-facing systems
2. Extranet-based collaboration
3. Electronic purchasing
4. Interoperability
5. Thin clients
6. Knowledge management
7. Smart products
8. Globalization

1. *Market-facing systems*. Many manufacturing organizations will need to make some profound decisions regarding how this important new capability fits into their current business operations. This is especially true for those businesses that sell through any sort of channel-based model. Can a company sell directly through an MFS and indirectly through channels at the same time? If so, how?

Market-facing systems affect more than just product sales. Similar dilemmas can occur on the service front. In many industries—cars, consumer electronics, appliances, computers—maintenance and repair services are often an important source of additional channel revenue and profit. What happens when some of these services can be better managed from a direct MFS-style approach?

2. *Extranet-based collaboration*. You hear it said so often it has almost become a cliché: Today's manufacturers need to treat their suppliers as partners to work with, not contractors to be squeezed. This increased emphasis on collaboration cuts across many functional areas—design, testing, inventory management, forecasting, cost cutting, even R and D. Chrysler's SCORE supplier management system featured in detail in Chapter 4 has already saved the company some $2.5 billion. The resounding success of McDonnell-Douglas's Aerotech subsidiary—"the virtual factory"—demonstrates how extranets are becoming the technological platform of choice in order to pursue worthy collaborative goals.

3. *Electronic purchasing*. In contrast to the broad capabilities of both market-facing systems and extranets, in this mission-critical area very specific efficiencies can be gained through automated on-line purchasing. Here, innovation is taking place on two main fronts: those specialized products needed as part of the actual manufacturing process, and those products that are more broadly needed to support virtually all businesses, for example, office supplies, furniture, computers, telephones, and similar essentials.

In this latter area, the typical corporate purchasing department has historically been a highly inefficient mix of paper forms and manual ordering processes. Forward-thinking companies want to be able to compare products and prices from all their suppliers, as well as to place and check the status of orders, electronically. Early evidence is that the cost savings, mostly in staff time, can be significant.

A number of software companies are working on the necessary standards and application software. Someday electronic purchasing of typical office supplies will be a standard business application. General Electric's ability to simply post its requirements on one of its Web sites and essentially seek out the lowest bidder is only the most prominent example. GE is even making a business by providing this service to other manufacturers. A start-up like QCS for on-line retail purchasing is another example of the same trend.

4. *Interoperability.* Few other industry sectors can match the manufacturing business's sheer diversity of systems and technologies—legacy mainframes and software, dedicated minicomputers, specialized factory floor equipment, and so on. In order to reach their full potential, these systems need to be able to communicate. Interoperability is even more difficult and important as companies enter into complex cross-enterprise environments. Making the necessary forms, data structures, and security checks work across multiple organizations has historically been prohibitively difficult.

This is why the manufacturing industry is showing such a strong interest in the Java programming language and also in the Java Beans object model. These two approaches are currently our best hope for achieving the necessary interoperability. The challenge for manufacturers and the IT industry is to bring the great interoperability of the Web to much more complex information handling requirements. Without this, collaborative progress will certainly stall.

5. *Thin clients.* Closely related to the interoperability issue is the strong manufacturing industry interest in network computers and other so-called "thin clients." A browser-based client approach is seen by many as the best way to assure compatible technologies while keeping device maintenance costs down. This is particularly true on the factory floor, where there is often little ability to manage and maintain today's powerful personal computers. This is why in many of these environments there are still large numbers of traditional computer terminals. This installed base of terminals composes a natural early market for today's network computer offerings. As a general rule, personal computers remain better suited to office environments.

Per our industry's usual pension for overstatement, we initially launched the network computer as a broader-based replacement for PCs. Not surprisingly, we have seen a slower than anticipated acceptance in the market. My point here, however, is that there are millions of dumb terminals that ultimately will be replaced at low cost with this kind of networked and intelligent device.

6. *Knowledge management.* This is an area critical to just about every business, but there is one reason why it is even more important to manufacturing. In many manufacturing sectors, the products themselves will need to become increasingly smart. In the not too distant future, most machinery and equipment will incorporate advanced electronics—self-diagnostics, sensors, even communications via the Internet. We see this today with cars, but it is easy to see it happening with many other products as well. The implications of this are clear: Manufacturers will need to acquire new bodies of digital expertise, and they will have to learn how to incorporate this new knowledge into their core design, manufacturing, and customer service operations. Clearly some companies will incorporate digital knowledge more effectively than others.

7. *Smart products.* To date, computers have largely performed in the world of data and digital information. They have relatively few links to the actual physical world. However, the next great frontier in computing will be the ability of products to accept, process, and make sense out of analog, sensory data: cars that give directions; air conditioners, heaters, and refrigerators that know when they are not running efficiently; smart cards that replace passwords and keys; exercise equipment that monitors bodily stress, and all manner of other health and medical diagnostics.

8. *Globalization.* Suffice to say, manufacturing today is the most global of all industries. Financial services and health care have unique national structures; entertainment often follows national tastes and languages; and most retail distribution is inherently local. In contrast, a great many manufactured products are built and sold identically all around the world. It is this relative level of product homogeneity that makes the manufacturing business so fiercely competitive.

Not only is the market for these products global but, of course, so are the production systems. Today's products are designed and built through increasingly complex global supply networks, to an extent simply not found in most other industries. The management of such global capabilities has become almost totally dependent upon modern information technologies. Building and sourcing products in the right places with the right logistics has become a daunting challenge and hence a major source of potential competitive advantage.

In short, the collaboration required to cost-effectively build, sell, and service smart products all around the world will define much of tomorrow's global manufacturing competition.

SUMMING UP

The four mini–case studies that have made up the bulk of this chapter should provide a strong sense of just how radically businesses are going to change—and going to *have* to change—in order to compete effectively in the coming network-centric, Web-based era. The good news is that advances in technology are opening as many windows of opportunity as they are threatening to close obsolete and outmoded ones.

CHAPTER 8

THE GREAT AMERICAN
ECONOMIC SURPRISE

---

*Signs of a major technological transformation of the economy are all
around us, and the benefits are evident not only in high-tech industries but
also in production processes that have long been part of our industrial
economy.*

—**U.S. Federal Reserve Board Chairman Alan Greenspan**
Testimony Before Congress June 10, 1998

IN JUNE 1998, AS THE AMERICAN ECONOMY entered its sixth
year of expansion, Federal Reserve Board Chairman Alan Greenspan—
not a man prone to outbursts of "irrational exuberance"—observed in an
upbeat statement to Congress, "The extent to which strong growth and
high resource utilization have been joined with low inflation over an extended period is extraordinary."

From a global perspective, particularly when viewed against a backdrop
of persistent market turbulence in Asia, the American economic position
on the global stage hadn't looked so strong since the 1960s. To a degree
just about unimaginable less than a decade before, the American economy
had—within a relatively brief period of time—become the envy of the
world.

Echoing Greenspan's judgment, most Americans have sensed for some
time that the economy has been improving significantly, but only recently
have a significant number of Americans credited information technology
with a critical role in this great and largely unexpected American turn-
around.

DISPARATE, NOT DESPERATE:
THE IT INDUSTRY IN THE 1980S

A decade ago, such a scenario would have been painfully hard to predict. Although the U.S. computer industry appeared in relatively good health compared to the overall economy, from the limited perspective of national IT usage and global IT competitiveness, the United States was beginning to look like an IT laggard. American firms never lost their dominance of the IT industry, but by the late 1980s the traditional American IT leaders—IBM, Digital, Unisys, Wang, and others—were all in serious trouble.

The question hovering—but often unvoiced—on many lips was whether relatively small, comparatively highly focused hardware companies like Intel, Seagate, Cisco, and 3Com would be able to stand up to the expected onslaught from Japanese giants Fujitsu, Hitachi, NEC, and Toshiba—or, even if these companies did withstand the Japanese assault, whether new challenges from Korea and Taiwan might be yet another harbinger of doom.

Fueling this era of widespread anxiety were significant shifts in the performance of domestic IT markets around the world. While growth in U.S. IT spending averaged just 7 percent per year from 1986 to 1991, in Europe the figure was 14 percent, and in Japan it hit an impressive 16 percent. Indeed, absurd as it may seem now, a number of serious industry forecasters were predicting that the Japanese IT market would soon equal that of the United States, despite a population of about half the size. True, America still was the world's most heavily IT-oriented economy, but the technology gap was narrowing rapidly.

Perhaps even more serious than the hard facts were the pervasively negative attitudes of even sophisticated business leaders and analysts toward the further implementation of IT. As America's perceived position declined, it had become increasingly commonplace to call into question the IT industry's ability to deliver on the potential of computers. It had become increasingly difficult to dispel the notion gaining ground in executive suites across the country that excessive competition between computer vendors had led to the development of discrete islands of computing, making it difficult for end users to take full advantage of ever improving information technology.

Whether the style of computing was mainframe-, minicomputer-, or PC-LAN-based, most systems ran on proprietary technologies and were thus largely incompatible with one another. Interoperability on the most basic systems-integration level seemed at best a distant pipe dream. Apparently perpetual efforts to standardize systems with new languages— UNIX, COBOL, ASCII—and other communications protocols failed more than they succeeded. In many ways, this chaotic, divisive, fragmented IT marketplace struck many people as just another example of American companies' obsession with short-term self-interest at the expense of long-term industry and customer benefits.

With a wide array of essentially incompatible systems, most organizations were hard-pressed to send messages or transfer files within their own organizations, let alone to partners, clients, or customers. This greatly complicated and substantially slowed the development of true enterprise information systems. Understandably, many business users, especially non-IT executives, had little patience with computer industry rationalizations and promises, and increasingly the IT industry (and even a company's own management information systems department) was viewed with skepticism, even cynicism. The IT industry's tendency to over-promise and under-deliver had become a commonplace customer sore point.

If anything, during the 1980s the blossoming of the personal computer industry accelerated these increasingly disparate and dissatisfied IT attitudes. PCs communicated awkwardly or not at all with existing mainframe-or mini-based systems. Even communications between PCs was difficult, as PC LAN technology took time to mature. As a result, the early years of the PC revolution focused heavily on the individual use of word processing, spreadsheets, graphics, databases, and other applications. Of course, I can't honestly cast a negative view upon that era, since Lotus was built and attained critical mass during this period. Still, like the BMW, the image of the souped up individual PC became one of the enduring symbols of what were seen as the overly individualistic 1980s. The PC's role as a communications and collaborative tool had yet to emerge.

By the late 1980s, the U.S. computer industry had achieved an unpleasantly polarized state of tense equilibrium. A weakened U.S. supplier base was divided into proprietary camps—IBM versus Digital, UNIX versus

Proprietary, MS-DOS PCs versus Apple. Within user organizations, tensions were rising between end users and corporate information systems (IS) departments, as well as between IS departments and their corporate superiors. Top management was not sold on the value of IT, and end users were not sold on the value of the central IS functions.

Things were clearly not on a healthy course, and underneath it all lay a single question, which was repeated constantly: *Was this huge and ongoing investment in information technology really worth it?*

A BRIEF HISTORY OF IT PRODUCTIVITY

Difficulties in identifying and measuring the productivity of IT investments have characterized our industry since its inception, but for whatever reasons, the issue, sort of like El Niño, periodically resurfaces, causes a great deal of turbulence, and then calms down for a while.

As IT use increased, it became increasingly more difficult to measure the return on IT investments, even as computers became ever more vital to a widening array of sectors. In other words, there appeared to be an inverse relationship between return on investment (ROI) measurement and the extent of IT usage. Put another way, the more embedded computers became in everyday work, the harder it became to measure what companies would be like without them.

Since the early 1970s, a steep and largely unexplained decline in the rate of productivity growth had become the main brake on economic growth in the United States. Although debates ranged and raged as to the reasons for this slump in productivity, without question the massive investments in IT made by American industry from the late 1940s on were becoming increasingly more difficult to justify on an ROI basis.

In the 1960s and 1970s, when computers were used mostly to automate existing back-office functions such as payroll, accounting, and inventory management, relatively discrete computer tasks were developed to enhance or replace existing punch card or entirely human-based systems. This meant that even though precise measurements were never easy, cost-benefit analyses reached a sufficient level of confidence to provide a rough sense of ROI. In contrast, computing in the 1980s tended to focus on front-office systems, which made measuring the ROI on such systems significantly more challenging. Not only had IT spread much more widely throughout the organization, but its very pervasiveness often made it nearly impossible to map discrete applications to particular IT costs.

What made the ROI question even more vexing was that most of the benefits of front-office automation were only remotely related to cost cutting or downsizing. As often as not, the goals of these systems were enhanced decision-making capabilities, improved customer service, faster business cycle times, and higher quality products and services. Often these strategic improvements were required either to maintain competitiveness or to create a market advantage, but they did not conform to traditional measures of productivity.

With the lack of any empirical evidence, perceptions of the value of computing tended to be shaped by the overall business climate. When U.S. business executives traveled the world, as they were increasingly inclined and compelled to do in a global economy, they saw that the United States was the most computer-intensive of nations; but it was also getting clobbered in many global markets. To many observers, the conclusion appeared obvious: Computers were clearly not providing the competitive advantage that had been promised, and so on an ROI basis, they were a waste of time and money.

Unfortunately, it became all too easy to deride or question the proposed productivity gains being promulgated by highly paid "knowledge" workers fiddling around with ever more highly formatted documents and often mind-bogglingly complex spreadsheets. Similarly, a new generation of client/server technologies proved so difficult to administer and justify that they became the butt of a thousand industry jokes. Indeed, the so-called slash (/) mark became one of the enduring symbols of an increasingly divided industry.

THE TOP TEN REASONS WHY THE CONVENTIONAL WISDOM WAS WRONG

Of course, with the benefit of hindsight it is now obvious that much of what was forecasted has proven wildly off base. Most broadly, perhaps the main reason American companies have become successful in spite of the predictions is that they have become so much more competitive. Indeed, *they have had to* become more competitive in order to survive. As the work of Michael Porter—a former Lotus board director—has shown, *countries with the most intensely competitive domestic markets tend to produce the most competitive vendors.* It's amazing what businesses will do when their very survival is threatened.

More specifically, let me outline ten explanations of where the predictions went wrong and of America's recent success:

1. Entrepreneurship
2. A change-oriented culture
3. Labor flexibility
4. Industry deregulation
5. More female workers
6. Immigration
7. Easier access to capital
8. Open flow of information
9. The end of the Cold War, and the peace dividend
10. The use of technology

It probably goes without saying that all ten factors have made substantial contributions to America's startling economic rejuvenation.

1. *Entrepreneurship.* Although one can certainly debate the causes, Americans have been considerably more likely to establish new businesses than citizens of other major industrialized economies, such as Germany, France, or Japan. Remarkably, *nearly 1 million new businesses are started in the United States each year.* The generally recognized reasons that the U.S. economy has developed this way are

- the psychic appeal of running your own business
- a culture more willing to accept risk and less likely to stigmatize failure
- relatively supportive bankruptcy laws
- relatively easy access to credit and capital

2. *A change-oriented culture.* America has always been fascinated— some would say obsessed—by the new. During periods when the pace of business change quickens, this becomes a critical asset. America's general lack of business and cultural formality has lent itself well to flattening corporate structures and to the reduced emphasis on traditional management hierarchies that such flattening implies.

3. *Labor flexibility.* This factor shows up in many areas: simpler hiring and firing laws, fewer union rules and restrictions, greater worker interest in changing jobs and companies, widespread acceptance of flex-time and part-time employment, and high employee interest in telecommuting. Few other major countries could have absorbed so easily the tremendous shifts in employment that have occurred in the United States over the last fifteen years. For better or for worse, having less than 20 percent of American employees as members of labor unions has clearly been an important pro-flexibility factor.

4. *Industry deregulation.* The massive and ongoing deregulation of the financial services, telecommunications, media, airline, and other industries has clearly provided an additional economic spur. Many of the world's major countries are now in the early stages of reforms that have taken place in the United States over the last twenty years. Not coincidentally, American companies tend to be world leaders in these newly competitive sectors. This leadership becomes additionally valuable as deregulation spreads around the globe, creating global markets in previously nation-centric businesses.

5. *More female workers.* To put it bluntly, America has taken better advantage of the skills and ambitions of its female labor force than most other major economies. The huge number of women entering the workforce between 1975 and 1990 has provided an enormous additional set of human resources. This is especially important in new or rapidly growing industries where large numbers of skilled workers are needed quickly.

6. *Immigration.* Although immigration will probably always remain a controversial issue, there is little doubt that relatively high U.S. immigration levels have contributed to U.S. competitiveness in at least two direct ways. First, a large supply of labor willing to work for relatively low wages clearly can help keep business costs down. Second, and perhaps more importantly, the large number of highly skilled immigrants entering the United States each year has also helped alleviate critical technical skill shortages in fields such as computers, health care, and general science and engineering. The Business Software Alliance has estimated this year that 300,000 IT jobs are currently unfilled in the United States, without a skilled population to match the requirement. Much to the concern of developing nations all around the world, America remains a strong magnet for international skills and talents.

7. *Access to capital*. Although many other countries are now eagerly trying to follow suit, the U.S. venture capital system remains unique in the world, and an ideal greenhouse for launching and nurturing new businesses. More than just raising money, venture firms provide critical strategic and managerial guidance, as well as highly valued recruiting assistance. They have effectively institutionalized the realization that the gains of a few big successes can easily outweigh the losses of a larger number of failures.

8. *Free flow of information*. Regular and in-depth disclosure policies enhance investor confidence and are often the first step in addressing serious problems. They are also a prerequisite for informed and active shareholders. In contrast, as has become clear in recent months, many Asian institutions have traditionally provided much more limited public information.

9. *The end of the Cold War, and the peace dividend*. Since the collapse of the Soviet Union, the U.S. defense budget has, in real terms, fallen by nearly 50 percent. This has forced the giant defense contractors—Lockheed, Raytheon, Loral, Rockwell, and so on—to focus increasingly on international and nondefense opportunities. More broadly, U.S. interests are now much more defined by economic than by military concerns.

10. *Use of technology*. The U.S. deployment of various emerging technologies—particularly information technology—has been significantly greater than that of all other major economies; it is, in fact, rivaled only by nations with significantly smaller populations, such as Sweden, Australia, and New Zealand. This gap has existed for virtually all of the IT industry's history, but over the last five years it has widened substantially.

Information technology has contributed to improved productivity and economic growth in another significant way: Many of the new engines of U.S. economic growth—communications, pharmaceuticals, media, entertainment, not to mention the IT industry itself—rely extensively upon computer-based systems. Thus America's strength in this one area has paid double dividends—both enabling other key growth industries and being a high growth sector itself.

A close look at these ten aspects of American economic success will reveal that technology is their common denominator. Technology has often been one of the major driving forces of *deregulation*, especially within the communications, financial services, and media businesses. Technology further fits in with America's *change-oriented culture*, its relative willingness to try new things, and its free-flowing attitudes toward *information distribution*. Similarly, *entrepreneurship, technological innovation,* and *venture capital* have traditionally been culturally linked. Less directly, but still importantly, the technology industry and *the use of technology* within user organizations has created exciting opportunities for large numbers of *female workers*, as well as highly skilled *immigrants*. And technology has certainly contributed to *the flexibility of labor*, as attested to by the increasing practice of telecommuting.

Finally, and perhaps most visibly, technology clearly played an important role in bringing about the collapse of communism and *the end of the Cold War*. Indeed, the decisive role of technology was never more visibly demonstrated than during the Gulf War, which, almost eerily, seems to have coincided precisely with the observable resurgence of the American economy. If nothing else, the Gulf War helped embed the image of America's technological prowess within the minds of the entire world. It has thus become almost second nature to associate America's other achievements with this advanced capability.

America's experience with the transformative power of information technology is, however, unique—as a brief look at the role of IT in other countries will make evident.

VARIATIONS IN WORLD
IT USAGE PATTERNS

One thing that e-mail and database have in common is that each tends to require substantial organizational change. Electronic mail, in the modern day context of advanced messaging systems like Lotus Notes or Microsoft Exchange, has enabled the flattening of organizations and the breakup of rigid country management structures. More advanced collaborative workflow solutions have served only to hasten this process.

Similarly, effective database utilization requires the breaking down of the functional barriers between sales, marketing, and customer service. In both cases, substantial business and cultural changes are required before meaningful benefits can accrue. In myriad ways organizations are being and have been reshaped to take advantage of IT. In order for this transformation to take place, a high degree of organizational and cultural flexibility is required.

Japan

In sharp contrast to the American experience, Japan—along with the rest of Asia—got off to a relatively slow start in terms of their overall utilization of IT. While American companies in the late 1980s and early 1990s were developing increasingly powerful PC networks, much of Japan remained committed to older mainframe computing styles and phone/fax modes of communication. In retrospect, there appear to be at least five clear reasons why this substantial gap developed:

1. *Culture.* Much of Japanese business and IT culture was oriented toward hardware. Emphasis on modern software and networking has consistently lagged. More broadly, much of Japan's business emphasis was on producing technology for export, not on using it at home.

2. *Language.* Until the more powerful PCs of recent years arrived, handling Japan's kanji characters was simply too difficult for most PC users. Consequently, many organizations relied on specialized Japanese language word processors, which were most often used by secretaries. This tended to give the use of computers an overly clerical image.

3. *Lack of standards.* Until 1993–1994, there was no clear PC standard in Japan; thus PCs from different vendors were often not interoperable with one another. This greatly held back overall usage as well as Japanese language software development.

4. *Weak infrastructure.* Japanese telecommunications services were heavily regulated and very expensive. Consequently, value-added network services for both businesses and consumers tended to develop much more slowly.

5. *Mainframe bias.* Most of Japan's leading IT vendors (Fujitsu, Hitachi, and NEC) also had large mainframe businesses. These vendors were reluctant to move customers away from these highly profitable platforms. Unlike the pattern in the United States, new start-up companies did not emerge to take advantage of the established vendors' reluctance.

Working under the influence of a combination of these five factors, Japanese workers had no effective access to modern voice mail and e-mail systems, even as late as 1995. For technical and cultural reasons, knowledge worker use of PCs was also quite limited. Even at the corporate level, heavy reliance on older, proprietary, mainframe technologies greatly limited the use of departmental, relational-style systems. In short, a technology gap of as large as three to five years developed in many areas.

At Lotus, the sharp difference between the pace of IT consumption in Japan and the pace in the United States has always hit very close to home. The fact is that we have always had a significantly larger share of the PC software market in Japan than in the United States, particularly in competition with Microsoft. A comparison of the relative market share of our SmartSuite—or "SuperOffice," as it's branded in Japan—with the market share of Microsoft Office makes this clear.

Although Lotus's popular 1–2–3 spreadsheet helped trigger the PC revolution, our early U.S. lead was eventually eclipsed by Microsoft, which optimized whole suites of personal productivity products and attached its distribution to its Windows platform. In contrast, Lotus withheld early support for Windows, in favor of IBM's OS/2. More than any technological dispute, it was this fierce competition and often bad blood between the two companies at that time that accounted for what was perhaps Lotus's largest, single strategic mistake.

But the rollout of Windows in Japan came considerably later than in the United States. This gave us the time we needed to develop our Windows products, and we never lost our early brand advantage. Today, Lotus and Microsoft enjoy roughly equivalent shares of the office suite business in Japan, whereas worldwide we have had to settle for just a 25 percent unit share. Certainly, there was more to our success in Japan than just market timing. Lotus has always had a very talented Japanese management team. Nevertheless, this story does provide a real-world example of how two major economies can be at very different stages of IT development.

It's also an excellent example of how management mind-sets can change. Today Microsoft and Lotus, while still highly competitive, have a pragmatic and workable relationship. Both Bill Gates and I frequently discuss our mutual responsibility to make sure that our customers don't get caught in the middle of our various industry food fights. The fact is that most of our customers use Windows and NT, and more than 30 million Microsoft customers use Lotus Notes. In fact, Lotus Domino is perhaps the single largest carrier of NT into the Fortune 2000. And let's face it, our earlier strategy to always take on Microsoft directly just flat-out didn't work. Customers want value, interoperability, and integration—not a mud wrestling contest from which they derive no benefit.

Europe

As American business travelers are almost always being reminded, there is no such place as Europe. Western Europe is a collection of many countries with sharply different economic, cultural, and demographic profiles. Consequently, European "averages" need to be used very carefully and are often best ignored altogether. This observation is nowhere more true than in the IT arena. Some European nations could be described as highly advanced and others as seriously lagging, with still others covering almost all stops in between. However, given the need to make some general observations, I think it is fair to divide Europe into three geographical regions and to then consider the status of IT in each region:

1. *Northern Europe.* Countries like Sweden, Denmark, Norway, Finland, and the Netherlands are some of the world's most developed IT users, with a wide variety of sophisticated voice and data applications often rivaling and sometimes even exceeding what is found in the United States. However, all of these countries have relatively small populations and thus have only a minor global economic impact. Switzerland also tends to be an honorary member of this group, even though its location is in central Europe.

2. *Central Europe.* The state of technology infrastructure in Germany, France, the United Kingdom, Belgium, and Austria runs modestly but consistently behind that of the United States. Not only does this description fit three of Europe's "Big Four" economies—Germany, France, the United Kingdom, and Italy—but only Britain has recently displayed a U.S.-like capability to deploy IT in order to restructure and reinvigorate its economy. Perhaps even more than IT successes in the United States, Britain's success is leading many of Europe's leaders to reconsider some of their traditional economic and social assumptions.

3. *Southern Europe.* Italy, Spain, Portugal, and Greece all tend to lag substantially behind the European averages in just about all technology categories. It's hard to avoid the view that in Europe there is often an inverse correlation between a nice climate and the intensive use of IT.

THE FUTURE OF IT:
MORE GLOBAL *AND* MORE LOCAL

So what do these usage patterns, when considered in conjunction with the success of the American IT experience, suggest about the future of the IT industry in a globally competitive world? One answer, I think, is that with the impact of the Web on various nations' deployment of IT to enhance productivity, the upcoming network-centric, Web-based era is likely to be both more global and more local.

The Web, it is often said, will have an enormous impact on traditional national borders. In the more extreme versions of this claim, Internet enthusiasts have gone so far as to predict sharp declines in national sovereignty, even the decline of the state itself. After all, from a technology perspective, the Net makes little distinction between national boundaries, laws, or cultures.

There is, of course, some solid logic behind this view. Individuals, businesses, and organizations will clearly have more global freedom and capacity than ever before. To an extent much greater than television, the Internet can in many ways bring about aspects of what Marshall McLuhan long ago labeled as the emerging "global village." Information, ideas, and discussion will surely flow more quickly and freely than ever before. Additionally, as more and more activities become embedded into packaged software, there will be an inclination to use these same software modules whenever possible. This will also tend to have a homogenizing global effect.

It would be a great mistake, however, to make too much of all of this. The reality is that an equally good argument can be marshaled for the claim that the Internet will tend to strengthen and reinforce local cultures, languages, and customs, not weaken them. This is certainly the lesson from history: The twentieth century has already witnessed several generations of technologies that inherently pay little heed to physical boundaries—airplanes, telephones, televisions, radios, satellites, and so on—yet over the course of this century the nation-state has remained as important as ever.

Contrary to common claims, when one examines the outlook for technology, business, consumers, education, government, and culture itself, many of the signs point inward. Indeed, the Net may well have the effect of making the world of the future more global and more local at the same time.

How can this be? Surely globalization will remain on the rise, but so will local and community issues. What is likely to be reduced is today's high level of individual isolation, as well as the passive broadcast spirit itself. In this sense, the profile of both local, community issues and global

issues can be raised. This is no idealistic vision but rather the natural consequence of the forces that have been set in motion. Technology doesn't
make people nicer, happier, or altruistic, but it does tend to shape how one
spends one's time. Take, for example, the automobile and television.

From the PC to the Web: Homogeneity and Diversity

One tends to think of information technology as a global force. Certainly,
this was true throughout the personal computer era. Hardware products—
microprocessors, disk drives, laser printers—as well as software packages—word processing, spreadsheets, relational databases, groupware,
and local area networking—tended to be pretty much the same all around
the world. From Munich to New York to Singapore, a PC was a PC.

The highly homogenous nature of these front-office era products made
it relatively easy for American companies to expand rapidly around the
world. American semiconductor, hardware, and software companies benefited greatly from their ability to sell more or less the same product in all
of the world's major markets, despite having to adapt to local business
practices, distribution channels, and sales and marketing idiosyncrasies.

It is easy to assume that with the emergence of the Internet homogeneity will continue to foster the global expansion of information technology.
But this will be only partly the case. Although critical Internet technologies such as routers, browsers, modems, and many types of Web server
hardware and related software will remain globally consistent products,
over the next decade other key areas of information technology will contain and sustain more purely local elements. Consider the following five
elements of evolving information technology:

1. *Communications infrastructure.* Today, *communications bandwidth*
has largely replaced *microprocessor speed* as the IT industry's main technology driver. However, unlike microprocessors, communications technology is highly fragmented and is not controlled by any single vendor or
even set of vendors. Consider that some countries have developed extensive cable TV networks, whereas others have not. Some nations will aggressively deploy fiber optics; others will not. Still others will rely more
on wireless technologies like PCS and satellite, whereas some nations will
look to telephone-based offerings such as DSL (digital subscriber line)

and ISDN (integrated services digital network). And still other countries will depend upon a mixture of all of the above.

Acronyms aside, there exists no widespread consensus on what a universal communications infrastructure should be. Since different countries have different needs and are starting from different places, a variety of infrastructures will emerge. Just as no two countries today possess the same mix of air, road, train, and truck transportation, no two communications infrastructures will be alike five or ten years down the road.

Perhaps even more critically, these diverse infrastructures will be owned and operated by an even more diverse set of vendors. Clearly, there will be far more diversity among telecommunications and Internet service providers (than exists in today's PC industry). Although some global consolidation is occurring, in the end relatively few countries will allow their critical information infrastructures to be owned and operated by foreign firms. Most nations will view their IT infrastructures as important national assets, in the same way they do their road, water, energy, and electrical systems.

The obvious implication of this diversity is that some infrastructures will be more capable than others. Some countries will collectively do a better job of choosing technologies; others will be more effectively managed. Still others will do a better job of working through the inevitable government and regulatory concerns. In other words, infrastructure development will be a major area of national competitive differentiation, a situation far different than with today's microprocessors, where the nation state plays essentially no role whatsoever.

2. *End User Devices.* End user devices connected to these infrastructures will, over time, vary considerably by country. Obviously, the whole issue of cable TV set-top boxes is of interest only in those countries with an active cable industry. Those without it are more likely to rely largely on PCs or a Web/TV-type device for Net access.

3. *NCs versus PCs.* In sharp contrast to personal computers, the outlook for network computers is also likely to vary considerably by country. The NC approach becomes increasingly viable as bandwidth increases. Those nations that provide the fastest consumer connections are likely to take advantage of NCs first. In contrast, countries that continue to rely on today's modem-class speeds will find NCs to be of much more limited use, at least in consumer markets.

4. *Wireless Networks.* The evolution of national wireless networks will play a critical role in shaping markets for personal digital assistants and other highly mobile devices. The effective establishment of the GSM (global system for mobile communications) cellular phone standard across Europe has already led to far more extensive and sophisticated cell phone use than in the highly fragmented U.S. market. This differentiation could easily be repeated for wireless Internet access and a variety of smart pagers, phones, and other wireless telecommunications devices and appliances.

5. *Applications.* The PC era was driven by a small but highly consistent set of applications—spreadsheets, word processing, presentation graphics, groupware, databases, file and print, and the like. Clearly, there will also be a number of important global Web applications—e-mail, search, audio, video, telephony, and so on. However, for many Web users the defining Web applications will be much more specific and varied.

With the Web's wide variety of news, entertainment, shopping, banking, health care, education, training, job searches, political or social involvement, and all manner of chat and personal services, the Web era will be much more diverse than the PC era, where an overwhelmingly strong sense of what a PC was and what it should be used for prevailed virtually across the board. In the Web era, a nation's or region's popular consensus of what makes the Net valuable will vary considerably around the world.

Tables 8.1 and 8.2 provide a summary of the shift from the global technologies and applications of the PC, front-office era to the diversity of local technologies and services of the network-centered, Web-based era.

From the Global to the Local: Convergence and Structure

From a broader perspective, changes in the very nature of what the IT industry is and what it consists of will also tend to make it substantially more local in nature. Consider Figure 8.1. On the left is a typical view of what is often described as IT industry convergence: the coming together of the four Cs—computers, communications, consumer electronics, and content. Clearly all four of these elements share an increasingly common digital foundation and therefore are overlapping and interacting in unprecedented ways. Essentially a new IT industry value chain is being created.

TABLE 8.1   From Global to Local Technologies

PC Era	Web Era
Microprocessors	Cable TV
Operating systems	Fiber optics
RDBMS	XDSL, ISDN
LANs	Carriers/ISPs
Servers	On-line services
Disk drives	ATM/gigabit Ethernet
Laser printers	Satellites/wireless

TABLE 8.2   From Global Applications to Local Services

PC Era	Web Era
Word processing	News/entertainment
Spreadsheets	Shopping/finance
Database	Health care
Graphics	Government
File and print	Education/training
	On-line expertise
	Classified ads
	Chat/personals

A broad sense of what this new structure will look like is provided in the image on the right side of Figure 8.1. In spite of their common service component, the hardware, software, and communications industries will likely remain distinct layers in the overarching industry of information technology, as is the case with today's computer business. For example, Compaq is not doing much in *software*; Lotus does virtually nothing in *hardware*; and AT&T has refocused almost entirely on *communications*. The right side of the figure displays the fact that each of these industries will remain distinct, even as each industry will also take on aspects of the others, as conveyed on the left side of the figure. Thus *hardware* will reflect the convergence of PCs and consumer electronics; *communications* will reflect the convergence of voice and data, and *content* will reflect the merger of multiple media—text, image, audio, and video.

FIGURE 8.1   The IT Industry: Convergence and Structure

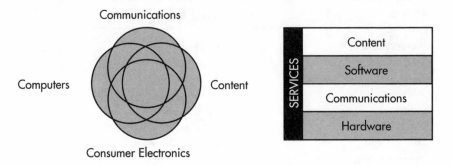

Software will reflect the convergence of multiple data types as well. It will come in two forms: structured and unstructured. Data will continue to be the central currency of the structured and relational database world, and the document will become the central currency of the unstructured software world. The document in software terms has and will continue to become increasingly complex, containing all manner of objects from rich text to graphics to sound waves and video.

One thing the figure does not portray is the continued separation of content and software. Despite repeated claims that the software and content industries are converging, this is really not the case. With the notable exception of Microsoft (which has more money than it knows what to do with), few if any other independent software vendors (ISVs) are moving seriously into the content business. ISVs continue to focus on software tools, applications, and related services.

Similarly, it's difficult to name any major content company—Time Warner, Disney, The News Corporation, Dow Jones—that has shown any real or sustained interest in expanding into the software industry. It is a totally different business, run by very different types of people, with little leverage between skills and competencies. Software and content companies will continue to partner in any number of important ways. But such partnerships are just another way of admitting that neither side can easily enter into the other's realm.

What does all of this have to do with localization? Well, consider the five main industry elements (the four layers in Figure 8.1 plus their common service component):

1. Hardware
2. Communications
3. Software
4. Content
5. Services

At the highest level, three of these layers—communications, content, and services—will be predominantly local or at most national in nature. Meanwhile, the other two layers—hardware and software—will prove predominantly global.

Now consider that during the PC era, hardware, software, and services defined most of the IT industry. This is why that period was so inherently global in nature. But now two important new dimensions have been added to the value chain—communications and content—and both happen to be much more locally defined. Thus from a broad structural perspective, increased localization is virtually certain. After all, local issues will determine the shape of three of the five main IT industry layers.

A Customer Perspective

Figure 8.2 portrays a similar shift from the global to the local, but this time from a customer perspective. The image on the left reflects what the IT industry of the 1980s looked like to a typical consumer. Basically, brand name vendors existed for the major hardware and software products; but beyond these two areas, customers were mostly dealing with various, generally highly fragmented service entities—be they a retail dealer, a value-added reseller (VAR), a systems integrator (SI), or a user MIS organization. Consequently, product vendors dominated both the industry news and the customer brand awareness.

In contrast, on the Web a new highly organized layer of network services is being built on top of a base of globally standard hardware and software products. "Network services" doesn't necessarily mean just Internet access and telecom-type offerings. Of much greater interest are the actual business, information, and entertainment services that exist in such great numbers on the Web. Is there any doubt that the Bank of America site or similar financial services compose their own unique layer of online value? These services define the actual consumer experience much

FIGURE 8.2   The Subordination of PC Products to Network Services

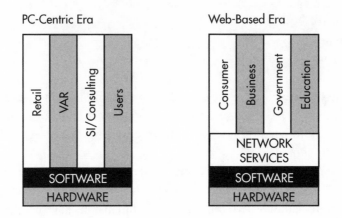

more so than the underlying hardware and software products, which in many cases are all but invisible.

So, be it from a consumer, business, educational, or government perspective, hardware and software products are steadily becoming subordinate to value-added network services. Since the vast majority of these services will be local or national in nature, they will also contribute significantly to the increased localization of the industry.

In short, the two most global parts of the business—hardware and software—are becoming increasingly subordinate and transparent, while the most visible segments, the actual Web-based services, are predominantly local in focus. Thus, from both an IT vendor and customer perspective, IT industry localization is clearly on the rise.

Fostering Global and Local Community:
AIDS Research and Education (HIV/TDP)

One splendid example of the power and potential for the Web to further local/global action and community is a collaborative research initiative coordinated by the American Association of Health Plans Foundation (AAHPF) and involving AIDS patients, their health care providers, and AIDS activists. Lotus got involved because some of our employees took the initiative to explore the possibility of leveraging Lotus technology both to enable local action and to demonstrate the capacity of collaborative technologies and MFEs to help address a critical crisis on a global scale.

For a person with AIDS, the culture of drug research and trial can be a real roller-coaster ride. First, literally thousands of drugs are purported to be effective at preventing HIV infection or managing its progression and symptoms. In the United States, these drugs must go through a great deal of testing before they are approved by the Food and Drug Administration. This is time not afforded easily by someone whose disease is rapidly progressing.

The HIV/TDP project proposes to collect self-reported clinical and administrative information directly from patients around the world and to aggregate representations of their success or frustration with many drugs and drug combinations. The idea is that the understanding of which drugs and combinations are a better bet can be speeded by this process.

Lotus employees have built a prototype interactive Web site that will facilitate the self-reporting of a variety of clinical measures, as well as health-related quality of life (specific to people with AIDS) and general patient satisfaction. The actual site will ultimately provide for this critical "community" and for information sharing in a secure environment, while also generating actionable knowledge—the core of KM—of an invaluable nature for individuals dealing with a critical health challenge.

LOOKING BEYOND
THE BUSINESS MARKET

In order for business automation to attain its full potential, the other major segments of society—consumers, schools, and government—will also need to be wired. Although a global business consensus is forming because of the competitive need to use IT effectively, no such broad consensus as yet exists within the consumer, education, and government sectors. In each of these three areas, the effective deployment of IT can help build critical mass while highlighting local diversity.

Education

Although we hear a lot about the importance of computers in the schools, within the academic world itself, this remains a topic of fierce debate. Not surprisingly, given the early stage of usage, there is only sketchy evidence as to whether the use of computers will actually improve K–12 education. And unfortunately history is not particularly encouraging in this regard.

It's hard to avoid the fact that television, cable television, VCRs, and CD-ROMs have all been touted as potentially great educational tools; and yet it is also the fact that the reality has proved disappointing. Understandably, many educators see the Internet as just another technology distraction. Many also believe that any new money would be better spent on new buildings, smaller classrooms, newer books, and of course, more qualified and available teachers. Only at a university level is there broad-based recognition of the true value of the Net and the Web as learning tools.

Education thus remains an area of potentially high international experimentation. No one really knows what the best approaches will be, and odds are, they will vary by culture anyway. Since basically everyone is at ground zero, it is one of the few areas where the United States does not have an important current advantage.

The Consumer Sector

The same range of mixed opinion and opportunities exists within the consumer sector. Whereas many consumers—particularly the well-off and well-educated—are sold on the idea of having at least one PC in the home, many others remain skeptical. Below are five of the main barriers to mass acceptance:

1. *Work at home.* This remains one of the top home PC applications, but obviously, it is only relevant to certain types of office workers. If your job happens to be landscaping, construction, painting, cooking, cleaning, electrical work, plumbing, aerobics instruction, or such, the work-at-home value of the Web is greatly limited.

2. *Entertainment.* Not everyone enjoys the isolated experience of surfing the Web; and until much higher levels of bandwidth are available, the multimedia capabilities needed for a compelling Web experience will remain somewhat elusive. With the exception of reading, most successful forms of entertainment are much more social in nature; and as we all know, surfing the Net is often more like watching TV than it is like reading.

3. *Convenience.* Despite all the Web's progress, it is still rare that it is more convenient to use the Web to check TV listings, pay a parking ticket,

reserve a theater seat, or look over one's financial accounts. In many areas, despite the increasing use of market-facing systems, pure convenience has yet to become a driving Web capability.

4. *Ease of use.* If you don't use a computer extensively at school or work, gaining the skills required to manage today's PCs is both frustrating and time-consuming. Although improvements continue to be made, PCs remain by far the most complex electronics product sold to the mass market, with levels of reliability considerably below those of other consumer electronics products. From an ease of use and maintenance perspective, PCs actually have much more in common with automobiles than consumer electronics.

5. *Cost.* Even with today's PCs in the $1,000 range, cost remains a significant barrier to entry. Understandably, many people can think of better things to do with this level of discretionary income, especially when PCs become obsolete after just three or four years.

Of course, even if all of these generic barriers are overcome around the world, the trend toward localization is likely to continue. In the end, geographical proximity doesn't matter much to *computers*, but it does matter to *people*. Families, friends, schools, community members, workplaces all tend to be relatively nearby. And who do people really want to communicate with?

Today, over 90 percent of U.S. consumer telephone traffic volumes are within the United States. There is little reason to think that the global picture is very different. This is not simply a result of historically high international phone rates; it's just that people are not—at least not yet—nearly as geographically dispersed as some high-tech nomads would have it. Most people don't have much reason to talk regularly with people in other countries. Of course, that may change, and already has changed, with the growth of on-line communities on the Web.

Overall, both the educational and consumer sectors have the potential— and probably the likelihood—of varying significantly by country and region. In business computing, competitive forces will tend to drive companies in a common direction, whereas with consumers and education, issues of taste, culture, choice, and even aesthetics will always come into play. Market forces alone cannot assure that all schools will be automated or that all consumers will enjoy the Web.

In addition to these variations in the extent of usage in both the education and consumer sectors, significant differences in types of activity are also highly likely to remain as World Wide Web usage increases. Working at home is much more appealing in America than, say, in many parts of Asia, where homes tend to be much smaller. Similarly, there is little reason to think that home banking, shopping, health care, classified and personal advertising, and so on will be consistently attractive aspects of the Web across nations. Differences in tastes and laws will clearly have a significant impact on Web use in ways largely irrelevant to the PC era. All of this will make predicting rates of consumer acceptance far more difficult than in the business sector.

To date, business computing and business transformation through market-facing systems are both dependent upon pervasive use of computers in homes. This creates a real dilemma for many companies: Unless one knows how many consumers are likely to be able to use an on-line service, planning new offerings and transitioning from older approaches becomes problematic.

Perhaps more than any other area, variations in consumer usage will determine variations in the overall national patterns. With no country today having PCs in more than 40 percent of its homes, usage remains one of the single most important wild cards. Indeed, perhaps only the communications infrastructure itself is more important.

Government

Nowhere is the evidence of growing local diversity more apparent than in the broadening role of government. This is especially ironic, since many globalists expect the power and scope of governments to shrink steadily over time. A brief analysis of the fundamentals will easily show why such shrinkage will not be the case, at least not for the next decade. If anything, technology and the role of the state will become increasingly intertwined. Local and national government decisions will have a great deal of impact on the evolution of the Web—and vice versa: Information technology and government will both transform and be transformed by each other.

The first thing to keep in mind is that the world economy is much more national than global. International trade rarely composes more than one-quarter of any country's economy, often considerably less. Fewer than 10 percent of all American workers ever live or work in another country. Although these numbers are increasing, they are doing so only slowly.

More specifically, a quick look at the basic functions of governments shows that the Web will change some, enhance others, and still others will be affected hardly at all. Consider the following ten functions of government, which taken together can provide a rough sense of the Net's overall impact on government activity:

1. *Finance and taxation.* Financial and currency issues were extensively globalized well before the Web ever came along. To be sure, the advent of global capital markets and instantly tradable floating currencies have placed new limitations on national monetary policies. Nevertheless, governments retain substantial financial power and responsibility. Just look at the role national governments are playing in cleaning up many of the bankruptcies in Asia or, closer to home, the U.S. Savings and Loan disasters of the late 1980s.

In contrast, with rapidly increasing levels of electronic commerce, taxation has emerged as a major new area of Internet controversy. There are serious issues as to how cyber-based businesses should be taxed, since physically a Web site could be located almost anywhere. But is this issue really new? Catalog sales commonly cut across state lines, and multinational corporations have long been able to shift activities and profits from one tax zone to another. One of the effects of this shift has been that governments have shifted the tax burden from corporations to individuals, who are far less mobile and fungible.

Although the Internet may well lead to more uniform taxation laws on sales, governments can always find other ways of raising money. Public sector spending as a share of national GDP continues to range anywhere from 20 to 70 percent. It will certainly continue to go up or down in particular countries, but probably not because of the Internet.

2. *Defense and law enforcement.* The impact of the Web on traditional military concerns is negligible, although the potential for so-called information warfare should not be minimized. But the Web has many interesting implications for law enforcement. Today, much of the debate has been about the role of encryption in either aiding or restricting government surveillance capabilities. This remains a potentially volatile issue that will almost definitely need to be addressed in a global forum.

On the other hand, the potential of the Web in terms of soliciting local citizen information, displaying wanted posters, providing warnings, and other forms of community interaction should not be underestimated. In the longer term, the increased use of smart cameras and sensors will also play a critical role, with high potential for significant national differentiation.

3. *Regulation.* Although much recent discussion has been preoccupied with various attempts to censor or restrict Web content, from a broader perspective a major government role is unavoidable. Just consider the prospect of solving the following problems in the absence of government intervention:

- How will the wireless spectrum be allocated?
- What sorts of media cross-ownership will be allowed?
- What, if any, subsidies will be allocated to help spur universal service?
- When will price controls on current monopoly services be lifted?
- Will telecommuters receive any tax incentives?

4. *Commerce development and promotion.* Governments have always helped spur commerce in selected sectors, especially technology-based areas such as computers, aerospace, and health and safety. As the Web economy unfolds, the following questions will need to be addressed by governments:

- What sorts of R&D will be sponsored?
- As a nation, will we invest in or oversee communications infrastructure development?
- Will special tax programs be set up to entice Web hosting services much like what has been done for manufacturing sites and software development centers?
- Will the government become an advanced user, demonstrating the Web's potential?

5. *Income redistribution.* For better or for worse, most governments already do this extensively and efficiently; there is little reason to think that the Web will change things substantially.

6. *Voting and political participation.* Here there are of course tremendous possibilities. It will be up to each nation to find its own balance between the advantages of receiving direct citizen feedback on specific is-

sues and the potential dangers of instantaneous majority decisions. There is little reason to expect anything resembling uniformity, but the potential to significantly increase citizen involvement is certainly there.

7. *Intellectual property rights.* This has certainly been one of the most highly publicized policy areas—cutting across privacy, decency, and copyright concerns. While the copyright protection/violation issue is today rightly seen mostly in global terms, both privacy and decency issues will be determined much more locally. A good example would be gambling. Sure, one can always place bets with an Internet gambling operation outside of one's country borders. But if a country decides to ban such gambling, a citizen from that country who accepts winnings from another country would be breaking the law and could face serious taxation and criminal issues. This would probably be enough of a disincentive to deter the great majority of law-abiding citizens.

Where a financial transaction trail exists, country regulation will remain viable. In contrast, where a financial transaction trail does not exist—as is often the case with pornography sites—regulation will prove more difficult. But of course, this has been true in this area for centuries.

8. *Personal privacy.* Perhaps more than either copyrights or decency, policies protecting individual privacy are likely to display the greatest regional and national variation. Laws on the use of citizen information already vary widely from country to country. There is little reason to expect any fundamental changes or shifts in this always controversial area. The reality is that the Web presents a complex privacy dilemma: If citizens want to receive customized information and services, they have to reveal their needs and interests.

This obviously implies a certain level of trust and risk. Here, national and regional differences around the world are likely to be significant because personal willingness to reveal or conceal certain "private" information as to needs and interests tends to be highly culturally determined. Such variations, of course, are already taken into account in such direct business-to-consumer realms as direct mail, telephone solicitation, and list rentals.

9. *Health and education.* To the extent the government is involved in these areas, there is tremendous room for discretion regarding how technology will be deployed. These two areas should be seen not just as essential public services but as major aspects of international competitive-

ness. It will certainly be very interesting to see how, over the next decade, public and private health care and educational institutions in various nations around the world manage to use or fail to use technology.

10. *Information and statistics.* As the Web enables dramatic new abilities in both collecting and disseminating information, it could breathe new life into this important but traditionally stodgy area of government activity. There are still many types of important data—employment, income, demographic—that only governments can effectively collect. Even in today's privatization environment, this is unlikely to change.

Overall, the advent of the Web provides a real opportunity for governments all around the world to make an important contribution to their country's technological competitiveness. In an era of widespread privatization and deregulation, it's sometimes easy to forget governments' many contributions. Over the next few years, perceptions will shift, and the need for business/government cooperation will become clearer.

CULTURE AND LANGUAGE

With the possible exception of those fearing the loss of their *jobs*, perhaps the most vociferous attacks on the dangers of globalization come from those who fear the loss of their *culture*. These worries inevitably stem from the fact that the early years of the Internet have been dominated by the English language in general and American content and values in particular. The fear, of course, is that the Internet as a major new media will contribute steadily to a loss of cultural and even linguistic identity.

There are, of course, a number of very real issues here. English has already become the world's common business language, and is well on the way to being the common citizens' language as well. The great majority of content on the Internet today is available only in English. More broadly, it is unarguable that over time the world's dominant language has periodically changed, and individual languages have come and gone. In the end, languages have always been in competition with each other. Learning any language requires work, and individuals naturally tend to gravitate toward those languages that offer the highest return on their time investment.

The Internet certainly didn't invent this pattern of change, but there is good reason to think that it will accelerate it. Companies wishing to reach the largest global audience for a book, newspaper, movie, or television program will be tempted to produce in English. Since these types of products essentially enjoy the economics of software, producing in high volumes enables powerful economies of scale. Television programs from the United States can be exported to another country for less money than the development of similar local programs in local languages. This can have the worrisome result of making certain local production noncompetitive.

From a consumer perspective, these trends tend to become mutually reinforcing. Learning English provides real opportunities for business, social, and cultural advancement. Additionally, the more forms of business and entertainment that use English, the stronger the incentives become. This is a dynamic that won't change anytime soon. In Europe, French, German, and English are still used in roughly equal measures. But in Asia, Latin America, and the Middle East, English is the overwhelming second language of choice.

There are, however, countervailing forces at work, even at a national level. What is really happening with both the Internet and television is that the total amount of *content space* is being increased dramatically. Whereas in the past, television was often limited by airwave capacities to just a few channels, in an era of cable and satellite, 500-channel systems can be available everywhere. Obviously, the Internet has an even broader content capacity.

Without sharing content from around the world, how would such capacity be utilized? Would it really be feasible to develop 500 TV channels in French, let alone Danish or Norwegian? No, only by leveraging programming from elsewhere can today's technology be fully taken advantage of. There really isn't anything new about this. The reality is that this pattern has been going on in smaller countries for years. The fact that it is not economical to translate many books into Danish (with a total population of just 3 million) became a major incentive for many Danes to learn to read in English or German.

It would be a mistake, however, to confuse *volume of content* with *cultural identity*. The evidence is overwhelming that when it comes to critical news, entertainment, and cultural expression, local languages and issues remain vital. Local programming might have to share the stage with more global content, but it will not be replaced by it. Depending upon your point of view, the ability to watch CNN, MTV, or the American Superbowl may be a luxury or a curse, but these programs don't cut to the core of any national culture, except possibly America's.

The Internet is also likely to contribute about as much as it takes away. For every Frenchman watching English programming, there might well be another French speaker in Canada, Southeast Asia, or Africa, tuning into French language programming that only the digital revolution could make available. This new global market for non-English programming is already catching on in America, where immigrants and expatriates from Asia, the Middle East, or Latin America have increased access to programming in their native languages. With facts like these, one can argue that the Internet might actually help preserve some languages that would otherwise decline.

The bottom line is this: Both sides have a point. Technology's global reach will further entrench the universal use of English because there will be a real need for a common denominator of usage; and Esperanto notwithstanding, at least for the time being there really are no viable alternative candidates available. One could argue that through sheer numbers Chinese might someday be the world's common tongue, but there are good reasons why no character-based language is likely ever to be dominant in a computer-driven world.

As a countervailing force to the likely domination of English on the Web, the total opportunity for local languages to proliferate and gain in usage and immediacy will also increase as markets move beyond national boundaries to reach anyone at any given time. Perhaps more importantly, as the Web matures, its global applications and services will become increasingly local in content and language, much as the most important forms of television and newspapers always have been. Today, well over half of the content on the Internet is in English. But this share is likely to fall steadily over the next five years.

In this sense, the Internet is making the world both more global and more local. When it comes to content, "more" really is the operative term.

CHAPTER 9

THE RACE FOR
GLOBAL LEADERSHIP

DURING THE 1990S, A POWERFUL SYNERGY developed between a number of economic and cultural characteristics prevalent in the United States and a number of powerful enterprise-enabling information technologies, including e-mail, voice mail, relational databases, and call centers.

The U.S. lead in adopting these technologies was significant compared to much of Europe, and dramatic compared to most of Asia. Not surprisingly, as we near the millennium and the cutting edge of technology shifts to other application areas, a new set of driving technologies has emerged. Today, network-based collaborative computing and the market-facing systems required to take advantage of the Web as a commercial medium are forging a new business climate.

Clearly, by nearly every standard measure, the United States is way out in front with regard to IT usage and implementation. And just as clearly, this lead has greatly contributed to the U.S. recovery of economic dominance in the developed world. But how does the United States really stack up in comparison to other countries?

MEASURING TODAY'S U.S. LEAD

International Data Corporation, the world leader in compiling information and statistics regarding global IT usage, has compiled some benchmark data regarding IT usage for the United States and Japan, as well as for the four largest European markets: Germany, France, Italy, and the

TABLE 9.1   Comparative IT Usage Statistics, 1997

	% of Employees with Web Access	No. of People Using the Web (in millions)	% Companies with Intranet	PCs/100 People	IT as % of GDP
U.S.	32%	29	23%	27	3.9%
Japan	23%	5.9	7%	20	2.0%
France	16%	1.2	2%	19	2.4%
Germany	24%	4.3	15%	21	1.9%
Italy	14%	0.8	2%	10	1.6%
U.K.	21%	3.1	5%	23	3.1%

United Kingdom (see Table 9.1). The IDC defines five IT usage categories:

1. Percentage of employees with Web access
2. Percentage of population with Web access
3. Percentage of companies with intranets
4. PCs per capita
5. IT expenditure as a percentage of a country's GDP

Of course, collecting precise and consistent information across national boundaries is never easy. Any attempt to compose a reliable picture of worldwide IT usage is further complicated by the fact that nearly every country listed has developed its own distinct IT culture. For example, the fact that France's Web usage numbers are as low as they are is at least partially a function of the strong presence of its unique minimal videotext system.

Nevertheless, the data provided by IDC sheds some light on comparative IT usage worldwide. It's worth noting at the start that in every category the United States has taken a substantial early lead, whereas Italy ranks last in all five areas. Now let's take a closer look at the data in each category:

1. *Employee Web access.* No country has reached anything approaching market saturation here. Companies face difficult questions in defining who needs Web access and who doesn't. But as intranets become the dominant mode of internal communications for medium as well as large orga-

nizations, the hardware and software required for intranet access will increasingly find its way to most workers' desks. Once this occurs, external access to the Web will become essentially a policy matter, roughly equivalent to allowing external phone calls—although perhaps harder to regulate.

2. *Web population.* Although this category is a mix of business, consumer, government, and education usage, the data tell a powerful story. By having both a much larger population and a much higher level of Web usage, the absolute U.S. numbers are anywhere from five to thirty times those of the world's other major economies. Given the powerful critical mass effects that the Web provides—remember Metcalfe's Law—the absolute advantages are probably even more important than the relative ones.

3. *Intranet use.* In nearly all countries, this factor varies greatly according to the size of the enterprise. For large Fortune 1000 class organizations in the Unites States, the number is now well over 70 percent and rising fast. For smaller organizations, however, the pace of change will remain much slower. Nevertheless, the gap between the United States and the other countries except Germany is striking. With the deployment of corporate intranets a virtual prerequisite toward widespread electronic commerce, this IT gap is significant.

4. *PCs per capita.* Since network computers and Web TV are still not installed in large numbers anywhere, PCs per capita is still perhaps the single most accurate and meaningful metric to compare relative IT pervasiveness. As the data demonstrate, the United States has generally maintained a four- to eight-point lead over the other countries, with the notable exception of Italy. On the other hand, the market is nowhere near the saturation point anywhere, particularly with regard to PC access in homes and schools. As is true in the United States as much as elsewhere, much lower prices and more user-friendly products remain badly needed to achieve more universal PC and Web availability.

5. *IT as a percent of GDP.* This is perhaps the most interesting macroeconomic indicator of all. It is, however, also notoriously difficult to measure. Measuring the internal spending of companies on internal information system staff, training, and related activity has proven practically impossible to calibrate accurately. Still, the sheer size of the U.S. lead in this realm is striking and reflects the often controversial, sustained dou-

ble-digit growth in IT spending over the course of the 1990s. In contrast, Japan's IT expenditures have fluctuated wildly between high, low, and no growth years, whereas European spending has expanded steadily but at a much lower rate than in the United States.

OTHER PLAYERS: ASIA (JAPAN, SINGAPORE, MALAYSIA)

What about other regions and countries? According to IDC, the six advanced countries depicted above account for 65 percent of the world's GDP and roughly 75 percent of the world's total IT spending. Other advanced computing countries include Canada, Australia, New Zealand, and in Europe, Denmark, Norway, Switzerland, and the Netherlands.

Asian investment levels are generally lower than those in Europe, with only Korea, Singapore, Malaysia, and Hong Kong joining Japan in IDC's list of the top thirty most computerized nations. Most of the so-called BEMs (big emerging markets), such as China, India, Brazil, Nigeria, and Indonesia, still rank far down the list. There is no debating the fact that the United States is the most developed major IT market today. But how likely is it to retain its paramount position? In an attempt to answer that question (or at least place it in context), let's look more closely at Asia and Japan.

The Asian Financial Crisis

From an IT industry point of view, Japan accounts for more than two-thirds of the entire Asian marketplace. Moreover, in a wide range of industries, Japan is the principal U.S. rival. For the better part of the last twenty years, U.S. and Japanese firms have tended to view their positions with respect to one another.

However, the Asian financial troubles that began in late 1997 have encouraged all observers to take a more regional perspective. Surely, it could not be an accident that Japan, Korea, Thailand, Indonesia, and Malaysia all have had serious economic and financial problems at roughly the same time. There are clearly some common forces at work.

What, you may ask, do recent headlines regarding "crony capitalism," insolvent banks, and collapsing currencies have to do with information technology? In fact, the relationship between the Asian financial crisis and

IT is much stronger than has been generally recognized. The reality is that a large part of today's financial crisis in the region stems from deeper competitive problems; and these competitive shortcomings are at least partially linked to lagging technology usage. Consider the following three factors:

1. *Corporate insolvency.* Many Asian companies have gotten into serious trouble by participating in all sorts of businesses in which they don't make any money. Without profits they can't pay off their loans. Why haven't they made any money? Often, in businesses from cars to PCs to investment banking, they have been beaten in global markets by more energetic competitors. In many industries today, only the top tier suppliers are profitable; the rest have to get by on revenues alone. At the end of the twentieth century, technology utilization has proven to be an unusually good indicator of the gap dividing leaders from followers.

2. *Market capitalization.* Many Asian companies have been heavily criticized because of their astronomical debt/equity ratios. A lack of profits has certainly been part of this problem, but a lack of confidence has played at least an equal role. Over the last few years, investor expectations have been steadily revised downward. This has led many to conclude that Asian stocks must have been seriously overvalued. But is this necessarily so?

Consider that during the late 1980s and early 1990s, many observers fully expected Japanese, Korean, and other Asian players to take ever higher shares of key global industries. If, for example, these vendors had gone on to dominate the markets for semiconductors, personal computers, data communications equipment, cellular phone devices, satellite technology, printers, storage, and related product areas, the valuations of the past might in retrospect now look cheap. In other words, the value many thought would accrue to Asia has actually gone largely to U.S. companies. In the technology sector alone, we are talking about something on the order of a *trillion* dollars in market capitalization that unexpectedly failed to materialize in Asia. This is how a competitive crisis (often directly tied to technology) has turned into a financial one. Once again, Asia's loss has been the flip side of the U.S. gain.

3. *Downsizing.* What's the remedy for the Asian crisis? Not surprisingly, the overriding message from Western creditors and from organizations such as the International Monetary Fund has been for Asian compa-

nies to get rid of their bad businesses and focus on the good ones. It's basically the same "downsizing and restructuring" recipe that, for all its pain and hardship, swept late-1980s America back into the winner's circle.

However, since downsizing and restructuring are often just euphemisms for wholesale layoffs, this is a prospect that most Asian companies and workers have a culturally determined difficulty taking seriously. Sometimes it seems as if some Japanese and Korean companies would rather close their doors altogether than carry out significant personnel cuts. That's how strong the sense of group identity is in the East.

In contrast, although they certainly weren't happy about it, IBM, the big three automakers, and others laid off hundreds of thousands of U.S. workers. Since they didn't see any other viable option, they took the heat and even the humiliation, and most eventually returned to prosperity. Now it appears to be Asia's turn to go through the same turmoil and anxiety. When they finally bite the bullet, they will undoubtedly turn to technology to fill the knowledge gaps in their leaner, flatter, "hollowed out" organizations.

Understandably, many in Asia (and, for that matter, in Europe) associate using technology to replace people with the least appealing aspects of American-style capitalism. Perhaps this is fair. On the other hand, radically shifting labor patterns tend to be an inherent component of any truly great technological revolution. Strangely, many people seem to have already forgotten that IBM, AT&T, and other U.S. giants also used to have de facto no layoff policies. Only when the pressure of the marketplace compelled them to change their traditional ways did they reluctantly comply.

Asians today are being warned that American-style change is inevitable. They are being told that their lifelong employment systems are now a source of weakness, rather than a source of strength. And they are being asked to accept this fundamental change in philosophy in a remarkably short period of time. More than anything else, the abruptness of this intimidating message has become a primary source of the region's confusion, fear, and increasingly, resentment. To the citizen on the street, this is what the Asian Contagion is really about.

Nevertheless, most observers see no real alternative. If Asia could find a successful way forward without the painful restructuring America has experienced, then we should all take note that perhaps there really is a better "Asian way." However, if it cannot find such a path (as seems increasingly likely), then we should all recognize that technology-driven restructuring is not just an American fad. In this critical sense, we are all technologists now.

In the late 1980s and early 1990s, when America was in sorry shape, expectations for Asia soared. If America had remained on a downward course, such expectations might well have proven justified indefinitely. But America roared back with unexpected strength. This is just another way of saying that Asia's relative position declined with unexpected speed. In America, a stock market boom created trillions in new wealth. Not surprisingly, falling markets in Asia have on occasion led to financial ruin. Such are the implications of global competition. And such is the awesome power of technology.

Technology Utilization in Japan

For a variety of technical, cultural, and linguistic reasons, IT usage in Japan evolved much more slowly than in the United States and other Western countries. Although there have been a number of positive developments in recent years, at least five barriers still exist to widespread IT adoption in Japan today.

1a. *Messaging (e-mail)*. Widespread use of electronic mail began to catch on in Japan around 1994 and has since gained considerable momentum. Today, it has become de rigueur for Japanese business people to have an e-mail address on their highly valued business cards, a sharp contrast to the early 1990s. Although there is still some resistance to typing among older executives, today's Japanese language keyboards and software handle phonetic to kanji translation effectively.

On the other hand, the use of remote and mobile access to corporate messaging systems is still much more limited than in the United States and elsewhere, if for no other reason than that most Japanese would rather stay late in the office than try to work extensively from home. Perhaps more importantly, the use of e-mail has not yet led directly to significant organizational flattening, largely due to a general lack of cost-cutting emphasis. However, e-mail has led to broader, more open corporate communications, an important change in a traditional, strongly hierarchical management system.

1b. *Messaging (voice mail).* The use of voice mail, however, is still relatively rare. The reasons for this vary. Japanese offices still tend to have much higher numbers of secretaries, and therefore fewer phones go unanswered. Some customers cite the high cost of such systems, but the real explanation seems to stem from the simple fact that in Japanese organizations it is common to pick up each other's phone, something that rarely happens in many American offices. To betray a personal bias, I'm a constant critic of voice mail as the lowest value form of electronic collaboration—so the Japanese may have a point there. What little voice mail exists is often found in those Japanese companies that enjoy an extensive multinational presence.

2. *The Internet and the Web.* Use of the Web in Japan remains at least eighteen to twenty-four months behind use in the United States. As of early 1998, the state of the market can generally be summarized as lingering at the "home page and e-mail" level. Surprisingly, a considerable number of user organizations still wonder if the Web isn't just some sort of fad that might well lose its luster over time.

More specifically, the big business initiatives driving the Web engine for corporate America—market-facing systems, intranets, and extranets, the development of fully integrated and enabled MFEs—are by and large not yet a presence on the Japanese scene. Consumer transactions over the Web remain quite limited (and legally more complex). Intranets are still limited and usually confined largely to internal information publishing. Extranets have failed to catch on, despite some natural affinities with Japan's intricate supply chain systems. More than one Japanese executive has told me that face-to-face interactions are still the preferred manufacturer/supplier business mode, particularly for those businesses centered in Tokyo.

3. *Knowledge management.* Many Japanese companies expect that in the long run knowledge management will emerge as one of their greatest competitive strengths. After all, Japanese business culture is centered around group process and information sharing, and collaborative work is deeply ingrained in the Japanese traditional approach to life in general. This, along with lifelong or near lifelong employment, is ideally suited for training, education, and knowledge development. However, the challenge in many Japanese organizations is to manage the often subtle transition from *tacit* to *explicit* knowledge. Information is often known and shared, but it is generally not written down and thus is still often distributed via face-to-face interaction.

4. *Infrastructure.* Only in the last year or so has a more open communications industry come to Japan, but at long last real competition is developing and prices have already started to fall. Although the long-term direction of Japan's telecommunications infrastructure remains unclear, more positive dynamics do seem to be emerging. At the time of this writing, a break-up of NTT's monopoly appears likely.

5. *Critical mass.* Overall, the number of PCs in use in Japan is rising, but a weak economy has prevented dramatic increases. Similarly, the low number of individuals accessing the Web limits the incentives for Japanese Web content developers. Many publishers and media companies have still made only modest commitments toward putting their most valuable information on line. This cycle can of course feed on itself. In addition, Japanese use of computers in K–12 schools is no better, and probably even worse, than in the United States.

Interestingly, in Japan, manufacturing companies are often the most advanced information users. These are the companies that participate in the most globally competitive markets and have been the most exposed to Western computing styles. In contrast, Japan's banking and insurance industries have been relatively isolated from world trends and thus have often not kept up technologically. As the Big Bang of financial deregulation begins to take effect in the latter half of 1998, many expect, or at least hope, that this situation will begin to change rapidly.

Japan remains a world leader in many industries—autos, electronics, steel and other metals, machinery, and textiles, to name just a few. It still has many of the world's largest banks and insurance companies. It's hard to imagine that these companies will not respond effectively to the technology challenges that lie ahead. But the clock is ticking, and progress to date has been surprisingly slow. More than anything else, Japan's ability to fundamentally change at a deep level has been called into question by its status as IT laggard.

Regional Generalizations

Although it's obviously difficult to make generalizations about a region as diverse as Asia, a close look at the region does seem to warrant four conclusions about the state of things.

1. *Build versus use.* As a general rule, much of the region (including Japan) has historically placed far more emphasis on *building* IT products

than *using* them. Taiwan, Korea, Malaysia, Thailand, Singapore, the Philippines, Indonesia, and increasingly, China have all become critical links in the IT industry's global supply chain. Developing a position in high-tech *production* has been considered consistently a critical commercial and national goal. However, only recently has the *deployment* of computers received similar attention. In many ways, the lack of IT in places like Taiwan and Korea is reminiscent of the old saw about the cobbler's children having no shoes.

2. *Language barriers.* As with Japan, developing efficient local language processing systems took considerably longer than, for instance, in Europe. This has proven especially true in Chinese-speaking nations where character-based systems are still difficult to operate. Indeed, in countries like Singapore and Hong Kong (with their strong British colonial influence), e-mail and many other forms of business communication are now often conducted mostly, or even entirely, in English. The use of English has reached such an extent that the use of Chinese—even by those for whom it is their native language—has demonstrably fallen off, especially in Singapore.

Obviously, in countries like China and Taiwan such changes are neither possible nor desirable, but difficulties in computing in Chinese remain a key implementation barrier. It is not an accident that Australia, New Zealand, Hong Kong, and Singapore are by most accounts the region's four most sophisticated IT markets.

3. *Protected information markets.* As with Japan, the most global companies in the region tend to be involved in manufacturing. In contrast, finance, insurance, media, and other service industries have often been either protected or otherwise relatively immune from direct global competition. Fortunately, and at least partially as a response to the region's recent economic troubles, this is changing. However, it may be some time before bit-based businesses become energized on the Web in anything approaching the way they have been transformed in the United States.

4. *Large infrastructure projects.* More than just about anywhere else in the world, Asian governments have displayed a strong inclination toward taking a direct role in their nations' telecommunications infrastructure development. This trend is most prominent in Malaysia and Singapore, but throughout the region government funding has been made available for advanced infrastructure projects. This investment in infrastructure is widely regarded as offering the best chance for the region and the nations

within it to catch up with or even leapfrog the West. Since this approach differs so sharply from the American philosophy, it is worth looking at both the Singapore and Malaysia experiences in somewhat more detail.

Infrastructure Leapfrog: Singapore and Malaysia

Over the last couple of years, both Singapore and Malaysia have made it clear that they intend to join the ranks of the world's knowledge-based economies. Both the Malaysian Multimedia Super Corridor (MSC) Project and Singapore ONE represent bold initiatives to develop and utilize advanced, high bandwidth infrastructures. Although both projects have received much local and international attention, the Malaysia story is particularly noteworthy since it has come from a country with little or no track record in technology leadership. In contrast, Singapore has long had one of Asia's most advanced telecommunications infrastructures and is the Asian headquarters of many multinational technology firms.

Despite coming from very different backgrounds and perspectives, the two projects do have at least four key themes in common:

1. *Government leadership.* The Malaysian project is heavily associated with Prime Minister Dato' Seri Mahathir Mohammed. The nation's top officials have fully grasped the significance of IT and have remained fully engaged in the project. These charismatic leaders are passionate visionaries leading by example with a crystal clear understanding of the significance of what the MSC can and will deliver to their people. Trust me, I've met with them many times, and this country is blessed with a real visionary in the form of its prime minister. I can't overstate how impressed I've been in my meetings on the MSC. In Singapore, the government's National Computer Board has long been the dominant force in shaping that nation's IT policies. I've spent several interesting and eye-opening hours with Stephen Yo, the head of the NCB, and found another eminently capable IT visionary.

2. *High bandwidth infrastructures.* As a large nation, Malaysia has chosen to focus on a single area roughly thirty miles long and ten miles wide, connecting Kuala Lumpur with a new business center (Cyberjaya) and a new seat of government (Putrajaya.) In contrast, as a small island state, Singapore plans to wire virtually the entire country using either ADSL or cable modem technology to link into its high-speed communications

backbone. In this sense, Singapore's approach is much more of a national strategy, while the Malaysia project is essentially a very special development zone, complete with tax breaks, looser employment policies, and intellectual property protection.

3. *Business and social applications.* Both nations have targeted a similar set of application priorities. Malaysia has identified seven flagship areas: research and development, electronic government, smart schools, borderless marketing, smart cards, manufacturing, and telemedicine. Singapore likes to stress electronic commerce, news and information, on-line education, games and entertainment, government services, videoconferencing, and fast Internet access. Overall, the Malaysia project is more focused on economic development, and Singapore's on providing a platform for national services.

4. *Competition for Asian investments.* As noted above, Singapore has benefited greatly by becoming the business hub of the southeast Asian region. In fulfilling this role, it has moved far beyond manufacturing and now has a large base of managerial and other knowledge workers. With lower costs and other incentives, Malaysia hopes to tap into a similar prosperity. As of December 1997, it had already attracted thirty-four world-class companies to the MSC project, including Microsoft, Lotus, Oracle, and Sun.

In addition, in both the Singapore and Malaysian examples there is an equal desire to foster the formation of local technology-driven companies. With its strength in computer audio, disk drives, and other areas, Singapore is already well on its way.

The most important aspect shared by both projects is their sense of long-term commitment. Despite the severe economic challenges in the region, Malaysia has made it clear that it tends to hold to its aggressive timelines. Singapore has been talking about becoming an "intelligent island" for nearly a decade and continues to make steady progress toward that goal. From a broader economic perspective, the rest of the world is watching to see how these government-driven initiatives develop, especially as compared to their more laissez-faire counterparts around the world.

Catching Up on IT

Beyond Singapore and Malaysia, virtually all of Asia has begun to develop a consensus that catching up with the West in IT usage must be a high national priority. The lack of IT might have been only a partial cause of the problems and challenges currently confronting the region, but a consensus has formed that this is one of a few necessary and positive paths forward. Perhaps the greatest challenge the region faces will be to continue to invest heavily in its technological capabilities even during the tight times ahead.

In the end, Asia is trying to avoid what otherwise might become a twenty-first century paradox. We are often told that the twenty-first century will be the age of Asia, but we are also told that the twenty-first century will be the age of information. Given the current IT gaps between East and West, both of these statements cannot be true.

Should Asia catch up to or surpass the West in information usage, the balance of world power would almost certainly shift. However, changes of such magnitude will clearly take some time to emerge and can only result from sustained IT commitment. The rate of progress in this area will likely prove to be one of the world's most important competitive determinants.

OTHER PLAYERS: EUROPE

The strengths of the European IT environment are not hard to identify. Like America—and unlike most of Asia—Europe has enjoyed a long history of sophisticated IT development and deployment, with expertise in software, services, and applications that are often unsurpassed. Europe's well-educated population and intensive involvement in knowledge and service industries are also well suited to developing an advanced information economy. Indeed, at present Europe represents the world's most bit-based society.

Several additional aspects of European society appear specifically well-suited to a Web-driven era. Europe's large public sectors could benefit greatly from more efficient delivery of various information and services. The European Union is, theoretically at least, well positioned to help solve the inevitable challenges that lie ahead, particularly with regard to building an international consensus in areas like security, privacy, electronic commerce, and taxation.

Since many European countries have relatively homogenous national cultures, they should be open to advanced knowledge management and business collaboration. With declining populations all but certain for the years ahead, the need to improve every worker's productivity is widely recognized.

Despite this abundance of promise, however, the 1990s have been largely a decade of lost opportunity (with the notable exception of what has occurred in the United Kingdom). The much ballyhooed economic integration of 1992 fizzled, as, unfortunately, did most of Europe's major economies. Slow growth, high unemployment, and declining international competitiveness became the sad watchwords of what has been a generally forgettable era.

Probably the only major bright spots were in cellular telephony and in business management software. In the case of the former, the wide acceptance of the GSM standard has enabled much more robust service than in the United States. (Partially as an offshoot of this activity, vendors such as Nokia and Ericsson have become global communications leaders.) In the case of the latter, the rise of Germany-based software contender SAP and, to a somewhat lesser extent, the Dutch firm Baan speaks to important European competencies in complex business process management software.

Otherwise, things look pretty dismal. European computer hardware vendors have all but disappeared, and most of Europe's software and service providers have failed to keep pace with their bigger, stronger U.S. rivals. In 1992, the European IT market was roughly equal in size to the U.S. market. Today, the U.S. IT market is nearly 50 percent larger. From an Internet and Web usage perspective, the bulk of Europe is probably still about two years behind the United States—a significant gap in this fast-moving business. In short, Europe probably can't afford another decade like this one.

Looking ahead, European leaders have identified a number of initiatives and opportunities to help reignite Europe's sluggish economic conditions. Interestingly, most of these have an important technology dimension, as is evident if we consider three of the key initiatives and opportunities these leaders singled out:

1. *Monetary integration.* After years of debate, much of continental Europe appears to be on track to move in unison toward a single European currency beginning January 1, 1999. Although most of the discussion has rightly focused on the Euro's impact on national political processes and even national sovereignty, at least two important technology dimensions are worth keeping in mind:

First, the conversion of virtually all existing information and transaction processing systems to support the Euro will likely constitute the largest software upgrade in history. This is almost certainly an even bigger challenge for Europe than the year 2000 (Y2K) problem. This is especially so, since there are still so many unknowns regarding the exact speed and scope of the process. Some countries may be running in parallel for quite some time. Pulling off such an unprecedented financial transformation will be the greatest test of the European Union's ability to function as a coherent entity. Computer technology will be a critical part of the process. The next few years will certainly be expensive and messy; the real challenge is simply to make it manageable.

Second, the emergence of a single European currency could be a real boon for the future of European electronic commerce in the all-important realm of critical mass. In today's fragmented European markets, reaching sufficient economies of scale is not always possible. A common currency and common commercial law could greatly increase the appeal of pan-European stock buying, travel services, banking, insurance, and other knowledge-intensive areas. Indeed, without the creation of a more homogenous market, prospects for many of these on-line opportunities might prove limited.

2. *Telecom deregulation.* Telecommunications deregulation is now the official policy of the European Union. Although long overdue, the impact of the current reforms should be dramatic. Unlike the process in the United States, local, long-distance, and international services are being deregulated simultaneously. Perhaps more importantly, since the whole of Europe has known about the January 1, 1999, changeover date for several years, substantial and concrete preparations are already well underway. Europe's often hideously high telecommunications rates should finally begin to trend down toward U.S. levels.

High telecommunications tariffs have historically prohibited high levels of network utilization. From 1994 to 1996, public access to the Internet was often three to five times more expensive than in the United States. Perhaps even more critically, it can't be just a coincidence that the countries with the most open telecommunications markets—the United Kingdom and much of Scandinavia—have also been those that have enjoyed the strongest economies. Certainly, most of Europe hopes that as telecommunications and other forms of deregulation spread across the continent, similar benefits will accrue elsewhere.

3. *Eastern Europe.* The steady economic development of all of the countries formerly under the control of the Soviet Union should provide Western Europe with a powerful long-term growth engine. Although many of these countries will continue to struggle with both their internal reform processes and the vagaries of free-market economies, their long-term need for Western European goods and services seems almost certain to provide a unique growth outlet to Europe's otherwise mostly mature markets.

THE CHALLENGES AHEAD

From an IT management perspective, perhaps the biggest challenges over the next few years will be obtaining resources and establishing priorities. Consider that before the end of the millennium, many major European corporations will ask their IT organizations to

- manage the year 2000 problem
- support the Euro (however it evolves)
- take advantage of telecommunications reform
- catch up with America in many areas of Web usage
- continue to upgrade and enhance mission-critical business

To make matters even more difficult, these IT organizations are being asked to do this within relatively tight budgets. Sometimes it is easy to forget how important money really is. But the fact remains that much of the current U.S. lead has been due to the fact that U.S. investments in IT spending have been increasing at double-digit rates for the last six years, and they show no serious signs of slowing down.

In sharp contrast, the forecasts for Europe generally hover in the 7 to 8 percent range. Although this represents a substantial improvement over recent years, given the enormities of the challenges ahead there is good reason to question whether these figures will prove sufficient. The Euro and the Y2K challenge alone could possibly consume most, if not all, of this incremental advance. And in this case, European Web usage will fall even farther behind.

Despite the wealth of business and technical challenges, however, the greatest challenges appear to be primarily cultural. In too many areas it would appear that much of Europe has resisted change rather than adapt to it. This resistance, of course, can take many forms—inflexible labor rules, excessive regulation/protection, lack of entrepreneurship—but the net effect remains clear. With a few significant exceptions, the overall rate of business and economic change has been demonstrably lower than in the United States, Asia, and many emerging economies as well.

Technology can only promise so much in the absence of significant change. Merely plopping a layer of technology on top of existing obsolete modes of operation and production will rarely achieve the necessary competitive improvements. Although this fact is easily and widely understood, the steps required are not easily or broadly implemented. Much of the challenge for Europe is to do many of the things it already knows need to get done.

CHAPTER 10

THE CHALLENGES AHEAD

To an increasing extent, the future of America—and of the world—and the future of technology have become inseparable. The great question now facing us all is, How long can this unique situation last?

The reality is that information technology is just one of the many complex social, economic, cultural, and political variables that affect business evolution. Many of these factors are far less predictable than ever more powerful advances in technology. Our world remains full of deep divisions and high barriers to cooperation. For information technology to reach its full potential, many obstacles must be resolved in a timely and predictable manner. The greatest risks and challenges that lie ahead can be divided into the following four areas:

1. *Technological and human limits.* It's nearly impossible to eliminate the risk that technology itself might not be able to deliver on the many promises it is making. Similarly, the demands of ever more sophisticated systems might one day outstrip the skills and talents of available workers.

2. *Failed standards.* Even if the technological capacity exists, a real risk remains that today's rising levels of product interoperability will prove a temporary illusion. The IT industry has yet to prove in a systemic sense that its particular style of competition can sustain a meaningful "open standards" process. The evidence of the last two years in this regard has been positive. But with the experience of the preceding two decades, there is every reason to be concerned that the industry dynamic could shift back to the direction of internecine warfare.

3. *Lack of demand.* It's also perfectly possible that no matter what technologies and standards emerge, two further problems could arise: Busi-

nesses might decide that there are limits to the value of automation, or consumers might decide that on-line services are simply not all that compelling. My personal sense on both counts is that the risk is fairly low; but with all our momentum and influence, it's critical that we never forget that it is the customer we must endeavor to satisfy, not ourselves.

4. *Government intervention.* For reasons of commerce, culture, politics, fairness, and security, some governments may seek to block largely unfettered use of the Internet. In this realm of Internet governance, I can foresee two main problems: restrictions on the flow of commerce and restrictions on the flow of information.

Let's take a look at each of these four areas of risk and challenge in more detail.

TECHNOLOGICAL AND HUMAN LIMITS

Although the necessary technologies are rapidly evolving, some limits may apply that will inhibit future development. These potential limits can be grouped into three basic areas: hardware, software, and telecommunications.

1. *Hardware.* Much of the computing power and storage capacity required to build the on-line enterprise of the future is available today. On the desktop, future increases in microprocessor power are likely to be aimed at helping computers to see, hear, and speak, or to display applications in three dimensions. We may see some important potential bonuses in the near future, but they will not be required for the further sequential development or proliferation of market-facing enterprises.

On the server level, processing power improvements are largely a matter of lowering costs. Very few applications today are limited by pure performance issues. Down the road, it appears likely that Moore's Law will hold true for at least another decade. By then, standard desktop microprocessors will be able to execute more than *1 billion* instructions per second. At that point, we can safely assume, these processors will pack more than enough processing power for most of us.

2. *Software.* Given the immense new needs created by the Internet, software innovation should continue at an extraordinary rate, with both today's leaders and a whole new range of start-up companies continuing to race ahead. On the other hand, three potentially serious technology risks lie ahead:

First, today's software systems are becoming so *complex* that no one person can truly understand them. Highly complex software projects have had a long history of serious management problems. Given today's often severe shortages of software professionals, some companies might find it very difficult to overcome ever more daunting software management challenges. The availability of qualified software engineers is also a very real issue. At the time of this writing, more than 300,000 IT jobs remain unfilled due to the scarcity of professionals equipped to fill them.

The real challenges here lie not so much in the complexity of the user interfaces, nor in the endless feature/function glut, but in the manageability and administration of increasingly complex software, much of which will come to be managed remotely. The total cost of ownership (TCO) is being attacked in these regards, and to meet the challenge, we need more intelligence at the back end and a thoroughly networked redistribution to the client. Keep in mind, however, that we often rush to complexity in our industry and then cyclically retreat to relative simplicity as we outstrip our ability to cope. There is no guarantee these cycles will always be addressable at the same pace. It is impossible to escape the fact that human limits will continue to affect the development of information technology.

Second, despite all that has been written about this subject, *the year 2000 debacle*, popularly known as Y2K, remains an unknown risk. No one will really know the full extent of the problem until we get there. Should the Y2K problem result in software and business chaos, it might take our industry several years to recover. The more likely outcome is the simple co-opting of available resources for a brief period. Still, given the pace of growth and innovation in the field, the opportunity cost of only a few lost quarters is certainly not negligible.

Third, although issues involving market-facing systems and other transaction style applications are quite well understood, the field of *knowledge management* is still relatively new. It is certainly possible that capturing the right knowledge at the right time could prove a quixotic challenge in many areas.

3. *Telecommunications*. Here, I can foresee two central challenges: reliability and bandwidth. The Internet is not a structured and managed system. In other words, unlike the top-down, highly engineered character of the phone system, the Internet has grown through a more bottom-up, organic approach. From 1995 to 1997, a fierce debate raged within the technical community as to whether a *reliable* network could emerge from such

a loosely constructed process. In fact, serious concerns were often voiced that the Internet might one day experience a massive collapse. The resiliency of the Net over the last few years has largely silenced this debate; but from a scientific perspective, the issue has never been resolved fully and in theory could resurface at any time.

As the reliability issue wanes, the need for more communications *bandwidth* will become the single greatest area of technological debate. However, in many ways this is not really a technical issue at all. The IT industry knows how to transmit data reliably at stunningly fast speeds measured in the billions of bits per second. The lack of bandwidth stems from the difficulty in upgrading today's massive telecommunications infrastructure to incorporate these more modern technologies. Thus, the bandwidth issue is inseparable from the challenge of moving toward a more competitive and deregulated communications industry. It is mainly a matter of industry convergence and structure.

It really isn't surprising that progress has been slow in this area. Countries around the world are desperately struggling to move from a centuries-old utility industry structure with pronounced monopolistic tendencies to a modern competitive business model. Although deregulation was able to proceed relatively rapidly in the banking and airline industries, the existence of an immense network of in-the-ground wires makes rapid telecommunications change nearly impossible. Governments may be criticized for moving too slowly, but the problems they face are formidable.

Every nation will need to solve the bandwidth problem for itself, and some will clearly do a better job than others. In the United States, it now appears that the combination of cable modems and DSL telephone adapters, along with ever improving compression technology and more sophisticated Internet routing techniques, will bring significant progress over the next few years. A decade from now, communications bandwidth should be as abundant as microprocessor performance is today. But if this does not happen, the overall pace of industry advancement is likely to be retarded.

A FAILURE OF STANDARDS

Closely related to technological advancement is the overall issue of standards. Individual progress in hardware, software, and telecommunications won't mean much unless each area can work effectively with the other. We all know that standards are what make today's Internet possible. We can visit a Web site because a computer understands the rules of electronic communication. Those rules are formalized in a protocol called TCP/IP. We can read a Web page because the computer understands the Web's rules of document structure, called HTML. As long as we follow the rules, it doesn't matter what sort of computer, nor what kind of operating system, browser, word processor, and so on, we're running.

As IT customers, we can all appreciate the value of this sort of standardization, since it assures a certain level of functionality and interoperability. Standards also protect our investments. If one vendor goes out of business or builds an inferior product, we can buy a similar or better product from another. In this sense, standards democratize computing on the Internet: Everyone can pretty much use everything in the same way, often regardless of the vendor.

But this is also why standards tend to run against the grain of vendor competition. Since product differentiation is often the key to establishing a competitive edge, companies are reluctant to abandon or degrade their efforts merely in order to "plug and play" with those from other companies. Why would any self-respecting businessperson want to sell a solution that interoperates with that of his or her competitors, when a complete, soup-to-nuts proprietary product would generate more profit? The answer, of course, is simply that this is what customers want to buy. But the tension between these conflicting goals remains.

In earlier periods of IT history, computer industry competition often led to proprietary islands of computing and various de facto standards controlled by a single vendor. It is important to remember that today's Internet standards did not come out of this process. The IT industry was fortunate that critical standards such as TCP/IP, HTML, and HTTP emerged from the government and university communities not concerned with the profit motive. The IT industry first adopted and then co-opted these efforts.

Now the evolution of these standards lies at the very heart of a multibillion-dollar vendor competition. Existing standards need to be enhanced and upgraded, while whole new areas—such as voice telephony, directories, and objects—will require similar interoperability. As we observe the intense vendor lobbying and bickering in areas such as Java and Internet domain names, we have to worry about whether the IT industry will revert to its old proprietary ways. Business executives outside the IT industry have a key role to play here. If they appropriately punish IT vendors who fail to play ball and fight for an open standard, then their level of influence as field referees for our food fights could be extraordinary.

Where, you might ask, do all these standards come from? In general, various IT industry groups with odd names—IETF, W3C, ISO, ANSI— are charged with identifying important areas of need, hammering out the detailed specifications, working out the compromises between groups, and then promulgating the standard. However, since standard proposals are often brought to these bodies by industry leaders like Lotus, Microsoft, Netscape, Intel, and Cisco, the very vendors who hope to benefit from particular adoptions are typically the authors and originators of the underlying codes.

Not surprisingly, this process can be slow, tedious, and occasionally contentious, but in the end a standard typically emerges on which all parties can agree and around which products can be built. Thus far, the process has worked remarkably well, but there is no guarantee that this will continue. Hence business executives outside the IT industry need to use their whistle and throw up a red flag if and when any of us get out of line.

I've found myself facing this issue on several occasions, and I've learned through hard personal experience that challenging an existing standard is a bit like arguing against motherhood and apple pie. At the same time, competition in the software industry is about ever more advanced functionality, hence the constant urge not just to embrace standards but to extend them to gain a market advantage. When you add to this competition the sophisticated marketing engines of Microsoft, Netscape, Lotus, and the rest, the stage is set for an ongoing tug-of-war that composes the weekly, monthly, and annual one-upmanship for which our industry is known but not always admired.

I can think of no better example of this one-upmanship than the hype, controversy, and self-serving positioning centered around Java. Indeed, it often seems that the more critical the concept, the more likely it is to be sucked into the vortex of today's standards-based competition. Whether a truly interoperable Java emerges will say a great deal about the future of the IT standards process.

Today's bottom line is that there are really two standards challenges. First and foremost, current levels of interoperability must be maintained. Fortunately, both businesses and consumers are becoming increasingly adept at recognizing and adopting only those products that remain within an overall sphere of interoperability. If that means passing up a certain innovation or function, then so be it. Secondly, and from a longer-term perspective, the IT industry needs to ensure that standards do not wind up becoming the technological equivalent of the lowest common denominator. If standards cannot evolve to incorporate ever improving technology, they will have failed to fulfill their role.

DEMAND:
WHAT IF WE GAVE A
TECHNOLOGY PARTY AND NO ONE CAME?

It would be naive to assume that if the IT industry keeps building better products and maintains today's interoperability momentum, then customers will automatically keep buying. Ultimately, every industry comes down to issues of supply and demand. Although current demand *seems* strong, it is not impossible to imagine how this environment could significantly change. What are the chances that business, consumer, and educational interest in IT could cool? Let's look at each of these three key sectors in turn.

1. *Business.* The underpinnings of business demand are essentially faith and resources. During the 1990s, the United States has deployed technology more extensively than other countries, and this deployment seems to have been vindicated by tangible competitive gains. Thus as we approach the end of the millennium, our once shaky faith in the merits and benefits of information technology has been restored.

But what if the United States were to slump suddenly into a steep economic downturn? Or what if rival nations seemed to be suddenly surging ahead? Either of these scenarios might reverse today's conventional wisdom and undermine the pro-IT business strategy that is becoming increasingly uniform throughout the world. In my opinion, neither scenario is likely.

But faith and enthusiasm are only half the story. Businesses also need the financial wherewithal to continue to expand their IT capabilities. A strong economy has enabled U.S. firms to increase their technology spending at double-digit rates, while Europe and Japan have lagged. An economic downturn in the United States would significantly slow the pace of today's technology adoption. As we find ourselves seven years into the U.S. economic expansion, it seems inevitable that some type of recession could eventually take hold, though this certainly doesn't seem to be a high-percentage bet.

Perhaps the real nightmare scenario would come from some combination of these two concerns. If a serious economic downturn was combined with, say, the resurgence of Japanese competition and greater than expected troubles from the year 2000 problem, U.S. business faith in the overriding importance of IT might be deeply shaken. Although today such a scenario seems unlikely, it certainly can't be ruled out. Business perceptions of technology, after all, have always had their ups and downs.

2. *Consumers.* Business enthusiasm is grounded in faith and resources, but consumer interest in IT remains much more concerned with cost and appeal. Whereas businesses are forced to make difficult theoretical assumptions about the relationship between IT and competitiveness, it's fairly easy for consumers to grasp whether computers are useful or entertaining enough to justify their cost.

In 1996, cost was the IT industry's main concern. We were never going to get to a world of a billion wired users if every household had to spend $2,000 for a powerful PC. But in 1997 and 1998, the progress on the cost front was remarkable. Inexpensive devices such as Web TV, cable set-top boxes, and eventually consumer NCs will soon make Net access available for just a few hundred dollars, and possibly less. Even PCs have fallen into the sub-$1,000 range.

Of perhaps even greater interest, services like free e-mail allow Net use even by those who don't own an access device. You can now, free of charge, send and receive e-mail from any browser-enabled device connected to the Web. These free e-mail accounts are proving a boon to schools, libraries, small businesses, and families. As mixed as my emotions may be about this development, I would be the first to concede that it's a socially and culturally significant trend, and what is more, it is just the sort of innovation needed to reach much larger proportions of the population. Even business people are attracted to the idea of these truly network-centric messaging systems.

As the issue of cost begins to recede, industry emphasis is shifting to the need to create compelling consumer applications. Here, the record has been mixed. Although important and interesting applications have emerged, for most people they are still nowhere near as vital as those of the telephone, the automobile, or the TV. Given the newness of the media, this isn't surprising. On the other hand, I think it is becoming clear that the "have and have-nots" of the Information Age might soon be more accurately called the "want and want-nots." With a range of low-cost devices now becoming available, the path toward universal service is coming into view; but only if people actually want to take advantage of it.

3. *Education.* Like businesses and consumers, the nation's schools have their own way of viewing technology. In this often vexing area, I would pose three main questions:

1. How important is IT to improving education?
2. Assuming that it *is* important, do schools have the cultural capacity to effectively incorporate it?
3. Assuming a "yes" answer to the first two questions, will there be enough money to fund the necessary investments?

To be perfectly frank, I don't believe that the education industry in the United States has fully evolved past the first of these questions. Many of the most prominent people in the field are firmly convinced that technology in general—audiovisual aids, TVs, telephones, radios, movies, film strips, slide projectors, VCRs, PCs, the Internet—has little or nothing to do with the learning process and the acquisition of critical thinking skills.

Unless this consensus changes, it may be pointless, and perhaps even counterproductive, to spend much time debating the second and third questions. Only at the university level does anything even resembling a consensus on the value of IT exist within the teaching profession. Accordingly, I believe that this is where the next wave of educational innovation is most likely to occur.

INTERVENTION: WILL GOVERNMENTS GET IN THE WAY?

The emergence of unencumbered global networking poses a number of significant concerns to law- and policymakers in virtually every nation. Although some of these issues will prove much more serious than others, how governments respond to them will be one of the more important factors shaping worldwide technology usage.

I see a number of areas where government/Internet collaboration will be required, including

- Taxation
- Money supply management
- Commercial law
- Media regulation
- Economic development
- Income redistribution
- Social equity
- Voting and political participation
- Free speech
- Research and development
- Intellectual property
- Individual privacy
- Health and educational welfare
- Cultural development and preservation
- Defense and law enforcement

As you can see at a glance, the list goes on and on. The sheer length of this list, combined with the size of the topics on it, should make it clear to even the most avid Webtopians that the question is not whether government should or shouldn't be involved, but whether the worlds of technology and the worlds of government will be able to work together to produce a better society.

The potential for conflict is obvious and exists on many fronts. But I believe that the issue at the end of the day distills down to two main areas of concern: restrictions on the flow of commerce, and restrictions on the flow of information. Surprisingly, although I believe that in principle our own government fully supports the free flow of commerce. I still have some serious reservations regarding the latter. Let me address commerce first.

Toward a Framework for Global Electronic Commerce

When it comes to issues of Internet trade and taxation, the Clinton administration is saying and doing all the right things. According to a special 1997 White House electronic commerce report, the administration believes the private sector should take the lead; governments should avoid undue restrictions; and where government involvement is required, its aim should be to enable a simple, consistent, and fair legal environment for Internet-based business. Recognizing the global nature of many of these challenges, the administration has been actively working with governments all around the world to build a global consensus around this broad strategic framework.

Of course, it's always much easier to talk about these general principles than it is to fully deliver on them. Both the U.S. government and the IT industry will undoubtedly face some serious obstacles in their efforts to transform this free-market vision into reality. Interestingly, these obstacles exist both within and beyond our own national borders.

Consider the taxation issue. In America, with some 30,000 separate state and local taxing jurisdictions, each jurisdiction reserves the right to establish its own taxation agenda. Although having a uniform Internet taxation policy would clearly make life easier for nationwide Internet businesses, it would essentially eliminate an important source of state and local power and revenue.

Not surprisingly, many less enlightened state governors oppose any restrictions upon their state's right to impose sales, excise, transmission, or other Internet taxes. Given our federal system, the administration will have to work very hard to carry the argument. Similarly, states can make their own laws regarding the distribution of alcohol, cigarettes, gambling, and many other products and services. This can have some surprising consequences. For example, a growing number of small California wineries hope to promote and sell their wares directly over the Internet. But in many states this is illegal because only specially licensed distributors are permitted to deliver alcohol within each state's boundaries. Although this might seem to be a trivial example, it illustrates an important point. State laws and borderless commerce will not always be in sync.

As I write, six bills are pending in the 105th Congress, each of which addresses the critical issue of Internet taxation, and each of which strikes a different balance between the authority of federal, state, and local governments to ban or impose a tax on Internet transactions. The Congress now needs to make some tough political calls in order to pass a bill and get one more piece of the blueprint for Internet commerce in place.

Despite these and many other similar obstacles, any government restrictions on electronic commerce in America are likely to prove manageable. Businesses are used to dealing with complex local, state, and national taxes. In addition, many distribution laws will eventually change due to both consumer and business pressure. In America, consumer demand counts for a lot, and consumers will have little sympathy for laws that restrict their ability to buy and sell on line.

Internationally, this picture is somewhat less optimistic. Governments in nearly every country (including the United States) have always reserved the right to grant certain protections and privileges within their own borders, and there are few signs that they are prepared to give up this important source of authority.

Let's go back to our core example of market-facing systems. Most companies selling products on line will want to be able to sell their wares to anyone, regardless of their national location. But consider these serious questions:

- Are nations really ready to permit the development of MFEs?
- Will citizens in one country really be able to buy stocks, airline tickets, computers, books, mortgages, insurance, or other products directly from a Web business in another country?
- Will consumers be able to shop around to get the best price, at the best exchange rate?

The answer to all of these questions could be "Yes"—*unless governments pass particular laws that make these things illegal or unattractive.* But because the reality is that many new laws, taxes, and regulations are likely to regulate the Internet, the answer to each of these questions is probably "No."

From a U.S. perspective, our domestic market is large enough that the speed of our Internet commerce evolution is not heavily dependent upon the ability to sell directly beyond our own vast borders. In other words, Amazon.com would be unhappy if it was prevented from selling books directly to people in China, but such a restriction would not be catastrophic. However, for countries with smaller populations, the ability to sell beyond their own borders could well be the only way to reach the required economies of scale.

In short, restrictions on electronic commerce will probably slow down the acceptance of on-line business. Nonetheless, these restrictions are unlikely to halt the momentum already underway. In the end, perhaps the only thing that could potentially derail this momentum are restrictions on the free flow of information itself.

The Great Encryption Debate

Of all the issues I have covered in this chapter so far, the debate over encryption is the most controversial, the most intractable, and potentially, the most damaging. And of all of the issues I have been compelled to get involved in personally, this has been far and away the most frustrating. All the support the Clinton administration has given the electronic commerce community will mean little unless the impasse in this area can be broken.

The essence of the problem is really quite simple. On one side sit the FBI and the National Security Agency (NSA). From their perspective, the Internet is just another communications technology. With appropriate warrants, U.S. law enforcement officials can search a house, open a file cabinet, or intercept a telephone call. Why, they ask, should computer-based communications be treated any differently?

On the other side sit executives from the Internet industry, from the world's leading software vendors, and from the global business community generally. From their perspective, unless secure communications can be assured, the potential of Internet commerce will not be realized. Additionally, even if law enforcement tries, it will not be successful in keeping powerful encryption technology out of the hands of terrorists, spies, organized crime, or other worrisome groups, since advanced encryption software is already freely available from many sources around the world. In other words, restrictions on U.S. products will do nothing other than harm U.S. vendors.

The roots of this problem run deep. Encryption has been treated historically by the U.S. government as a form of munitions, and therefore it has come under the purview of the NSA, which oversees the granting of encryption export licenses. Indeed, the history of the encryption debate has certainly revealed its share of Cold War thinking. Even today, it is still the law that products with strong encryption technology can be used within the United States, but only the much weaker 40-bit products can be exported by U.S. companies.

This is precisely the same type of policy that was used fairly successfully during the Cold War to limit the export of many types of weapons systems and even IT hardware such as supercomputers. But for software products, this approach cannot work. First of all, and for instance, you could easily buy a copy of Lotus Notes in the United States, take it out of the country, and then copy it. You can also legally download a full 128-bit encryption source from a Web-connected PC in Canada. In other words, and this is the point, any sixteen-year-old can easily download a full encryption algorithm. The genie is really out of the bottle, and the current U.S. administration wants the IT industry to work some magic and put it back. This is not only illogical but outright foolhardy.

Second, and more importantly, software needs to move in the opposite direction; that is, software needs to be designed to ensure privacy rather than to ensure the equivalent of wire taps. Powerful encryption must be built into even the simplest browser. This is the only way that everybody can have the ability to conduct secure electronic communications.

In short, for software companies, encryption software is a necessary utility that should be distributed as freely and widely as possible. But the FBI believes that the pervasive use of strong encryption could eventually eliminate law enforcement's ability to conduct effective surveillance of voice, text, and data communications. Software vendors, of course, express dismay at the apparent lack of real-world software understanding that accompanies this belief. But law enforcement officials offer the hard-to-answer "if you knew what we knew" argument. The IT industry and U.S. law enforcement couldn't be much farther apart on this issue.

Indeed, there is too little logic and too much political posturing driving this debate and widening the gulf between industry and government (or law enforcement). Trying to restrict encryption software is analogous to asking nuclear scientists to retroactively de-invent the nuclear age. It's not possible to put the genie back in the bottle. What makes the FBI think that by prohibiting U.S. software companies from exporting strong encryption software they will somehow prevent criminals from using the strong protection that is freely available elsewhere in the world?

The complexity of the problem is further compounded by the success and size of the U.S. software industry. On the one hand, the software industry notes its dependence on international sales, as well as the link between these sales and thousands of U.S. jobs. These jobs could be put at risk if American software companies are put at a unilateral competitive disadvantage. In contrast, law enforcement agencies cite these very same statistics as evidence of the continuing dominance of U.S. vendors, arguing that these vendors clearly are not being hurt by the current rules.

The messy debate between U.S. law enforcement agencies and U.S. software vendors has made other nations doubly wary, as they try to sort out their own encryption and security positions. Not surprisingly, a number of countries have either launched or talked about launching their own initiatives. Having multiple, incompatible systems would be the worst of all possible outcomes from the business perspective. In few other areas is there more need for a consistent global approach.

In the midst of this fierce disagreement, the Clinton administration has been pulled in many directions. From an economic perspective, it fully sympathizes with the software industry's concerns. However, since no one wants to be soft on crime, it understandably pays especially close attention to the requests of the law enforcement community. Not surprisingly, positions sometimes shift with the political winds. Certainly, there is little doubt that the law enforcement position has strengthened since the Republicans took control of Congress in the 1994 elections.

As has been said often, politics is the art of compromise; and the Clinton administration has eagerly looked for some sort of common ground. However, thus far no workable solution has emerged. The administration has floated the idea of a so-called key escrow system. In this approach, the key to a specific encryption algorithm would be held in escrow by either a private or government entity. Unfortunately, no one has come up with any workable way of implementing this across millions of businesses and with the trust and support of the international community. Nevertheless, the key escrow approach remains the preferred political solution.

It is not, however, the preferred approach of the IT industry. One small problem is that according to a current estimate, the cost to be passed on to consumers for this scheme may be as high as $7 billion per year. A second and larger problem is that it won't scale—in other words, it won't work. Key escrow is the equivalent of asking the IT industry to develop a global white pages phone directory, while continuously updating the billions of entries to remain current at any one point in time. In short, if you're wait-ing for key escrow to solve the problem, don't hold your breath.

As time drifts by, the consequences of inaction become ever more se-vere. Today's 40-bit systems have become increasingly easy to crack, and law-abiding businesses must worry about the security of their global com-munications systems. Additionally, any law enforcement hopes for a global restriction on strong encryption software effectively collapsed with the 1997 decision of the Canadian government to allow Canadian firms to export software products with full-strength, 128-bit encryption.

The correct path is now more clear than ever and is indicated by the fact *encryption technology is a genie that cannot be put back in the bottle*—to say it again. If the U.S. government insists on restricting the use of pow-erful encryption software, the only people who will be hurt will be U.S. software companies and their law-abiding global customers. Criminal el-ements will continue to have a wide array of security options. As much as I sympathize with the needs of law enforcement, it seems highly unlikely that the spread of powerful encryption software can or should be stopped.

What makes the situation doubly difficult is that the current administra-tion is right about so many other things. I was present in June 1997 when President Clinton affirmed his administration's desire to support the growth of the Internet through limited or no regulatory intervention. I can personally attest to the genuine zeal with which the President delivered this message.

On a wide range of issues—financial (such as customs and taxation), electronic payments, governance of contracts, intellectual property pro-tection, control over content, and implementation of technical standards—the administration believes that existing regulatory and legal controls in concert with the invisible hand of the marketplace will best meet society's needs.

But when it comes to encryption, the current administration makes a philosophical exception, insisting that the government play a major role in controlling the use and distribution of encrypted data. Thus, we are stuck with the current paradox. We have, on the one hand, a president who reg-ularly touts the wonders of the Internet and a vice president deeply and publicly committed to the development and growth of the U.S. technology industry. On the other hand, we have this same administration, apparently under the sway of the FBI and the intelligence community, supporting legislation that might be the single biggest threat to the software industry's very prosperity.

In a business where agreement among competitors is rare, this issue has unified software companies unlike any other. The CEOs of nearly all the major software companies have expressed unanimous agreement on the need to end export controls on encryption software. That the commitment is being made at the CEO level reflects the importance all of us place on this one issue. I have participated in several forums with members of Congress, the Senate, and the White House at which were present a dedicated group of independent, type A personalities from the software industry. This group was absolutely united and outspoken. Witnessing this solidarity was and is a rare pleasure. Our ongoing and very public concurrence may be our best hope for changing these destructive approaches to what we all recognize as a legitimate government concern.

A visit by the principal IT industry CEOs to Washington in the second half of 1998 showed a much clearer understanding on the part of the House and Senate leadership on both sides of party lines, so there is hope. Although the debate on how best to manage encryption technology has become extremely polarized, I see some signs that industry and government may be groping toward at least the beginnings of a common ground. It was, for example, encouraging to hear the house Republican leadership acknowledge that we are in a new world order when it comes to communications technologies. An invitation was issued to industry technologists to sit down with the House leadership and think through how this new world order will operate, and what tools law enforcement will need to be effective in combating crime at home and abroad. A serious discussion of the implications of the absence of strong encryption products for our national communications infrastructure also took place.

Similarly, representatives from industry and from a number of different branches of the administration continue to be engaged in discussions aimed at creating a clearer understanding of how industry and government can together address some of the most serious concerns of law enforcement in the digital age. If these dialogues produce an improved atmosphere of cooperation, it still may be possible for both parties to move closer to an agreement that will allow both continued U.S. leadership in the global encryption market and an approach that will satisfy the technical needs of law enforcement and national security.

THE NEXT WAVE:
REVIEWING THE PAST AND
ASSESSING THE FUTURE

As I look at the risks and challenges that lie ahead—from the possibility of economic downturns and technological limits to potential YK2 disasters and failed standards to the realities of government intervention and the always uncertain character of demand—I realize that I would be some technology tub-thumper if I were to suggest that technical progress will always be smooth, or even steady. Given the variety, number, and size of the potholes that I myself know about, there are bound to be a few big bumps along the road, and as we all know, the future will no doubt bring forth surprises as yet unimagined.

The emergence of the species we call Homo sapiens took billions of years of earthly evolution, with humanity as we know it starting to take shape only a few million years ago. In contrast, written human language has flowered only over the last ten thousand years, with the widespread availability of printed materials occurring a mere five centuries ago.

Today, leapfrog advances in communications take at most a matter of decades. Telephony, radio, television, computers, networks, and wireless technologies were all invented and deployed in the same century. The cycle times of human communications advancement are compounding rapidly. The process is now self-reinforcing, and even autocatalytic.

The fundamental sources of human well-being are also evolving at a breakneck pace. Land and other natural resources, although precious, can no longer assure the ongoing prosperity of the world's population. Many of our planet's most resource-rich nations remain poor, while a few resource-poor nations advance dramatically, due almost entirely to the efforts and ingenuity of their own people.

More than ever before in human history, our world is limited only by its ideas. We are living in an age of almost infinite possibility. Fears of resource depletion and overpopulation have largely receded, giving rise to a new sense that the future can be entirely what we as a species decide to make of it. Today, the scarcest commodity of all is time.

It's become clear by now that the speed of social evolution and the pace of technological change are deeply intertwined and largely inseparable. Given that extraordinary technological advances are likely to continue at a rapid pace, we can be sure that human communications will continue to be transformed at the most fundamental levels indefinitely.

As the worlds of information, entertainment, communications, and finances become ever more swept up into the digital domain, the speed, range, and breadth of technological innovation and deployment have grown greater than anything the world has ever seen. Sometime early in the next century, the volume of data communications between computers will begin to dwarf the total amount of voice communications among and between us.

This is just the beginning of a profoundly transformative process. Ever more powerful single-chip computers will bring all manner of products into the information processing realm, as smart machines, appliances, cameras, and sensors constantly communicate with each other without the slightest need of human intervention. Machine-to-machine interaction will provide the next great stage of communications evolution. Human communication will, of course, continue to evolve simultaneously. Communication will become more *global*, less *hierarchical*, and perhaps most important of all, more *constant*. For better or for worse, we're heading into an increasingly wired and wireless world. Business forces will require it; consumer demands will encourage it; the momentum of technical change will see to it. We can, of course, debate the specifics and ponder questions of timing, but the overall direction is now clear. And it is worth reviewing, here at the end, how things came to be this way.

The greatest success of the network era was to turn *data* into *information*, and then to turn *information* into *knowledge*. Knowledge workers discovered that groupware provided them with more than a means to move beyond e-mail. Once the networks necessary to support an effective culture of knowledge management were up and running, organizations found themselves faced with a major piece of knowledge to be managed. To remain competitive in the cyberspace market, they needed to maximize their organizational *know-how*. And to do that, they had to grasp—*collectively* grasp—that real knowledge management is not so much about technology as it is about people, and not so much about networks in the technical sense as about networks in the metaphysical sense.

Knowledge management, in short, is about people and culture, not about technology and machines. For these would-be MFEs of the future, these leaner, smarter, thinking companies—fully integrated and enterprise-enabled—to thrive, they needed to install and maintain a new culture of information *discovery, distribution, and application,* requiring an entirely new level of workgroup and even company-wide cohesion.

Over the next decade, while the *internal* focus of digital networks shifted toward an *external*—or market-facing—emphasis, organizations had to learn how to work closely, cooperatively, and collaboratively with customers, suppliers, partners, and other allies. And once this goal was achieved, they had to learn how to extend this cultural enterprise beyond the boundaries of the traditional organization to the public at large—the customers and clients of the future, anywhere in the world.

And in order to do *that,* organizations had to learn that although at one time they could operate as if in a vacuum with regard to technology, over the next decade the level of development of the *national* and *global* information infrastructure would become perhaps the most critical single factor in determining the broad direction and pace of enterprise evolution.

I can attest from personal experience that the PC user of the future will experience the fruits of this evolution as freedom and mobility. No more being tied to the desktop, no more pick it up, boot it up, and ready, get set, go—because soon we will be using computers in much the same way that we use a telephone today. "Instant on," after all, will be a Windows 98 support feature, and key technologies like Notes's base replication will make technology for the era of the mobile user that much more transparent and productive.

More and more of the productive portions of our computing time are spent in airplanes or Red Carpet Clubs or hotels, which means that we in the IT industry are truly dealing with the absolute necessity of developing an occasionally connected computing model. Let me offer an example.

I was in Tokyo recently, speaking at an IT industry conference called Comdex. When I left, I drove straight to the airport at Norita, on the outskirts of Tokyo, and repaired to the nearest Red Carpet Club to get a little bit of work done before boarding my flight. Now my particular collaborative network solution—it's called Lotus Notes, which shouldn't shock any of my readers here—is, from a mobility standpoint, the industry's killer app (I would be kidding you if I didn't simply confess this). Notes can be instructed to go out and search the Web automatically for key words and indicators in any of millions of Web sites out there, so that wherever I am and wherever I go the information I need to keep track of my business—

and my competitors' business—is made available to me at a moment's no-
tice, automatically.

On this particular day, after getting a pager signal that on a particular
Web page posted to a particular competitor's Web site there was something that I had better take a look at, I found the fax machine, like I always
do in Red Carpet Clubs, hung my jacket over it, took out the wire, and in
Lotus-speak replicated and cached all this information locally so I could
review it on the plane. (Note: Before I get a gazillion e-mails, I have my
AT&T credit card preface encoded in my dial-up setting, so I don't end up
ripping off United Airlines.)

On this day, as on others, the bad news was that my flight was delayed.
The good news was that we eventually ascended to cruising altitude, tol-
erated the meal service, and made it to that point in the flight where everyone in the front of the plane always whips out their systems and, somewhere over the darkening Pacific, gets down to work.

I pulled my Think Pad out, and as it happened the gentleman to my left
on the aisle took out his as well. I opened my Notes database and started
working my way through all of those competitors' Web pages that I'd
downloaded a few minutes before. This work would soon be followed by
responding to a few hundred new e-mail messages that were waiting for
me locally as well. After a while I started getting the oddest look from the
guy to my left, who after a few minutes, with jaws agape, finally screwed
up his courage to tap me gently on the shoulder.

"I had no idea," he said in a hushed tone, "that the infrared devices in
these Think Pads are so powerful that you can connect directly to a Web
site from 30,000 feet using a wireless connection."

I have to admit, I thought about this question for about half a second,
but then I shot back, adopting his covertly respectful, conspiratorial tone:
"Well, you have to have a window seat, and if there's turbulence, you can
really screw up your connection, but most of the time if I point the port in
the right direction, I can download these Web pages pretty well."

Much as I'll readily admit that I was just having a little late night
transPacific fun at this poor guy's expense, I can distinctly remember that
after shutting the lid of my Think Pad I mused to myself: "That's not really so crazy. This is, to be fair, a case of being so deep in the forest, you
can't see the trees, or possibly of being so deeply embedded in the tree
bark itself that you can't see the beetles. It may not be the way that every-

body interacts today with their information, but it sure is the way I live today, not to mention the wave of the future for most of us." Then as an afterthought, I asked myself, who was doing the forward-looking thinking: the guy on the aisle making the honest mistake or me in the window seat having my little joke?

After reading this book, you should be able to answer that question for yourself. After all, *Enterprise.com* was not written for the techie, but for every poor Joe or Jane in a Red Carpet Club, bleary eyed and suffering from time-zone meltdown, who wants to know precisely what's going on at a certain moment in time and in a certain place or space—even a digital or virtual one—half way around the world.

In the Web-connected collaborative world of the future, we'll all be able to wrap our eyeballs around that information, and—I hope—we'll all be able to count upon being supplied with the tools required to turn that information into actionable, explicit knowledge, wherever and whenever we want it or need it.

So now I turn this work over to you as an ongoing exercise in knowledge management. It takes data gathered from various sources—including a number of very smart people's heads other than my own—and transforms it into what I hope is useful knowledge, usable at any time, in any place.

And to my old seatmate in 4A on United Flight 633 from Narita to New York—just kidding. Next time, I'll let your Think Pad download the information from my Think Pad using that little infrared port—they work like a charm!—which will be a distinctive collaborative network solution. And don't worry—that warmed over pasta entrée will be on me. I never touch the stuff anyway. Although airline food may not have advanced all that much, in so many other respects, we truly are real-time participants in a quantum leap in the way civilization works.

It's our world, and welcome to it.

INDEX